AZTLAN

ĀZTLĀN

An Anthology
of Mexican American
Literature

EDITED BY
LUIS VALDEZ
AND STAN STEINER

Alfred A. Knopf   New York   1973

THIS IS A BORZOI BOOK
PUBLISHED BY ALFRED A. KNOPF, INC.

Library of Congress Cataloging in Publication Data

Valdez, Luis, comp.
  Aztlan: an anthology of Mexican American
literature.

  1. Mexican Americans—Collections. 2. Mexicans
in the United States—Collections. 3. Indians of
Mexico—Collections. I. Steiner, Stanley, joint
comp. II. Title.
E184.M5V3 1972   917′.003   76-171138
ISBN 0-394-47369-8

Acknowledgments for the selections are to be found at the back of the book.

Manufactured in the United States of America

Published June 14, 1972
Second Printing, August 1973

CONTENTS

IV. THE GODS OF WAR: DEATH TO THE GRINGOS!

INTRODUCTION: "LA PLEBE"

by Luis Valdez

Aun cuando el "pelado" mexicano sea completa-
mente desgraciado, se consuela con gritar a todo el
mundo que tiene "muchos huevos" (asi llama a los
testiculos). Lo importante es advertir que en este
organo no hace residir solamente una especie de
potencia, la sexual, sino toda clase de potencia
humana.

—SAMUEL RAMOS

It is the task of all literature to present illuminating images of mankind. This, as most writers are surely aware, is
not easy to do. It takes the clearest, most unassuming effort on the part of the poet to speak for Man. This effort
is very often confused and frustrated when the writer is
a victim of racism and colonization. His birthright to
speak as Man has been forcibly taken from him. To his
conqueror he is patently subhuman, uncivilized, backward, or culturally deprived. The poet in him flounders in a
morass of lies and distortions about his conquered people.
He loses his identity with mankind, and self-consciously
struggles to regain his one-to-one relationship with human
existence. It is a long way back.

Such is the condition of the Chicano. Our people are a
colonized race, and the root of their uniqueness as Man
lies buried in the dust of conquest. In order to regain our

corazon, our soul, we must reach deep into our people, into the tenderest memory of their beginning.

Alurista, a Chicano poet, writes:

> . . . razgos indigenas
> the scars of history on my face
>   and the veins of my body
> that aches
>   vomito sangre
> y lloro libertad
>   I do not ask for freedom
> I AM freedom . . .

Man has been in the Americas for more than 38,000 years. White men have been around for less than five hundred. It is presumptuous, even dangerous, for anyone to pretend that the Chicano, the "Mexican-American," is only one more in the long line of hyphenated-immigrants to the New World. *We are the New World.*

Our insistence on calling ourselves Chicanos stems from a realization that we are not just one more minority group in the United States. We reject the semantic games of sociologists and whitewashed Mexicans who frantically identify us as Mexican-Americans, Spanish-Americans, Latin-Americans, Spanish-speaking, Spanish-surname, Americans of Mexican descent, etc. We further reject efforts to make us disappear into the white melting pot, only to be hauled out again when it is convenient or profitable for *gabacho* (*gringo*) politicans. Some of us are as dark as *zapote,* but we are casually labeled Caucasian.

We are, to begin with, *Mestizos*—a powerful blend of Indigenous America with European-Arabian Spain, usually recognizable for the natural bronze tone it lends to human skin. Having no specific race of our own, we used poetry and labeled ourselves centuries ago as La Raza, the

Race, albeit a race of half-breeds, misfits, and mongrels. Centuries of interbreeding further obfuscated our lineage, and La Raza gave itself other labels—*la plebe, el vulgo, la palomía.* Such is the natural poetry of our people. One thing, however, was never obscured: that the Raza was basically Indio, for that was borne out by our acts rather than mere words, beginning with the act of birth.

During the three hundred years of Nueva España, only 300,000 gachupines settled in the New World. And most of these were men. There were so few white people at first, that ten years after the Conquest in 1531, there were more black men in Mexico than white. Negroes were brought in as slaves, but they soon intermarried and "disappeared." Intermarriage resulted in an incredible *mestizaje,* a true melting pot. Whites with Indios produced *mestizos.* Indios with blacks produced *zambos.* Blacks with whites produced mulattoes. *Pardos, cambujos, tercernones, salta atrases,* and other types were born out of mestizos with zambos and mulattoes with Indios, and vice versa. Miscegenation went joyously wild, creating the many shapes, sizes, and hues of La Raza. But the predominant strain of the mestizaje remained Indio. By the turn of the nineteenth century, most of the people in Mexico were mestizos with a great deal of Indian blood.

The presence of the Indio in La Raza is as real as the barrio. Tortillas, tamales, chile, marijuana, la curandera, el empacho, el molcajete, atole, La Virgen de Guadalupe —these are hard-core realities for our people. These and thousands of other little human customs and traditions are interwoven into the fiber of our daily life. América Indigena is not ancient history. It exists today in the barrio, having survived even the subversive onslaught of the twentieth-century neon gabacho commercialism that passes for American culture.

Yet the barrio is a colony of the white man's world. Our life there is second hand, full of chingaderas imitating the way of the patrón. The used cars, rented houses, old radio and TV sets, stale grocery stores, plastic flowers—all the trash of the white man's world mixes with the bits and pieces of that other life, the Indio life, to create the barrio. Frijoles and tortillas remain, but the totality of the Indio's vision is gone. Curanderas make use of plants and herbs as popular .cures, without knowing that their knowledge is what remains of a great medical science. Devout Catholics pray to the Virgen de Guadalupe, without realizing that they are worshipping an Aztec goddess, Tonatzin.

The barrio came into being with the birth of the first mestizo. Before we imitated the gringo, we imitated the hacendado; before the hacendado, the gachupin. Before we lived in the Westside, Chinatown, the Flats, Dogtown, Sal Si Puedes, and El Hoyo, we lived in Camargo, Reynosa, Guamuchil, Cuautla, Tepoztlán. Before the Southwest, there was México; before México, Nueva España. The barrio goes all the way back to 1521, and the Conquest.

> We are Indian, blood and soul; the language and civilization are Spanish.
>
> —JOSE VASCONCELOS

Imagine the Conquistadores looking upon this continent for the first time. Imagine Pedro de Alvarado, Hernando Cortes! Fifty-foot caballeros with golden huevos, bringing the greed of little Europe to our jungle-ridden, god-haunted world. They saw the land and with a sweep of an arm and a solemn prayer claimed this earth for the Spanish crown, pronouncing it with Catholic inflection and Ciglo de Oro majesty, Nueva España. *New* Spain. Imagine now a fine white Spanish veil falling over the cactus mountains, volcanoes, valleys, deserts, and jungles; over the chirimoya, quetzal, ocelotl, nopal. Imagine, finally, white men marching into the light and darkness of a very old world and calling it new.

This was not a new world at all. It was an ancient world civilization based on a distinct concept of the universe. Tula, Teotihuacan, Monte Alban, Uxmal, Chichen Itzá, México-Tenochtitlan were all great centers of learning, having shared the wisdom of thousands of generations of pre-Columbian man. The Mayans had discovered the concept of zero a thousand years before the Hebrews, and so could calculate to infinity, a profound basis of their religious concepts. They had operated on the human brain, and had evolved a mathematical system which allowed them to chart the stars. That system was vigesimal, meaning it was based on a root of twenty rather than ten, because they had started by counting on their fingers and toes instead of just their fingers as in the decimal system.

It was the Mayans who created the countless stone stellae, studded with numerical symbols utilizing the human skull as number ten. Did this imply a link between mathematics and the cycle of life and death? There is no telling. Much about the Mayans is mysterious, but it is clear they had more going for them than frijoles and tortillas.

Then there were the Toltecs, Mixtecs, Totonacs, Zapotecs, Aztecs, and hundreds of other tribes. They too were creators of this very old new world. The Aztecs practiced a form of "plastic" surgery, among other great achievements in medicine. If a warrior, an Eagle or Ocelot Knight, had his nose destroyed in battle, Aztec surgeons could replace it with an artificial one. They also operated on other parts of the body and stitched up the cut with human hair.

All cures, of course, were not surgical, for the Aztec had a profound knowledge of botany, not to speak of zoology, astronomy, hieroglyphics, architecture, irrigation, mining, and city planning. The design of entire cities was an ancient art in the Americas when Madrid, London, and Paris were suffocating in their own crowded stench.

As a matter of fact, it came as a shock to the Spaniards to discover that the inhabitants of Tenochtitlan bathed daily; and that Moctezuma Xocoyotzin II, the Uei Tlatoani, Chief Speaker, bathed twice a day. Any European would have been just as shocked, for bathing was less than encouraged in Europe at that time. Perfume, of course, was already used in France.

The sight and smell of human blood on the altars and stone steps of the temples shocked the Conquistadores more than anything else. In the teocalli, the great central square of Tenochtitlan, stood a gigantic rack with a hundred thousand human skulls. It was a monument to another aspect of América Indigena, human sacrifice. How terrifying yet fascinating it must have seemed to the Conquistador. How alien yet familiar. Astonished by the ritualistic cannibalism of Aztec priests, the Spaniard went to mass and ate the ritualistic body and blood of Jesus Christ in Holy Communion.

América Indigena was obsessed with death. Or was it life? Man was a flower. A mortal, subject to the fugacity of all natural things. Nezahualcoyotl, Chief of Texcoco (1402–72), was a philosopher king and one of the greatest poets América has ever produced. His poem "Fugacidad Universal" pondered the philosophical question of temporal existence. *An nochipa tlaltipac: zan achica ye nican.* His words lose much in a double translation from the Nahuatl to Spanish, then English:

It is true we exist on this earth?
Not forever on this earth: only a brief moment here
even jade shatters
even gold tears
even the plumage of quetzal falls apart
not forever on this earth: only a brief moment here.

Man was born, blossomed, then deteriorated unto death. He was an intrinsic part of the cosmic cycle of life and death, of being becoming non-being, then back again. Coatlicue, Aztec goddess of fertility, was sculpted as a poet's vision in stone: with a death's head, scales like a serpent, and a belt of human hands and hearts. She was the embodiment of the nature of existence. Death becoming life; life becoming death. Fertility.

Life on earth was ephemeral, but impossible without the sacrifice of other living things. Did man not survive by devouring death, the dead bodies of animals and plants? Was he not in turn devoured and disintegrated by the earth? Even Tonatiuh, the Sun God, must eat, so man offered Him human hearts as sustenance, and thus became deified.

The religion of Ancient America abounds in natural symbols of the flux of life. Feathers and scales, birds and snakes, symbols of heaven and earth, of the spiritual and the material. The blue of the waters and the green of jungles combined to make turquoise and jade more precious to the Indio than gold. Yet the yellow brilliance of gold reminded him of the sun, so he valued it and learned to work with it, to mold it into the symbols of his belief. So too with feathers, especially the green feathers of the sacred Quetzal bird, which only the Uei Tlatoani, the Chief, could wear in his headdress. So too with crystal, a symbol of water and therefore of life. The most outstanding achievement of Aztec sculpture is a beautiful crystal cut with incomparable skill into the shape of a human skull. The duality of life and death again.

The *Popol Vuh,* sacred book of the Ancient Quiche Maya, describes Creation as American man saw it thousands of generations ago:

. . . There was only immobility and silence in the darkness, in the night. Only the Creator, the Maker, Tepeu, Cucumatz, the Forefathers, were in the water surrounded with light. They were hidden under green and blue feathers, and were therefore called Cucumatz.

How natural, how fitting, how deep is this Indio vision of genesis! Where else could life have begun but in the water? And with the Creator hidden under *blue and green feathers!* The sophisticated use of natural life symbols is so profound that the Catholic Conquistador, confident in his ignorance, must have thought it naïve.

None of the achievements of Indigenous America meant very much to the Conquistador. Nor was he content to merely exploit its physical strength. He sought to possess its mind, heart, and soul. He stuck his bloody fingers into the Indian brain, and at the point of the sword, gun, and cross ripped away a vision of human existence. He forced the Indio to accept his world, his reality, his scheme of things, in which the Indio and his descendants would forever be something less than men in Nueva España's hierarchy of living things. Murder and Christianity worked hand in hand to destroy the ancient cities, temples, clothes, music, language, poetry. The women were raped, and the universe, el Quinto Sol, the world of the Earthquake Sun, was shattered.

Desgraciada raza mexicana, obedecer no quieres,
gobernar no puedes.

—AMADO NERVO

In the twilight of the Conquest, the Mestizo was born into
colonization. Rejected as a bastard by his Spanish father,
he clung to his Indian mother and shared the misery of
her people, the overwhelming sense of loss:

Nothing but flowers and songs of sorrow are left in Mexico
and Tlaltelolco, where once we saw warriors and wise men.

Soon there was not even that. Death overtook all who remembered what it had been like, and colonization set in
for three hundred years.

Our dark people looked into one another's eyes. The
image reflected there was one the white man had given us.
We were savage, Indio, Mestizo, half-breed: always something less than simple men. Men, after all, have a tendency
to create God in their own image. No, men we could never
be, because only the patrón could be a god. We were born
to be his instrument, his peon, his child, his whore—this
he told us again and again through his religion, literature,
science, politics, economics. He taught us that his approach to the world, his logical disciplines of human
knowledge, was truth itself. That everything else was barbaric superstition. Even our belief in God. In time there
was nothing left in our hearts but an empty desire, a longing for something we could no longer define.

Still, for all the ferocity of the Conquest, the Mestizo
cannot totally condemn the Spaniard. He might as well
condemn his own blood. Anglos particularly are very fond
of alluding to the black legend of the Conquistador in
Mexico, perhaps to mask the even more inhuman treat-

ment of the Indian in the United States. The gachupin
offered the Indio colonization; the Anglo, annihilation.
There is no question that Nueva España was more human
to América Indigena than New England.

Some white men, such as Fray Bartolomé de las Casas,
saw the evils of New Spain and denounced them:

All the wars called conquests were and are most unjust and
truly tyrannical. We have usurped all the kingdoms and lordships of the Indies.

Others, like Sahagun and Motolinia, saved what they
could of ancient chronicles, *los codices de la tinta negra y
roja,* the life thought of a dispossessed world civilization.

It is doubtful, however, that any white man in colonial
Mexico or New England was aware of the ultimate importance of the Mestizo. As the real new man of the Americas,
he was the least likely candidate to be called an American.
The reason may be that the name *America* was an imported European title, and reserved therefore only for
European types. By right of discovery, the honor afforded
to Amerigo Vespucci should have gone to Christopher
Columbus. Yet *Columbia* would have been just as alien to
the native people of this land as *America.* The naming of
the continent had nothing to do with the Indios or their
Mestizo children. It was strictly an amusement of white,
western European man.

Once America was named, Europe yawned and went on
with the dull but profitable business of exploitation and
colonization. Wherever possible, North and South America
were built or rebuilt in the image of Europe. Spain gorged
itself on the gold of New Spain; and England did a brisk
trade on the tobacco of New England. Aside from mer-
cantile ventures, the Old World was so uninterested in
the New that even white colonists felt neglected.

It took a revolution in the thirteen colonies of New England to again raise the issue of America. Once again the Indios and Mestizos were forgotten. In 1776 the United States of America usurped the name of a continental people for a basically white, English-speaking, middle-class minority. It revealed, perhaps, the continental ambitions of that minority. But an American was henceforth defined as a white citizen of the U.S.A. The numerous brown Quiche, Nahuatl, and Spanish-speaking peoples to the south were given secondary status as Latin Americans, Spanish Americans, and South Americans. It was a historical snow job. The descendants of América Indigena were now foreigners in the continent of their birth.

Gabacho America, however, was not to touch the Mestizo for at least another half century. While the Monroe Doctrine and Manifest Destiny were being hatched in Washington, D.C., the Mestizo was still living in Nueva España. During the colonial period, he easily achieved numerical superiority over the white man. But the dominant culture remained Spanish. So the Mestizo stood at a cultural crossroads, not unlike the one he later encountered in the United States: choose the way of Mexico Indio and share degradation; or go the way of the white man and become Hispanicized.

The choice was given as early as 1598, when Don Juan de Oñate arrived in the Southwest to settle and claim New Mexico, "from the edge of the mountains to the stones and sand in the rivers, and the leaves of trees." With him came four hundred Mestizos and Indios as soldiers. Many of the Hispanos, or Spanish Americans living in New Mexico today, are descended directly from those first settlers. Their regional name reveals the cultural choice their ancestors made; but it also reveals a reluctance to choose, for Hispano to some New Mexicans also means Indiohispano. In

1598 there was not, of course, national status for Mestizos as Mexicanos. Even so, after Independence, Hispanos refused to identify with the racial, cultural, and political confusions of Mexico.

The internal conflicts of nineteenth-century Mexico resulted from a clash of races as well as classes. Conservative Criollos and the clergy usurped the War of Independence against Spain; after 1810, the bronze mass of Indios and Mestizos continued to be exploited by a white minority. Avarice and individual ambition superseded the importance of national unity. Coups and *pronunciamentos* became commonplace, and further weakened the new nation. Mexico did not belong to her people.

Watching the internal struggles south of the border, the United States circled around Texas and hovered above California like a buzzard. Mexico was ill-equipped to defend either state. When rebels struck at the Alamo, President Antonio López de Santa Ana unfortunately decided to rout them out personally. Leaving General don José Maria Tornel in charge of the government, he drafted an army of six thousand. Through forced loans from businessmen, he equipped them poorly, and with promises of land in Texas won their allegiance. The long march to Texas was painful and costly. Supplies, animals, ammunition, and hundreds of soldiers were lost due to the rigors of winter. Inept as a general, Santa Ana despotically ordered the worst routes for his convoys. He almost accomplished the failure of the expedition before even reaching Texas.

The rest is "American" history. The rebels lost the Alamo, but regrouped under Samuel Houston to finally defeat Santa Ana at San Jacinto. Some important historical facts, however, are never mentioned in U.S. classrooms. After the fall of the Alamo and San Antonio Bejar, the rebels resorted to guerrilla warfare. They destroyed crops and burned towns, so that the Mexican troops would have no place to get supplies. They in turn received weapons, food, and men from the United States. The South particularly was interested in Texas as a future slave state. Mexico had outlawed slavery in 1824, but some of the defenders of freedom at the Alamo died for the freedom of holding black slaves.

Slavery was foremost in the minds of the Mexican signers of the Treaty of Guadalupe Hidalgo in 1848. Ceding fully half of the national territory of Mexico to the United States, they were concerned about the 75,000 Mexican citizens about to be absorbed into an alien country. They feared that the dark Mexican Mestizo would share the fate of the black man in America. They asked for guarantees that Mexican families would not lose their ancestral lands, that civil and cultural rights would be respected. But the United States, still hot from its first major imperialistic venture, was not ready to guarantee anything.

Witness the memoirs of Ulysses S. Grant, who was with General Zachary Taylor at the Rio Grande, which admit that the United States had goaded Mexico into "attacking first." No stretch of the imagination can explain why Mexico, bleeding from internal conflict, would want to provoke war with the U.S. Known as *la invasion norteamericana* in Mexico, the Mexican War polluted the moral climate of America. Abraham Lincoln debated with Stephen Douglas over the ultimate wisdom and morality of the war. It was an early-day version of Vietnam. Manifest Destiny won the day, however, and the U.S. acquired the Southwest. When the Treaty of Guadalupe Hidalgo came before Congress for ratification, Article Nine was replaced and Article Ten was stricken out. The two Articles dealt, respectively, with civil rights and land guarantees.

The no-nonsense attitude of American politics merged

with white racism to create the stereotype of the Mexican greaser. Carrying the added stigma of defeat in battle, the Mestizo was considered cowardly, lazy, and treacherous. Anglo America was barely willing to recognize his basic humanity, much less the nobility of his pre-Columbian origins. He was a Mexican, and that was it. But contrary to the myth of the Sleeping Giant, the Mexican in the Southwest did not suffer the abuses of the gringo by remaining inert.

In 1859 Juan N. Cortina declared war on the gringos in Texas. On November 23 from his camp in the Rancho del Carmen, County of Cameron, he released a proclamation:

Mexicans! When the State of Texas began to receive the new organization which its sovereignty required as an integrant part of the Union, flocks of vampires, in the guise of men, came and scattered themselves in the settlements . . . many of you have been robbed of your property, incarcerated, chased, murdered, and hunted like wild beasts, because your labor was fruitful, and because your industry excited the vile avarice which led them. A voice infernal said, from the bottom of their soul, "kill them; the greater will be our gain!"

The document was intense but despairing for a real solution to the problem of gringo domination. Cortina proposed to fight to the death if need be, and offered La Raza in Texas the protection of a secret society sworn to defend them. He addressed his people as Mexicanos, but the fact remains that they were no longer citizens of Mexico. They were Mestizos cast adrift in the hellish limbo of Anglo America. Cortina got his war, and lost.

There were others, before and after Cortina, who waged guerrilla warfare from the mountains of the Southwest. In California, from 1850 to 1875, Joaquín Murieta and Tiburcio Vásquez span a period of unmitigated struggle. History dismissed them as bandits; asinine romanticized accounts of their "exploits" have totally distorted the underlying political significance of their rebellion.

Bandits in Mexico, meanwhile, were on the verge of creating the first major revolution of the twentieth century. The Revolution of 1910. The revolution of Emiliano Zapata and Pancho Villa. *El indio y el mestizo*. At Independence, only one fifth of Mexico's population had been white. A century later, it was less than one thirteenth. In the hundred years between Independence and the Revolution, the number of Mestizos had *quadrupled*. In 1910 they numbered fifty-three percent of the total population, while the Indios had remained fairly stable at close to forty percent. Yet white men ruled, while the blood and flesh of Mexico went hungry.

A new motivating force was behind the Revolution of 1910, and that force was La Raza, la plebe, los de abajo. Indigenous Mexico discovered itself and so arose with all the fury that four hundred years of oppression can create. The bloodroot of la patria exploded, and Mestizos and Indios fought to the death to make Mexico what it had not been since Cuauhtemoc: a unique creation of native will. La plebe burst into the private halls and dining rooms of the rich; it broke down the great walls of the haciendas and smashed the giant doors of holy cathedrals, shouting obscenities and laughing, crying, yelling, sweating, loving, killing, and singing:

> La Cucaracha, La Cucaracha
> Ya no puede caminar
> Porque le falta, porque no tiene
> Marijuana que fumar!

It was a revolution with few restraints, and La Raza expressed itself as never before. A half-breed cultural maelstrom swept across Mexico in the form of corridos, bad language, vulgar topics, disrespectful gestures, *pleberías*. It was all a glorious affront to the aristocracy, which, wrapped in their crucifixes and fine Spanish laces, had been licking the boots of American and British speculators for a lifetime. In 1916, when Woodrow Wilson sent Pershing into Mexican territory on a "punitive" expedition, looking for Pancho Villa, U.S. intervention had already seriously crippled the Revolution. Pershing failed to find Villa, but la plebe launched a corrido against the gringo:

Que pensarían esos gringos tan patones que nuestro suelo pretenden conquistar. Si ellos tienen cañones de amontones aquí tenemos lo mero principal!

Three years later Emiliano Zapata was dead in Chinameca, and the terrible reality of a dying Revolution began to settle on the people. In 1923 Pancho Villa was assassinated by a savage hail of bullets in the dusty streets of Parral, Chihuahua. That same year, almost 64,000 Mexicans crossed the fictitious border into the United States. During the following years 89,000 poured across, and the U.S., alarmed by the sudden influx, organized the border patrol. This was the first time the boundary between Mexico and the Southwest had ever been drawn, but now it was set, firmly and unequivocally. Even so, ten percent of Mexico's population made it across, *pa' este lado*. La plebe crossed the border, and their remembrance of the patria was forever stained by memories of bloody violence, festering poverty, and hopeless misery. For all their hopes of material gain, their migration (and it was only a short migration into the Southwest) meant a spiritual regression, for them and for their sons—a legacy of shame for being of Mexican descent in the land of the gringo.

Yet the *Revolución* would persist, in memory, in song, in cuentos. It would reach into the barrio, through two generations of Mexicanos, to create the Chicano.

The Chicano is the grandson, or perhaps even the son, of the Mexican *pelado*. Who is the *pelado*? He is the Mestizo, the colonized man of Mexico, literally, the "stripped one." La Raza is the *pelado en masse*. He is almost inevitably dirt poor, cynical about politics, and barely manages to live. He earns his immediate survival day by day, through any number of ingenious schemes, or *movidas*. During the last thirty years or so, he has been epitomized in the cine mexicano by the genius of Mario Moreno's Cantinflas. Yet he is hardly a mere comic figure. The humor in his life is born of such deep misfortune that the comedy takes on cosmic proportions and so becomes tragedy.

The pelado is the creator of the corrido and the eternal patron of mariachi. His music, in turn, inspires him to express all his joy and sorrow in a single cry. So he lets out a grito that tells you he feels life and death in the same breath. *"Viva la Raza, hijos de la chingada!"*

In Mexican history, the pelado undoubtedly gave voice to the "Grito de Dolores" in 1810, and then went off with Miguel Hidalgo y Costilla to fight the War of Independence against Spain. In other generations, the pelado took orders from Santa Ana at the Alamo, and probably finished off Davy Crockett. He also fought with Don Benito Juárez during *La Reforma*, and most certainly rode with Pancho Villa. It was the pelado who crossed the border into the United States, only to be viciously stereotyped as the sleeping Mexican, leaning against a cactus.

There is no understanding of the pelado in the literature of the United States. None, that is, except for the embryonic works of Chicano literature. Comadres, compadres, pachucos, and campesinos begin to emerge from the pen of the Chicano poet: people of the rural and urban barrios of the Southwest, with names like Nacho, la Chata, Tito, Little Man, Pete Fonesca, and "el Louie Rodriquez, carnal del Candi y el Ponchi." Some are sketched, some are fully drawn, but they are all intimately real—a far cry from the racist stereotypes of the John Steinbeck past.

Yet they are all drawn against the background of the barrio, replete with the spiritual and material chingaderas of colonization. Beset by all the pain and confusion of life in los estados unidos, the pelados in Chicano literature take drugs, fight, drink, despair, go hungry, and kill each other. Some resist the racism of the gringo, and become pachucos. Some acculturate and sell out as Mexican Americans. Some are drawn from a distant twenty-year-old memory, and some are as real as today. But they are not to be confused with the writers that created them, for they are Chicanos.

The Chicano is not a pelado. His very effort to cut through nearly five centuries of colonization defines him as a new man. This effort is so total, in fact, that it is characteristic of Chicano writers to also be teachers, community organizers, and political leaders. In one sense, *being Chicano* means the utilization of one's total potentialities in the liberation of our people. In another sense, it means that Indio mysticism is merging with modern technology to create *un nuevo hombre*. A new man. A new reality, rooted in the origins of civilization in this half of the world.

Neither a pelado nor a Mexican American, the Chicano can no longer totally accept as reality the white, western European concept of the universe. Reason and logic are not enough to explain the modern world; why should it suffice to explain the ancient world of our ancestors? The sciences of archeology and anthropology may unearth the buried ruins of América Indigena, but they will never comprehend, through logic alone, its most basic truth: that man *is* a flower. For there is poetry in reality itself.

In an effort to recapture the soul-giving myth of La Raza, the Chicano is forced to re-examine the facts of history, and suffuse them with his own blood—to make them tell his reality. The truth of historical documents can sometimes approach poetic truth. So the Chicano poet becomes historian, digging up lost documents and proclamations other men saw fit to ignore. Yet he will inevitably write his own gestalt vision of history, his own *mitos*. And he will do it bilingually, for that is the mundane and cosmic reality of his life.

Anglo America, no doubt, will resent the bilingualism of the Chicano. The average educated gabacho will probably interpret bilingual Chicano literature as reflecting the temporary bicultural confusion of the "Mexican American." He will be reluctant to accept in the Chicano poet what he proudly accepts in a T. S. Eliot. Both are bilingual, or even multilingual poets; but the former intersperses his English with mere Spanish, while the latter alludes in the "highly sophisticated" Latin or French.

If the Anglo cannot accept the coming reality of America, *que se lo lleve la jodida*. Otherwise, he can learn Spanish, which is the language of most of the people in América.

The time has come to redefine all things American. If our bilingualism has prompted gabachos to wonder if we are "talking about them," in the street, in school, at work, this time, the Chicano literature, we certainly are discussing them. If Anglos insist on calling us Mexican Americans, then we must insist on asking: What is an American? Nobody pursues the title with such vehemence as the white man in the United States. He does on occasion recognize the existence of "Latin" America, and so calls himself a *norteamericano*. Still, North American does not define him clearly enough. After all, North America is not only the United States. It is also Mexico, Jamaica, Haiti, Puerto Rico, Canada, and Cuba. Fidel Castro is a *norteamericano*.

Who then is this resident of the United States known by the Chicano as an Anglo, gringo, yanqui, bolillo, or gabacho? Who is this person whose immediate ancestors were so incapable of living with Indigenous America that they tried to annihilate it?

He is the eternal foreigner, suffering from the immigrant complex. He is a transplanted European, with pretensions of native origins. His culture, like his name for this continent, is imported. For generations, despite furious assertions of his originality, the "American" has aped the ways of the Old Country, while exploiting the real native peoples of the New. His most patriotic cry is basically the retort of one immigrant to another. Feeling truly American only when he is no longer the latest foreigner, he brandishes his Americanism by threatening the new arrival: "America, love or leave it!" Or, "If you don't like it here, go back where you came from!"

Now the gringo is trying to impose the immigrant complex on the Chicano, pretending that we "Mexican Americans" are the most recent arrivals. It will not work. His melting pot concept is a sham: it is a crucible that scientifically disintegrates the human spirit, melting down entire cultures into a thin white residue the average gabacho can harmlessly absorb. That is why the Anglo cannot conceive of the Chicano, the Mexican Mestizo, in all his ancient human fullness. He recognizes him as a Mexican, but only to the extent that he is "American"; and he accepts Mexican culture only to the extent that it has been Americanized, sanitized, sterilized, and made safe for democracy, as with taco bars, chile con carne, the Mexican hat dance, Cantinflas in *Pepe,* the Frito Bandito, and grammar school renditions of *Ay Chiapanecas Ay, Ay* (Clap, clap, children).

But we will not be deceived. In the final analysis, frijoles, tortillas, y chile are more American than the hamburger; and the pelado a more profound founding father of America than the pilgrim. No, we do not suffer from the immigrant complex. We suffered from it as its victims, but history does not record the same desperation among our people that twisted and distorted the European foreigner, that made the white immigrant the gringo.

We left no teeming shore in Europe, hungry and eager to reach the New World. We crossed no ocean in an overcrowded boat, impatient and eager to arrive at Ellis Island in New York. No Statue of Liberty ever greeted our arrival in this country, and left us with the notion that the land was free, even though Mexicans and Indians already lived on it. We did not kill, rape, and steal under the pretext of Manifest Destiny and Western Expansion. We did not, in fact, come to the United States at all. The United States came to us.

We have been in América a long time. Somewhere in the twelfth century, our Aztec ancestors left their homeland of Aztlán, and migrated south to Anáhuac, "the place by the waters," where they built their great city of México-Tenochtitlan. It was a long journey, for as their guiding deity Huitzilopochtli had prophesied, the elders of the tribe died en route and their children grew old. Aztlán was left far behind, somewhere "in the north," but it was never forgotten.

Aztlán is now the name of our Mestizo nation, existing to the north of Mexico, within the borders of the United States. Chicano poets sing of it, and their *flor y canto* points toward a new yet very ancient way of life and social order, toward new yet very ancient gods. The natural revolutionary turn of things is overthrowing outmoded concepts in the life of man, even as it does in nature; churning them around in the great spin of Creation, merging the very ancient with the very new to create new forms.

The rise of the Chicano is part of the irrevocable birth of América, born of the blood, flesh, and life spirit of this ancient continent. Beyond the two-thousand-mile border between Mexico and the U.S.A. we see our universal race extending to the very tip of South America. We see millions upon millions of bronze people, living in Mestizo nations, some free, some yet to be freed, but existing: Mexicanos, Guatemaltecos, Peruanos, Chilenos, Cubanos, Bolivianos, Puertoriqueños. A new world race born of the racial and cultural blending of centuries. La Raza Cosmica, the true American people.

I. WHERE ARE THE ROOTS OF MEN? THE ORIGINS OF MEXICO

THE HEART OF EARTH

from Popol Vuh:
The Sacred Book of the Ancient Quiche Maya

One of the noble civilizations of mankind, the high culture of the Maya, was thought by Victor von Hagan (*The World of the Maya*) to have begun about 2000 B.C. In the *Popol Vuh*, the highland Quiche Maya of the Yucatan relate their origins to eternity. As in Genesis, in the Mayan beginning there was a void, darkness, and "Then came the word" and the Creator made man, who too soon knew too much. "They know everything," the Creator complained of the Maya; "we must curb their desires." So history began, even in the Yucatan. The *Popol Vuh* was set down by the Spaniards, in 1550, a "literal translation from a Maya painted book" (von Hagan). (*Popol Vuh: The Sacred Book of the Ancient Quiche Maya*, English translation by D. Goetz and S. Morley, from the Spanish of Adrian Recinos, Norman, Okla., University of Oklahoma Press, 1950.)

This is the account of how all was in suspense, all calm, in silence; all motionless, still, and the expanse of the sky was empty.

This is the first account, the first narrative. There was neither man, nor animal, birds, fishes, crabs, trees, stones, caves, ravines, grasses, nor forests; there was only the sky.

The surface of the earth had not appeared. There was only the calm sea and the great expanse of the sky.

There was nothing brought together, nothing which could make a noise, nor anything which might move, or tremble, or could make noise in the sky.

There was nothing standing; only the calm water, the placid sea, alone and tranquil. Nothing existed.

There was only immobility and silence in the darkness, in the night. Only the Creator, the Maker, Tepeu, Gucumatz, the Forefathers were in the water surrounded with light. They were hidden under green and blue feathers, and were therefore called Gucumatz. By nature they were great sages and great thinkers. In this manner the sky existed and also the Heart of Heaven, which is the name of God and thus He is called.

Then came the word. Tepeu and Gucumatz came together in the darkness, in the night, and Tepeu and Gucumatz talked together. They talked then, discussing and deliberating; they agreed, they united their words and their thoughts.

Then while they meditated, it became clear to them that when dawn would break, man must appear. Then they planned the creation, and the growth of the trees and the thickets and the birth of life and the creation of man. Thus it was arranged in the darkness and in the night by the Heart of Heaven who is called Huracan.

The first is called Caculha Huracan. The second is Chipi-Caculha. The third is Raxa-Caculha. And these three are the Heart of Heaven.

Then Tepeu and Gucumatz came together; then they conferred about life and light, what they would do so that there would be light and dawn, who it would be who would provide food and sustenance.

Thus let it be done! Let the emptiness be filled! Let the water recede and make a void, let the earth appear and become solid; let it be done. Thus they spoke. Let there be light, let there be dawn in the sky and on the earth! There shall be neither glory nor grandeur in our creation and formation until the human being is made, man is formed. So they spoke.

Then the earth was created by them. So it was, in truth, that they created the earth. Earth! they said, and instantly it was made.

Like the mist, like a cloud, and like a cloud of dust was the creation, when the mountains appeared from the water; and instantly the mountains grew.

Only by a miracle, only by magic art were the mountains and valleys formed; and instantly the groves of cypresses and pines put forth shoots together on the surface of the earth.

And thus Gucumatz was filled with joy, and exclaimed: "Your coming has been fruitful, Heart of Heaven; and you, Huracan, and you Chipi-Caculha, Raxa-Caculha!"

"Our work, our creation shall be finished," they answered.

First the earth was formed, the mountains and the valleys; the currents of water were divided, the rivulets were running freely between the hills, and the water was separated when the high mountains appeared.

Thus was the earth created, when it was formed by the Heart of Heaven, the Heart of Earth, as they are called who first made it fruitful, when the sky was in suspense, and the earth was submerged in the water.

So it was that they made perfect the work, when they did it after thinking and meditating upon it.

IN A TIME NOBODY
EXACTLY REMEMBERS: THE OLMECS

by Miguel Leon-Portilla

> Landing at Veracruz with Hernando Cortez, the
> chronicler of the Conquest, Father Bernal Diaz del
> Castillo, was most amazed by "the many books of
> paper" he found in the temples of the Totonacs. Writ-
> ten in abstract ideographs and polyglyphs, the books
> of pre-Columbian Mexico dealt with a wide range of
> subjects: history and philosophy, science and art. Not
> only did the Maya and Aztecs have a written litera-
> ture, so too did the Totonacs, the Mixtecs, and the Ol-
> mecs—a people who lived in a region the Aztecs
> called "Rubberland," on the Gulf of Mexico. (*Pre-Co-
> lumbian Literatures of Mexico* by Miguel Leon-Por-
> tilla, translated by Grace Lobanov and the author,
> Norman, Okla., University of Oklahoma Press, 1969.)

Along the coast of the Gulf of Mexico, in the modern Mexican states of Veracruz and Tabasco, a region known to the
Aztecs as Rubberland was the home of the Olmecs. These
people dated back more than nine hundred years before
Christ. Having identified certain characteristic traits in
many of their works, archaeologists have found traces of
their presence or at least influence in many other areas,
some far away from Rubberland. The oldest inscriptions discovered in Mexico up to now all show some relation to the
Olmecs. Among these are the "C" stele found in Tres Za-
potes, Veracruz, the inscriptions on the famous Tuxtla jade
figurine, and the still more ancient glyphs on the steles at
the ceremonial center of Monte Alban in Oaxaca which, as
already mentioned, antedate the splendor of Zapotec culture. These Olmec-type inscriptions all point to an inven-

tion of the art of recording the past. Alfonso Caso sums up concisely what is known to date about the origins of writing and the calendar in ancient Mexico as a result of archaeological findings:

According to the Carbon 14 test, it has been determined that there was writing and a calendar system in Mesoamerica at least as early as 600 B.C. But since the calendar of that time shows an extraordinary perfection and is already related to many other aspects of Mesoamerican culture (ceramics, sculpture in stone, jade, pyramids, palaces, and so forth), it can be stated positively that it was the result of a long process of development which began many centuries before the Christian era.

Apparently the same Aztec elders who rescued many texts and poems also knew of the antiquity of the invention of writing and the calendar. In a text in which they speak of the origin of their culture, they say that "in a time which nobody can reckon and about which nobody exactly remembers," many years before the building of Teotihuacan, along the shores of the Gulf of Mexico lived a people whose wise men and priests possessed many painted books and a knowledge of measuring time. These people appeared in the north, not far from the mouth of the Panuco River, and among them were

> Those who
> carried with them
> the black and red ink,
> the manuscripts and painted books,
> the wisdom.
> They brought everything with them,
> the annals,
> the books of song, and their flutes.

These wise men cannot be positively identified as the Ol-mecs, to whom archaeology has ascribed the oldest writing. However, archaeological discoveries give some support to the Aztec belief that before the days of Teotihuacan there was a people along the Gulf Coast who possessed the art of writing and the calendar. The accepted fact is that the methods of preserving knowledge and memories of the past among the native groups of Mexico have been carried in a cultural sequence with roots over two thousand years old.

THE CITY OF TENOCHTITLAN

When the Spaniards and the Indians "discovered" one another, in the sixteenth century, the society of the Aztecs had developed "into the governmental com-plexity of a populous and highly complicated city-state" (George C. Vaillant, *Aztecs of Mexico*, New York, Doubleday, 1962). The urban culture of the Az-tecs in some aspects surpassed that of Renaissance Spain, as can be seen in the incredulous dispatch of Hernando Cortez to Charles I ("What Greater Gran-deur," *Conquest: Dispatches of Cortes from the New World*, edited by Irwin R. Blacker and Harry H. Rosen, New York, Grosset & Dunlap, 1962) and Fa-ther Bernal Diaz's report ("Greater than Constantino-ple and Rome," *The Discovery and Conquest of Mex-ico, 1517–1521*, edited by Gennaro Garcia, translated by A. P. Maudsley, New York, Farrar, Straus & Cud-ahy, 1956).

What Greater Grandeur

from the Dispatches of Hernando Cortez

This great city of Temixtitan is built on the salt lake, and from the mainland to the city is a distance of two leagues, from any side from which you enter. It has four approaches by means of artificial causeways, two cavalry lances in width. The city is as large as Seville or Cordoba. The principal streets are very broad and straight; some of these are one half land and the other half water on which they go about in canoes. All the streets have openings at regular intervals, to let the water flow from one to the other. At all these openings, some of which are very broad, there are bridges, very large, strong, and well constructed. Over many of them ten horsemen can ride abreast. . . .

The city has many squares where markets are held and trading is carried on. There is one square twice as large as that of Salamanca, all surrounded by arcades where there are daily more than sixty thousand souls buying and selling. Every kind of merchandise produced in these countries is to be found there. . . .

One street is set apart for the sale of herbs, including every sort of root and medicinal herb which grows in that country. There are houses like apothecary shops where prepared medicines are sold as well as liquids, ointments, and plasters. They have places like our barbers' shops, where they wash and shave their heads, and houses where they supply food and drink for payment. . . .

There are skeins of different kinds of spun cotton in all colors, so that it seems quite like one of the silk markets of Granada, although it is on a greater scale; also as many different colors for painters as can be found in Spain, and they are just as good. They sell deer skins of different colors with all the hair tanned on them, excellent earthenware, many sorts of pots, large and small, pitchers, large tiles, an infinite variety of vases of very singular clay, most of them glazed and painted. They sell maize, both in the grain and made into bread, which is very superior to that of the other islands and the mainland; pies of birds, and of fish; also much fish—fresh, salted, cooked, and raw; eggs of hens and geese and other birds, and cakes made of eggs.

Each kind of merchandise is sold in its respective street, and they do not mix the different kinds of merchandise so that they preserve perfect order. Everything is sold by a kind of measure, and, until now, we have not seen anything sold by weight. . . .

There are many large and handsome houses because all the lords of the country live in the city a great part of the year; there are also many rich citizens who have fine houses.

Along one of the causeways which lead to the city, there are two conduits of masonry, each two paces broad and five feet deep. Through one of these there flows into the heart of the city a volume of very good fresh water. The other, which is empty, brings the water they use to clean the first conduit. Conduits as large around as an ox's body bring the fresh water across the bridges, thereby avoiding the channels through which the salt water flows. The whole city is supplied in this way, and everybody has water to drink. Canoes also peddle the water through all the streets. They get the water by stopping under the bridges where the conduits cross and where men are stationed who are paid to fill them. . . .

Considering that these people were barbarous, so cut off from the knowledge of God and from other civilized peoples, it is admirable to see to what they attained in every respect. As far as the service surrounding Montezuma is concerned and the admirable attributes of his greatness and state, there is so much to write that I assure Your Highness I do not know where to begin. For what greater grandeur can there be than that a barbarian monarch should have imitations in gold, silver, stones, and feather-work of all the things existing under heaven in his dominion; things so much like nature that there is not a silversmith in the world who could do better? As for the stones, there is no imagination which can divine the instruments with which they were so perfectly executed; and as for the feather-work, neither in wax, nor in embroidery could nature be so marvellously imitated.

Greater Than Constantinople and Rome

by Father Bernal Diaz del Castillo

When we arrived there Montezuma came out of an oratory where his cursed idols were, at the summit of the great Cue, and two priests came with him, and after paying great reverence to Cortes and to all of us he said: "You must be tired Senor Malinche, from ascending this our great Cue," and Cortes replied through our interpreters who were with us that he and his companions were never tired by anything. Then Montezuma took him by the hand and told him to look at his great city and all the other cities that were standing in the water, and the many other towns on the land round the lake, and that if he had not seen the great market place well, from where they were they could see it better.

So we stood looking about us, for that huge and cursed temple stood so high that from it one could see over everything very well, and we saw the three causeways which led into Mexico, that is the causeway of Iztapalapa by which we had entered four days before, and that of Tacuba, and that of Tepeaquilla, and we saw fresh water that comes from Chapultepec which supplies the city, and we saw the bridges on the three causeways which were built at certain distances apart through which the water of the lake flowed in and out from one side to the other, and we beheld on that great lake a great multitude of canoes, some coming with supplies of food and others returning loaded with cargoes of merchandise; and we saw that from every house of that great city and of all the other cities that were built in the water it was impossible to pass from house to house, except by drawbridges which were made of wood or in canoes; and we saw in those cities Cues and oratories like towers and fortresses and all gleaming white, and it was a wonderful thing to behold; then the houses with flat roofs, and on the causeways other small towers and oratories which were like fortresses.

After having examined and considered all that we had seen we turned to look at the great market place and the crowds of people that were in it, some buying and others selling, so that the murmur and hum of their voices and words that they used could be heard more than a league off. Some of the soldiers among us who had been in many parts of the world, in Constantinople, and all over Italy, and in Rome, said that so large a market place and so full of people, and so well regulated and arranged, they had never beheld before.

LIFE OF THE AZTECS

By conquering the Toltecs and taking their gods, the Aztecs enshrined a holy duality. Ometeolt, the Lord of Life, was female and male, darkness and light. Coatlicue, the Mother Earth was Mother Famine. Tlazolteotl, the Goddess of Fertility, was Lady of Filth and Eater of Feces. In everyday life good and evil were religiously embraced. The agrarian communalism, "in theory completely democratic" (G. C. Vaillant), humanistically described by the Aztec writer, Icazbalceta ("Aztec Democracy: In Favor of the Common Man," *Aztec Thought and Culture, a Study of the Ancient Nahuatl Mind* by Miguel Leon-Portilla, translated by Jack Emory Davis, Norman, Okla., University of Oklahoma Press, 1963), was equaled by the inhumanism of a society where theft was punished by slavery, and human sacrifice was the highest absolution ("Aztec Imperialism: Tlacaelel and Human Sacrifice," *Aztec Thought and Culture*).

Aztec Democracy: In Favor of the Common Man

by Icazbalceta

At dawn the judges would be seated on their mats, and soon people would begin to arrive with their quarrels. Somewhat early, food would be brought from the palace. After eating the judges would rest a while, and then they would continue to listen until two hours before the sun set. In matters of appeal there were twelve judges who had jurisdiction over all the others, and they used to sentence with the sanction of the ruler.

Every twelve days the ruler would meet with all of the judges to consider all of the difficult cases. . . . Everything that was taken before him was to have been already carefully examined and discussed. The people who testified would tell the truth because of an oath which they took, but also because of the fear of the judges, who were very skilled at arguing and had a great sagacity for examination and cross-examination. And they would punish rigorously those who did not tell the truth.

The judges received no gifts in large or small quantities. They made no distinction between people, important or common, rich or poor, and in their judgments they exercised the utmost honesty with all. And the same was true of the other administrators of the law.

If it were found that one of them had accepted a gift or misbehaved because of drinking, or if it were felt that he was negligent . . . the other judges themselves would reprehend him harshly. And if he did not correct his ways, after the third time they would have his head shorn. And with great publicity and shame for him they would remove him from office. This was to them a great disgrace. . . . And because one judge showed favoritism in a dispute toward an important Indian against a common man and gave a false account to the lord of Tezcoco, it was ordered that he be strangled and that the trial begin anew. And thus it was done, and the verdict was in favor of the common man.

Aztec Imperialism:
Tlacaelel and Human Sacrifice

by Miguel Leon-Portilla

The seeds of the Conquest of Mexico were laid long before the arrival of Hernan Cortez and his soldiers. The man who sowed and even nurtured these fatal seeds was the fifteenth-century Aztec *political* figure, Tlacaelel: the great counselor and *Cihuacoatl* to Itazcoatl, Motecuhzoma I [Montezuma I], and Axayacatl. With cold-blooded brilliance, his religio-political machinations re-established human sacrifice as a means of intimidating conquered tribes into facile obedience. The coronation of Axayacatl alone devoured 20,000 victims, all for the glory of Huitzilopochtli. It was this disdain for human life—so characteristic of Tlacaelel himself—that eventually turned the tribes of Mexico into an alliance with Cortez against Tenochtitlan.

A haunting question remains concerning the depth of Tlacaelel's religious belief: what motivated him to thrust a minor tribal god, Huitzilopochtli, into the supreme echelon of the Aztec pantheon, usurping the place and mythology of Quetzalcoatl (who was ironically avenged through the Conquest) and even becoming identified with the Sun God Himself? Miguel León y Portilla states that without exaggeration, Tlacaelel "may be called the creator of the mysticomilitaristic conception of the Aztecs as 'people of the Sun.' " This much is also clear: Tlacaelel was either a supreme politically motivated atheist or an extreme religious fanatic. Perhaps he was both. The duality of the Aztec universe pierces through history with frightening clarity: for without Tlacaelel, Tenochtitlan would not have achieved greatness; and with him, it fell to inevitable destruction. . . .

Notes by Luis Valdez

It was Tlacaelel who insisted on—perhaps originated—the idea that the life of the Sun, Huitzilopochtli, had to be maintained by the red and precious liquid. Human sacrifice undoubtedly existed before the Aztecs, but was probably not practiced as frequently. Perhaps explanation lies in Tlacaelel's ability to convince the various Aztec rulers that their mission was to extend the dominions of Huitzilopochtli, simultaneously preserving the life of the Sun. . . . Construction of a great temple, rich and sumptuous, was begun in honor of Huitzilopochtli, at the suggestion of Tlacaelel, and many victims were sacrificed in his honor. . . .

There shall be no lack of men to inaugurate the temple when it is finished. I have considered what later is to be done. And what is later to be done, it is best to do now. Rather, let a convenient market be sought where our god may go with his army to buy victims and people to eat as if he were to go to a nearby place to buy tortillas . . . whenever he wishes or feels like it. And may our people go to this place with their armies to buy their blood, their heads, and with their hearts and lives, those precious stones, jade and brilliant and wide plumes . . . for the service of the admirable Huitzilopochtli.

Specifying where such a market might be established where the Sun might "buy" his nourishment by means of war, Tlacaelel continued:

This market, say I, Tlacaelel, let it be situated in Tlaxcala, Huexotzinco, Cholula, Atlixco, Tliliuhquitepec, and Tecoac. For if we situate it farther away, in such places as Yopitzinco or Michoacan or in the region of the Huaxtecs, all of which are already under our domination, their remoteness would be more than our armies could endure. They are too far, and, besides the flesh of those barbaric people is not to the liking of our god. They are like old and stale tortillas, because as I say, they speak strange languages and they are barbarians. For this reason it is more convenient that our fair and markets be in the six cities that I have mentioned. . . . Our god will feed himself with them as though he were eating warm tortillas, soft and tasty, straight out of the oven. . . . And this war should be of such a nature that we do not endeavor to destroy the others totally. War must continue, so that each time and whenever we wish and our god wishes to eat and feast, we may go there as one who goes to market to buy something to eat . . . organized to obtain victims to offer our god Huitzilopochtli.

In this manner, the *guerra florida,* "flowery war," was viewed by Tlacaelel. Not only did he introduce reforms in thought and religion, but he also transformed . . . the juridical system, the service of the royal house of Motecuhzoma, the army, and the organization of the merchants. We know little of his artistic knowledge, but history assigns to him the creation of the botanical gardens, including the splendid park of Oaxtepec in present-day Morelos. . . . In this way Tlacaelel led the Aztecs to greatness. Although he was offered the throne after the deaths of Itzcoatl and Mote-cuhzoma, he never accepted. Still it was he who always inspired the plans and ideals of the people of the Sun.

THE COSMOS AND MAN: AZTEC HUMANISM

In the Calmecacs, the academies of the Aztecs, the wise men, the Tlamatinime (The Men with Words), were both poets and philosophers. They believed man was born "faceless": "He is born without an identity; he is born anonymous" (Leon-Portilla). It was the duty of the Tlamatinime "to humanize the will of the people" and "to them he gives a face (an identity)," unlike the "false wise man" who was "a destroyer of faces." The Tlamatinime taught by poetry, asking the cosmic question "Is There Any Truth in Man?" ("Where Are the Roots of Men?", *Pre-Columbian Literatures of Mexico*, Leon-Portilla; "Does Man Possess Any Truth?", "One Day We Must Go," and "Who Am I?", *Aztec Thought and Culture*, Leon-Portilla).

Where Are the Roots of Men?

Where are the roots of men?
Are they real?
No one can know completely

what is Your richness, what are Your flowers,
oh Inventor of Yourself!
We leave things unfinished.
For this I weep,
I lament.
Here with flowers I interweave my friends.
Let us rejoice!
Our common house is the earth.
In the place of mystery, beyond,
is it also like this?
Truly, it is not the same.
On earth: flowers and songs.
Let us live here!

Does Man Possess Any Truth?

Does man possess any truth?
If not, our song is no longer true.
Is anything stable and lasting?
What reaches its aim?

One Day We Must Go

One day we must go,
one night we will descend into the region of mys-
    tery.
Here, we only come to know ourselves;
only in passing are we here on earth.
In peace and pleasure let us spend our lives;
    come, let us enjoy ourselves.
Let not the angry do so; the earth is vast indeed!
Would that one lived forever;
Would that one were not to die!

Who Am I?

Who am I?
As a bird I fly about,
I sing of flowers;
I compose songs,
butterflies of song.
Let them burst forth from my soul!
Let my heart be delighted with them!

THE BLOOD WAS FULFILLED

from the Chilam Balam of Chumayel

Among the Indians of Mexico there were many
prophecies of "the bearded men who (will) come from
the east . . . the man-priest will come; he will bring
the sign of God." The awe of the Conquistadors was
quickly displaced by horror, however, when the "man-
priest" looted and destroyed the cities and temples of
the Aztec and Maya civilizations. In the Mayan Chilam Balam of Chumayel the fulfillment and betrayal of
the prophecy is related. (*The Book of the Chilam
Balam of Chumayel*, edited and translated by Ralph L.
Roys, Carnegie Institute of Washington, 1933; new
edition, Norman, Okla., University of Oklahoma Press,
1967.)

They did not wish to join with the foreigners, nor did they
desire Christianity. They did not know that they would have
to pay tribute. The lords of the birds, the lords of the precious stones, the lords of the carved stones, the lords of the
tigers had always guided them and protected them. One
thousand six hundred years and three hundred years more

and then their life had to come to an end! For they had always known within themselves the length of their days.

The moon, the year, the day and the night, the breath of life were fulfilled and they passed. The blood was fulfilled and came to the place of its rest, as also it had come to its power and its dignity. During their time they had repeated the good prayers; they had sought the lucky days when the good stars watched over them. Then they kept vigil, when the good stars watched over them. Then all was good.

In them there was wisdom. Then was no sin. In them there was holy devotion. Life was wholesome. There was no sickness then; there was no aching of the bones; there was no fever for them; there was no smallpox; there was no burning in the chest; there was no pain in the stomach; there was no consumption. Raised up straight was the body then. It was not thus the foreigners did after they came here. They brought shameful things when they came. Everything was lost in carnal sin. No more lucky days were granted us. This was the cause of our sickness.

> The foreigners made it different
> when they arrived here.
> They brought shameful things
> when they came here . . .
> No fortunate days
> were granted to us then . . .
> This was the cause of our sickness.
> No more fortunate days for us,
> no more just decisions.
> And in the end we lost our vision,
> it was our shame.
> Everything shall be revealed!

DEATH EMERGES FROM LIFE, LIFE EMERGES FROM DEATH

by Domingo Martinez Paredes

In contemporary Mexico, a group of Indianist revivalists have sought modern relevance in the ancient beliefs. Diego Rivera and David Siqueiros gave impetus to this movement in their frescoes and murals. The cosmology of the Maya and duality of the Aztecs have now been uniquely combined in the philosophy of Domingo Martinez Paredes, whose work has found an audience among the young intellectuals of the Chicano movement in the Southwest. (*El Popol Vuh Tiene Razon: Teoria sobre la Cosmogonia Preamericana* by Domingo Martinez Paredes, Mexico, Editorial Orion, 1968; this selection translated by Luis Valdez.)

We feel it is necessary to present some ideas as to why we think about the possibility that the Mayan COSMOGONY approaches or approximates ATOMIC THEORY. Of course, we are not trying to "assert emphatically" that the Mayans were the precursors of atomism, or that they had cyclotrons, nor that they discovered the nuclear bomb. Here we merely disclose "something" that may have been a simple speculation, or indeed—why not?—a study, an investigation by *pre-American*° man. Given that the Greek philosophers arrived at the ATOM by intuition, as the ultimate manifestation of MATTER, could not the Mayans, who knew more about cosmic life than those same Greeks, have arrived at similar or superior conclusions? Denying such an intellectual capacity to the men who were capable of inventing ZERO, creating MAIZE, having the mathematical concept of the Absolute Being . . . seems absurd, especially since the Popol Vuh is

° The emphasis is ours—eds.

telling us this by expounding the theory of the NEBULOUS. And if this theory has nothing to do with ENERGY and the CONDENSATION OF MATTER, what made possible the presence of the planet EARTH? . . .

Once comparisons are established between what the Mayan COSMOGONY explains and what the (modern) savants explain about what is supposed to be happening in that cellular microcosmos in which a true WHIRLWIND of energy operates and multiplies ELEMENTS that are gyrating at fantastic velocities precisely as a condition for the MOLECULE to conserve its form, and those forces upon being bombarded and separated release energy that may be captured and utilized for good or evil, then we establish a certain comparison between that and what the Popol Vuh explains about TEPEU, GUCUMATZ, and HURACAN: does it not seem that a certain similarity exists between both phenomena? But we would not clarify anything if we continue on the level of simple suppositions; to clarify, we need to explain some ideas about ATOMIC THEORY. . . .

When we grasp the significance of what is called the ATOM (and how human intelligence was able to discover what it contains and to unchain the ENERGY that every particle entraps) that once was believed to be INDIVISIBLE and which represents the BASIC POINT of something unimaginable, since it constitutes the formidable pool whose liberated contents form the atomic bomb . . . then we understand that it is MATTER, identified with ENERGY in the atomic theory, that has exploded in the nuclear reaction. Every body is constituted of ATOMS that are organized energy of ELECTRONIC particles, i.e., the electrons, ions, cations, neutrons that MOVE in orbits of special form for every element, that is, for every simple body: e.g., Hydrogen, ION H; Oxygen, ION O; Iron, ION FE; Gold, ION AU; these ELEMENTS obey GEOMETRIC forms maintained by true patterns of ENERGY

VIBRATIONS. The ATOMS make up UNITS OF MOLECULES which, in turn, form bodies. This nuclear composition is subject to a MOVEMENT. These electrons are not found in a fixed position, since they gyrate around the nucleus at tremendous velocities. It is calculated that the electron closest to the nucleus gyrates at a velocity of no less than 2,200 km. per second—a true WHIRLWIND, a HURRICANE—HURACAN— of energy. . . .

Physics and chemistry enter into all of the compositions that result in that atomic disintegration, matter converted into ENERGY, and here we encounter a great truth that the Mayan philosophers pronounced in ingenious form: DEATH EMERGES FROM LIFE; LIFE EMERGES FROM DEATH, and this magnificent sentence is proven when human intelligence rips away the secret of the ATOM . . . from there men have taken the terrifying forces disposed to annihilate all life on the planet once they are LIBERATED. And all of the PROPITIOUS ELEMENTS to elaborate the lethal weapon are provided by NATURE since nothing has been brought from other worlds, other planets, in order to complete that DESTRUCTION; instead, ALL has been taken from the physical and chemical elements combined by nature herself or provoked by man in a moment in which his passion and his spirit, distorted by war, by the desire of conquest, of dominion of man over man, provoked that march toward the field of investigation which permitted him to surprise that frightful secret of LIFE AND DEATH, that IMPRISONED ENERGY of the atoms . . . of that marvelous phenomenon that the MAYAN COSMOGONY describes upon speaking of CREATION, of what HURACAN did, as the Heart of Heaven: AGITATING, DISPERSING in the gigantic WHIRLWIND that CLOUD to RECAPTURE IT GRAIN BY GRAIN afterward and ENTRAP IT in molecules, changing them by CONDENSATION into MATTER that became the planet Earth, the plants, the animals.

And so totally opposed actions are presented for human consideration. The Mayan philosophers arrived at the marvelous conclusion that ENERGY was the origin of MATTER, and that of the atomic theory, that has been used to EXTRACT NUCLEAR ENERGY from MATTER. These have been proven by modern science.

It has been thousands of years since Mayan man spoke in a sincere and clear manner through his COSMOGONY in deific symbols, how CREATION WAS LIKE A MIST, LIKE A CLOUD, LIKE A CLOUD OF DUST, in which HURACAN was the symbol of electricity, since he was the thunderbolt and lightning in the midst of the CREATIVE WHIRLWIND produced by the CLASH OF ELEMENTS in the process of CONDENSATION. And this is clearly explained when we know that METEOROLOGY is principally a physical science, although one with chemical implications, because the LIGHTNING synthesized hydrogen and oxygen in order to create WATER electrochemically: H_2O. Also, when the ELECTRIC FORCES OF LIGHTNING synthesize or analyze, they SEPARATE or DISSOCIATE the ELEMENTS.

And in the drama of the CREATION as told in the Popol Vuh, we must note that there is no mention of WATER, as such, nor of AIR, neither HA nor IK'; and not until the DISAPPEARANCE OF THE WHIRLWIND, that Cloud, that Mist, that Cloud of Dust, does the Earth emerge within the WATER. The Aristotelian ideas of the elements of nature are better explained in the Popol Vuh, since it explains the origin of the planet Earth, BASED ON ENERGY, with the presence of chemical and physical elements: TEPEU, GUCUMATZ, AND HURACAN—HEART OF HEAVEN, HEART OF EARTH.

In this form, so simple and sincere, our *pre-American*° ancestors left us a scientific note concerning ENERGY and MATTER. The Popol Vuh continues to make sense.

° The emphasis is ours—eds.

▼▼▼▼▼▼▼▼▼▼▼▼▼▼▼▼▼▼▼▼▼▼

II. THE CONQUEST: FLOWERS AND SONGS OF SORROW

NO, IT IS NOT A DREAM

from the Aztec Codices

In the codices, or "painted books," of the Aztecs the accounts of the Conquest "contain many passages whose dramatic interest is equal to that of the great classical epics" (Miguel Leon-Portilla). On November 8, 1519, when Emperor Motecuhzoma (Montezuma)° and Hernando Cortez met (the date was recorded by the Aztec prince Ixtlilxochitl), their vows of friendship were inscribed with royal graciousness ("We Come as Friends: The Meeting of Motecuhzoma and Cortes," *The Broken Spears: The Aztec Account of the Conquest of Mexico,* edited by Miguel Leon-Portilla, Boston, Beacon Press, 1966), but a somber threnody filled Ixtlilxochitl's account of the slaughter two years later ("The Fall of Tenochtitlan," *The Broken Spears,* by Leon-Portilla).

We Come as Friends:
The Meeting of Motecuhzoma and Cortez

When Motecuhzoma had given necklaces to each one, Cortes asked him: "Are you Motecuhzoma? Are you the

° In English Montezuma is a simplified version of the emperor's true name, which in the language of Nahuatl was pronounced with a glottal stop that sounds something like "cuh," or a coughed-up "k"; so his name was really Motecuhzoma.

king? Is it true that you are the king of Motecuhzoma?"

And the king said: "Yes, I am Motecuhzoma." Then he stood up to welcome Cortes; he came forward, bowed his head low and addressed him in these words: "Our lord, you are weary. The journey has tired you, but now you have arrived on the earth. You have come to your city, Mexico. You have come here to sit on your throne, to sit under its canopy.

"The kings who have gone before, your representatives, guarded it and preserved it for your coming. The kings Itzcoatl, Motecuhzoma the Elder, Axayacatl, Tizoc and Ahuitzol ruled for you in the City of Mexico. The people were protected by their swords and sheltered by their shields.

"Do the kings know the destiny of those they left behind, their posterity? If only they are watching! If only they can see what I see!

"No, it is not a dream. I am not walking in my sleep. I am not seeing you in my dreams. . . . I have seen you at last! I have met you face to face! I was in agony for five days, for ten days, with my eyes fixed on the Region of the Mystery. And now you have come out of the clouds and mists to sit on your throne again.

"This was foretold by the kings who governed your city, and now it has taken place. You have come back to us; you have come down from the sky. Rest now, and take possession of your royal houses. Welcome to your land, my lords!"

When Motecuhzoma had finished, La Malinche translated his address into Spanish so that the Captain could understand it. Cortes replied in his strange and savage tongue, speaking first to La Malinche: "Tell Motecuhzoma that we are his friends. There is nothing to fear. We have wanted to see him for a long time, and now we have seen his face and heard his words. Tell him that we love him well and that our hearts are contented."

Then he said to Motecuhzoma: "We have come to your house in Mexico as friends. There is nothing to fear."

La Malinche translated this speech and the Spaniards grasped Motecuhzoma's hands and patted his back to show their affection for him.

The Fall of Tenochtitlan

On the day that Tenochtitlan was taken, the Spaniards committed some of the most brutal acts ever inflicted upon the unfortunate people of this land. The cries of the helpless women and children were heart-rending. The Tlaxcaltecas and the other enemies of the Aztecs revenged themselves pitilessly for old offenses and robbed them of everything they could find. Only Prince Ixtlilxochitl of Tezcoco, ally of Cortes, felt compassion for the Aztecs, because they were of his own homeland. He kept his followers from maltreating the women and children as cruelly as did Cortes and the Spaniards.

At nightfall the invading forces retired again. Prince Ixtlilxochitl, Cortes and the other captains agreed to complete the conquest of the city on the following day, the day of St. Hippolytus the Martyr. Shortly after daybreak, they approached the place where the remnants of the enemy were gathered. Cortes marched through the streets, but Ixtlilxochitl and Sandoval, the captain of the brigantines, approached by water. Ixtlilxochitl had been informed that Cuauhtemoc and his followers were assembling for escape in their canoes.

The anguish and bewilderment of our foes was pitiful to see. The warriors gathered on the rooftops and stared at the ruins of their city in a dazed silence, and the women and children and old men were all weeping. . . .

Cuauhtemoc, seeing that the enemy was overtaking him, ordered the boatman to turn the canoe toward our barkentine and prepare to attack it. He grasped his shield and *macana* and was determined to give battle. But when he realized that the enemy could overwhelm him with crossbows and muskets, he put down his arms and surrendered.

Garcia de Olguin brought him before Cortes, who received him with all the respect due to a king. Cuauhtemoc placed his hand on the Captain's dagger and said: "I have done everything in my power to save my kingdom from your hands. Since fortune has been against me, I now beg you to take my life. This would put an end to the kingship of Mexico, and it would be just and right, for you have already destroyed my city and killed my people." He spoke other grief-stricken words, which touched the heart of everyone who heard them.

Cortes consoled him and asked him to command his warriors to surrender. Cuauhtemoc immediately climbed onto a high tower and shouted to them to cease fighting, for everything had fallen to the enemy. Of the 300,000 warriors who had defended the city, 60,000 were left. When they heard their king, they laid down their arms and the nobles came forward to comfort him. . . .

The siege of Tenochtitlan, according to the histories, paintings and chronicles, lasted exactly eighty days. Thirty thousand men from the kingdom of Tezcoco were killed during this time, of the more than 200,000 who fought on the side of the Spaniards. Of the Aztecs, more than 240,000 were killed. Almost all of the nobility perished: there remained alive only a few lords and knights and the little children.

THE DIRGES

The "trauma of the Conquest" (Dr. Angel Maria Garibay) was voiced in the laments of the Aztecs. Slaughter, rapine, and disease brought by the Conquistadors had decimated the ancient kingdoms. It was estimated by the Spanish census that two centuries after the Conquest the Indian population of Mexico had fallen from four and a half million to one and a half million. Literally, the world of the Aztecs ended in laments. The first song was written by an unknown Aztec poet Tlaltelulco, in 1528 ("Broken Spears," *The Broken Spears: The Aztec Account of the Conquest of Mexico*, edited by Miguel Leon-Portilla, Boston, Beacon Press, 1962). The second song was probably composed that same year by another unknown Aztec poet and was preserved in *Cantares Mexicanos* by Antonio Penafiel in 1904 ("Flowers and Songs of Sorrow," *The Broken Spears*).

Broken Spears

Broken spears lie in the roads;
we have torn our hair in our grief.
The houses are roofless now, and their walls
are red with blood.

Worms are swarming in the streets and plazas,
and the walls are splattered with gore.
The water has turned red, as if it were dyed,
and when we drink it,
it has the taste of brine.

We have pounded our hands in despair
against the adobe walls,

for our inheritance, our city, is lost and dead.
The shields of our warriors were its defense,
but they could not save it.

We have chewed dry twigs and salt grasses;
we have filled our mouths with dust and bits of adobe;
we have eaten lizards, rats and worms. . . .

Flowers and Songs of Sorrow

Nothing but flowers and songs of sorrow
are left in Mexico and Tlaltelulco,
where once we saw warriors and wise men.

We know it is true
that we must perish,
for we are mortal men.
You, the Giver of Life,
you have ordained it.

We wander here and there
in our desolate poverty.
We are mortal men.
We have seen bloodshed and pain
where once we saw beauty and valor.

We are crushed to the ground;
we lie in ruins.
There is nothing but grief and suffering
in Mexico and Tlaltelulco,
where once we saw beauty and valor.

Have you grown weary of your servants?
Are you angry with your servants,
O Giver of Life?

ALL WARS OF CONQUEST ARE UNJUST

by Father Bartolome de las Casas

The Catholicism of Renaissance Spain was a paradox of "humanist learning" and "religious nationalization" (*Spain in America* by Charles Gibson, New York, Harper & Row, 1966). In spite of the Inquisition, the "Black Legend," and "religious slavery," the Spanish Church early recognized the "immortal soul of the Indians" and in the Law of the Indies persuaded the crown to acknowledge the human rights of the natives. Father Bartolome de las Casas, born in Seville in 1474, exemplified this Catholic humanism. In his writings he condemned not only the excesses of the Conquest, but all conquests ("The Last Judgment," *The Life and Writings of Bartolome de las Casas* by Henry Raup Wagner with Helen Rand Parish, Albuquerque, N. Mex., University of New Mexico Press, 1967), and in his "Twelve Doubts" he was the first advocate of reparations to the oppressed ("The King Must Pay," *The Life and Writings* . . .).

The Last Judgment

All the wars called conquests were and are most unjust and truly tyrannical.

We have usurped all the kingdoms and lordships of the Indies.

The encomiendas or allotments of Indians are most iniquitous, evil per se and therefore tyrannical, as is such a form of government.

All who grant them sin mortally and those who hold them are always in mortal sin and cannot be saved unless they give them up.

The King our lord, whom prosper and keep, with all the power God gave him, cannot justify the wars and robberies against these people, nor the said allotments of encomiendas, any more than the wars and robberies of Turks against Christians can be justified.

All the gold and silver, pearls and other riches, brought to Spain and traded among Spaniards in the Indies—all is stolen, save perhaps a very little that came from the islands and places we have already depopulated.

Those who stole it and today steal it by conquests and allotments or encomiendas, and who participate therein, cannot be saved unless they restore it.

The natives in any or all the regions we have invaded in the Indies have acquired the right to make just war upon us and erase us from the face of the earth, and this right will last until the Day of Judgment.

The King Must Pay

By natural and divine and human law, the Indians—as infidels of the fourth category who never harmed nor were subject to Christians—freely possess and rule their own lands, and no King or Emperor or Pope can make just war upon them.

The papal Bull of Donation was issued solely for the conversion of the Indians and did not dispossess the native lords. Rather, the Spanish kings must pay the costs of this conversion, and they need the free consent of the natives to acquire justly the sovereignty granted them over the Indies.

From the beginning till now [January 1564], Spain's entire invasion and misgovernment of the Indies has been wrong and tyrannical; and from 1510 on, no Spaniard there can claim good faith as an excuse for wars, discoveries, the slave trade, or the munitions business.

IT IS NOT PROPER THAT
THIS BOOK BE PUBLISHED

A Royal Cedula of Philip II

To obliterate the history and culture of the Maya and Aztecs, the Spaniards burned thousands of books. "We burned them all!" rejoiced the Franciscan monk Fray Diego de Landa after the burning of the Maya libraries in 1562; for, he said, the books told "lies of the devil." Fray Bernardino de Sahagun did not agree; he believed the wisdom of the Indians must be preserved. And in 1547, in Tepepulco, Mexico, he began the monumental task of gathering the history and knowledge of the Aztecs from the surviving elders of Motecuhzoma's courts. The church hierarchy in Spain was outraged; in 1577 they prevailed on the king to ban Sahagun's many volumed *Historia General de las Cosas Nueva Espana.* ("It Is Not Proper That This Book Be Published: A Royal Cedula of Philip II," *Aztec Thought and Culture,* Leon-Portilla.)

From letters written in those provinces we have learned that Fray Bernardino de Sahagun of the Order of Saint Francis has composed a Universal History of the most noteworthy things in New Spain. It is an abundant collection of all the rites, ceremonies, and idolatries practiced by the Indians when they were unbelievers, divided into twelve volumes and written in the native language. Although it is understood that the zeal of said Fray Bernardino has been commendable, and that his intention was for the book to bear wholesome fruit, it seems that it is not proper that this book be published or disseminated in those places, for several reasons. We thus command that, upon receiving this Cedula, you obtain these books with great care and diligence; that you make sure that no original or copy of them is left there; and that you have them sent in good hands at the first opportunity to our Council of Indies in order that they may be examined there. And you are warned absolutely not to allow any person to write concerning the superstitions and ways of life of these Indians in any language, for this is not proper to God's service and to Ours.

III. THE GENESIS OF THE CHICANOS

THE JOURNALS OF NUNEZ CABEZA DE VACA

In 1528 the first expedition of Spaniards came to the Southwest—not Conquistadors, but four barefoot and naked men, one of whom was the black Moorish slave Estavancio. Survivors of the ill-fated Narvaez expedition that had been shipwrecked on the Texas shore, the ragged crew was led by Nunez Cabeza de Vaca. For eight years they walked through the deserts. On reaching Mexico City, de Vaca wrote to the king of the humility he had learned from the Indians ("The Thoughts That Clothe the Soul of a European," from *Interlinear to Cabeza de Vaca: His Relation of the Journey, Florida to the Pacific, 1528–1536*, edited by Haniel Long, Buffalo, N.Y., Frontier Press, 1969) and of the arrogance of the Conquistadors whom he met on the way ("Our Countrymen, These Slave Catchers," from *Interlinear to Cabeza de Vaca*).

The Thoughts That Clothe the Soul of a European

Somewhere on that coast a handful of us crawled ashore, and were fed and tended by kindly Indians till we regathered nervous vitality for the hopeless voyage to Cuba. We stript and launched the boat, first putting our clothes aboard her. But a great comber [wave] capsized the rotten heavy hulk, imprisoning and drowning three of us. The others emerged mother-naked on the beach, shivering in the November wind of that overcast afternoon.

The Indians came back and found us as naked as they were, and our barge gone, and in tears. They sat down beside us and cried, too. I cried all the harder, to think people so miserable had pity for us. . . . That evening, for fear we might die on the way, the Indians made fires at intervals along the path to their village, warming us at each fire. That night and many nights after we slept beside them on the oyster shells which floor their huts, wrapt in hides against the cold winds from the sea.

While we were subjects of your Majesty, we had everything life offers, and now we had nothing. To understand what it means to have nothing one must have nothing. No clothing against the weather might appear the worst. But for us poor skeletons who survived it, it was not.

The worst lay in parting little by little with the thoughts that clothe the soul of the European, and most of all of the idea that a man attains his strength through dirk and dagger, and serving in your Majesty's guard. We had to surrender such fantasies till our inward nakedness was the nakedness of an unborn babe, starting life anew in a womb of sensations which in themselves can mysteriously nourish. Several years went by before I could relax in that living plexus for which even now I have no name; but only when at last I relaxed, could I see the possibilities of a life in which to be deprived of Europe was not to be deprived of too much.

Our Countrymen, These Slave Catchers

Then [came] a day when Indians said that on the night before they had watched the Christians from behind some trees. They saw them take along many persons in chains.

Our countrymen, these slave-catchers, were startled when they saw us approaching. Yet almost with their first words they began to recite their troubles. For many days they had been unable to find Indians to capture. They did not know what to do, and were on the point of starvation. The idea of enslaving our Indians occurred to them in due course, and they were vexed at us for preventing it. . . .

Your Majesty will remember my indignation in my first narrative, that Christians should be so wicked, especially such as had the advantages of being your subjects. I did not at the time understand the true source of my indignation. I do now, and I will explain it. In facing these marauders I was compelled to face the Spanish gentleman I myself had been eight years before. It was not easy to think of it. Andres and Alonso agreed that it was not easy. What, your Majesty, is so melancholy as to confront one's former un-thinking and unfeeling self? . . .

At first I did not notice other ways in which our ancient civilisation was affecting me. Yet soon I observed a certain reluctance in me to do good to others. . . . If a man need a cloak, we do not give it to him if we have our wits about us; nor are we to be caught stretching out our finger in aid of a miserable woman. Someone else will do it, we say. Our communal life dries up our milk: we are barren as the fields of Castile. We regard our native land as a power which acts of itself, and relieves us each of exertion. While with them I thought only about doing the Indians good. But back among my fellow countrymen, I had to be on guard not to do them positive harm. If one lives where all suffer and starve, one acts on one's own impulse to help. But where plenty abounds, we surrender our generosity, believing that our country replaces us each and several. This is not so, and indeed a delusion. On the contrary the power of maintaining life in others, lives within each of us, and from each of us does it recede when unused. It is a concentrated power. If you are not acquainted with it, your Majesty can have no inkling of what it is like, what it portends, or the ways in which it slips from one. In the name of God, your Majesty.

FROM THE EDGE OF THE MOUNTAINS TO THE STONES AND SAND IN THE RIVERS
The Proclamation of Don Juan de Onate

Often called "the first Spanish settler" of New Mexico, Don Juan de Onate led a caravan of 130 families and several thousand head of livestock across the Rio Grande in 1598. Onate was born in Mexico, an *Espagnol mexicano,* and wedded to the great-granddaughter of Emperor Motecuhzoma. His religious mysticism and his reverence for the earth was expressed in the proclamation he nailed to a tree, with a cross, before crossing the Rio Grande into New Mexico's Jornada del Muerto (the Journey of the Dead) on Ascension Day, April 30, 1598. ("How Onate Took Possession of the Newly Discovered Land," from *A History of New Mexico* by Gaspar Perez de Villagra, Chicago, Rio Grande Press, 1962.)

In the name of the most holy Trinity, and of the eternal Unity, Deity, and Majesty, God the Father, the Son, and the Holy Ghost, three persons in the one and only true God, who by His eternal will, almighty power and infinite wisdom, rules, directs, and governs from sea to sea, from one end to another, as the beginning and the end of all things; in whose hands are the eternal pontificate, the priesthoods, empires, kingdoms, principalities, dynasties, republics, elders, minors, families, and all persons, as the eternal priest, emperor, and king of all; king of emperors, lord of lords, creator of the heavens and the earth, the elements, the birds and fishes, animals, and plants, and of all creatures, spiritual and corporeal, rational and irrational, from the highest cherubim to the lowliest ant and the smallest butterfly; and in honor of His most holy and venerable Mother, the holy Virgin Mary, our lady, gate of heaven, ark of the covenant, in whom the manna of heaven, the divine rod of justice, and the arm of God, and His law of grace and love were placed, as the mother of God, sun, moon, north star, and guide and advocate of all human kind; and in the name of the most blessed Father, Saint Francis, image of Christ, God in body and soul, His royal ensign and patriarch of the poor whom I adopt as my patrons, advocates, and intercessors that they may intercede with God himself, that all my thoughts, deeds, and actions may be directed to the service of His infinite majesty to increase the number of the faithful and the extension of the holy mother church, and to the service of the most Christian of kings, Don Philip, our lord, pillar of the Catholic faith. May God guard him many years for the crown of Castile, and the prosperity of his kingdoms and provinces. . . .

Be it known, therefore, that in the name of the most Christian king, Don Philip, our lord, the defender and protector of the holy church, and its true son, and in the name of the crown of Castile, and of the kings that from its glorious progeny may reign therein, and for my said government, I take possession, once, twice, and thrice, and all the times I can and must, of the actual jurisdiction, civil as well as criminal, of the lands of the said Rio del Norte, without exception whatsoever, with all its meadows and pasture grounds and passes. And this possession is to include all other lands, pueblos, cities, villas, of whatsoever nature now founded in the kingdom and province of New Mexico, and all the neighboring and adjoining lands thereto, with all its mountains, valleys, passes, and all its native Indians who are now included therein.

I take all jurisdiction, civil as well as criminal, high as well as low, from the edge of the mountains to the stones and sand in the rivers, and the leaves of the trees.

THE VOW OF POVERTY

by Father Jeronimo de Zarate Salmeron

"And not only have the settlers of New Mexico not enjoyed riches, but the scourge of God has been on them always, and they are the most oppressed and enslaved people in the world," wrote Father Jeronimo de Zarate Salmeron in 1626. In the arid Southwest, the naturalness of Indian life and the humility of the Franciscan monks were integrated into what the Franciscan historian Fray Angelico Chavez has called "a philosophy of simplicity." The seventeenth-century missionary, Fray Zarate Salmeron, describes its origins. (*Relaciones: An Account of Things Seen and Learned by Father Jeronimo de Zarate Salmeron*, translated by Alicia Ronstadt Milich, Boston, Horn & Wallace, 1966.)

In all the provinces the people are pleasant, settled, and they helped the Spaniards with their supplies and appeased their hunger, and they helped them to build their houses, and everything else, and of course they gave their allegiance to His Majesty. Concerning the quality of the land, it is cold and healthful, with the climate of Spain. Its healthfulness is attested by the fact that the Indians reach the age of more than 100 years, for I have seen them. It is a fertile land with fine crystalline waters and much major and minor livestock is raised, and if it were not for the greediness of the governors who have taken them all out to sell, the fields would now be covered with them. A great supply of wheat and corn and all kinds of vegetables is gathered. As far as saying that it is poor, I answer that there never has been discovered in the world a land with more mines of every quality, good and bad, than in New Mexico. . . . More than anything else, there are mines, and there is no place that does not have them; the Spaniards who are there are the poor ones who have no means to work them and they have less enthusiasm, and are enemies of all kinds of work, and in the land we have seen silver, copper, lead, magnet stone, copperas, alum, sulphur, and turquoise mines that the Indians work with their talent, since for them, they are diamonds and precious stones. The Spaniards who are there laugh at all this; as long as they have a good supply of tobacco to smoke, they are very contented, and they do not want any more riches, for it seems as if they had made the vow of poverty, which is a great deal for being Spaniards, who because of greediness for silver and gold will enter Hell itself to obtain them.

SONORA IS OUR MOTHERLAND

by Arnold R. Rojas

In Old Mexico the villagers of the "Borderlands" were thought of as uncouth, at best, and *barbaros* (barbarians), at worst—both the Spaniards and the Indians. The villagers of northern Mexico and what is now the southwestern United States reacted with fierce independence and provincial pride to the governments of Imperial Spain, and later the Republic of Mexico. So-

nora, which once embraced much of California and
Arizona, was and still is a center of these feelings. (*The
Vaquero* by Arnold R. Rojas, Santa Barbara, Cal.,
McNally & Loftin, 1964.)

I do not come from an "Old Spanish Family." Old Spanish
families are an invention of the gringos. . . .

My father was of Sonoran stock and of clerical people,
that is to say, there had been priests and nuns in his family.
. . . My mother's mother, Rita Ruiz, was born in Los Angeles and had come to Rancho San Pasqual (which is now
the city of Pasadena) after the gringos had dispossessed her.
. . . My grandmother's parents had come from the old colonial town of Alamos, Sonora, while Don Pablo Sola, the last
Spanish governor of California, was still in office.

There were two Spaniards from Extremadura, and two
Yaqui women on my father's side of the family, two Cata-
lans and two Maya women on my mother's side. So if I now
and then take a dig at the Spaniards or at the Indians, I am
exercising an inalienable right. I am speaking about my own
family.

The Spanish spoken in California was a dialect of old Cas-
tilian which was brought by the Catalonian soldiers who accompanied the missionaries into this part of New Spain.
Even today the paisano counts his money in *reales*. Often
the vaquero adopted terms to suit the occasion or circumstance. The word *nuqueador*—one who slaughtered cattle
by stabbing them at the base of the neck, the *nuca*—is an
example.

Many of the words used here had gone out of use in Spain
long before the gringos came in 1846. From that time the
paisano's language began to die out in California. Few of
the old people could read or write, but spoke a clean, simple
Spanish; and it was not until the gringos erected schools and

the paisano sent his children to them that the young ones began to interlard their speech with English words. Those who retain fragments of Spanish today speak it with a Yankee accent.

The children did not have a chance. In the hands of that peerless civilizer, the Yankee schoolmarm, they were taught the three R's—and to think in English. It is safe to say that the school, more than the barbed-wire fence or the plowing up of the range, was responsible for the decline of the vaquero.

The *Californiano*—writers on California to the contrary —called himself a *Sonoreno*. I have heard third or fourth generation descendants of members of the De Anza expedition (Don Jose Jesus Lopez for one) say, *"Nosotros somos Sonorenos. Sonora es nuestra tierra."* We are Sonorans. Sonora is our motherland.

THE SIMPLE PASTORAL LIFE (TEXAS)
by Americo Paredes

In the fertile valley of the Lower Rio Grande the *tejanos* had herds of millions of cattle, which later formed the basis of the Texas cattle industry. The region was so prosperous that at the time of the American Revolution the town of Reynosa was as large as Philadelphia. The people, like those throughout the rural Southwest, were stubbornly individualistic; so much so that the Mexican government disarmed them before the outbreak of the War against Mexico. Professor Americo Paredes of the University of Texas describes the vibrant social and economic life of the *tejanos* under Mexican rule. (*With His Pistol in His Hand: A Border Ballad and Its Hero* by Americo Paredes, Austin, Tex., University of Texas Press, 1958.)

The Lower Rio Grande Border is the area lying along the river, from its mouth to the two Laredos. A map, especially one made some thirty or forty years ago, would show a clustering of towns and villages along both river banks, with lonely gaps to the north and to the south. This was the heart of the old Spanish province of Nuevo Santander, colonized in 1749 by Jose de Escandon. . . .

The Indians seem to have given little trouble. They were neither exterminated in the English manner, nor enslaved according to the usual Spanish way. They lived in the same small towns as the Spanish settlers, under much the same conditions, and were given a measure of self-government.

By 1775, a bare six years after the founding of Nuevo Santander, there were only 146 soldiers still on duty among 8,993 settlers. There were 3,413 Indians in the towns, not counting those that still remained in a wild state. In succeeding generations the Indians, who began as vaqueros and sheepherders for the colonists, were absorbed into the blood and the culture of the Spanish settlers. Also absorbed into the basically Spanish culture were many non-Spanish Europeans, so that on the Border one finds men who prefer Spanish to English, who sometimes talk scornfully about the "Gringos," and who bear English, Scottish, Irish, or other non-Spanish names.

By 1755 towns had been founded near the present site of Laredo—the only north-bank settlement of the time—and at Guerrero, Mier, Camargo, and Reynosa on the south bank. The colonists were pushing into the Nueces-Rio Grande area in search of pasturage for their rapidly increasing herds. Don Blas Maria Falcon, the founder of Camargo, established a ranch called La Petronila at the mouth of the Nueces at about this time.

By 1835 there were three million head of livestock in the

Rio Grande-Nueces area, according to the assessments of the towns along the Rio Grande. Matamoros, founded near the river mouth in 1765 by people from Reynosa, had grown into the metropolis of the colony with 15,000 inhabitants. The other riverbank towns, though not so large, were correspondingly prosperous. The old province of Nuevo Santander was about to emerge from almost a century of isolation and growth, when war in Texas opened the period of border strife.

Most of the Border people did not live in the towns. The typical community was the ranch or the ranching village. Here lived small, tightly knit groups whose basic social structure was the family or the clan. The early settlements had begun as great ranches, but succeeding generations multiplied the number of owners of each of the original land grants. The earliest practice was to divide the grant among the original owner's children. Later many descendants simply held the land in common, grouping their houses in small villages around what had been the ancestral home. In time almost everyone in any given area came to be related to everyone else. . . .

The simple pastoral life led by most Border people fostered a natural equality among men. Much has been written about the democratizing influence of a horse culture. More important was the fact that on the Border the landowner lived and worked upon his land. There was almost no gap between the owner and his cowhand, who often was related to him anyway. The simplicity of the life led by both employer and employee also helped make them feel that they were not different kinds of men, even if one was richer than the other.

Border economy was largely self-sufficient. Corn, beans, melons, and vegetables were planted on the fertile, easily irrigated lands at the river's edge. Sheep and goats were also raised in quantity. For these more menial, pedestrian tasks the peon was employed in earlier days. The peon was usually a *fuereno,* an "outsider" from central Mexico, but on the Border he was not a serf. *Peon* in Nuevo Santander had preserved much of its old meaning of "man on foot." The gap between the peon and the vaquero was not extreme, though the man on horseback had a job with more prestige, one which was considered to involve more danger and more skill.

THE VAQUERO

by Arnold R. Rojas

The mythology of the West is largely northern Mexican in origin. As the word cowboy is a translation of *vaquero,* so his life-style and equipment—lariat (from *la reata*), chaps (from *chaparreras*), rodeo, ramada, adobes, patios, ranches (from *ranchos*)—reveal his origins. But the *vaquero* was not simply Mexican, as Sr. Rojas indicates: "The blood of caballeros, bullfighters, Jews, Moors, Basques, and Indian heroes ran in the *vaquero's* veins." Arabian horses from Spain and Indian bravado created the character paradoxically re-created by Will Hart and John Wayne. In a sense, the *vaquero* was the ancestor of the contemporary Chicano. (*The Vaquero,* by Rojas.)

In speaking of the origins of the vaquero we must not forget to mention in passing the first horses to come from Spain. They came with the first Armada, and were such faithful, heroic horses and played so important, though innocent, a part in the conquest, that a list of them should be included in all books on the American horse. There were sixteen mares and stallions, mostly grays and sorrels, in the original conquest of the New World.

Bernal Diaz gives their colors and the names of the most outstanding. Two were of the famed Valenzuela breed of Spain. There were *El Harriero*, the Driver; *Motilla*, Little Tuft; *El Romo*, the Roman Nosed One; *La Rabona*, the Rat-tailed One (she was the "good gray mare" of Velasquez de Leon). *La Rabona* was probably an appaloosa because the rat, or stub tail, is a characteristic of that type of horse, and prevails on the appaloosa from Tierra del Fuego through South America, Mexico and western United States to Canada. Diaz called her a gray; but there are many shades of gray and some of the appaloosas are a mottled color which closely approaches, or is, gray. The "blunt old soldier" says of *La Rabona*, "when the battle was going against the Spaniards and the men were weakening, Velasquez de Leon would appear on his good gray mare, and the men would take courage."

The Indians' belief that man and horse were one (the centaur myth) was true in the sense that there existed a perfect affinity between horse and rider. This affinity has never been better exemplified than in the Conquest, where man and horse made one terrible creature.

The fabulous amount of gold which the Spaniards took from the New World had at least one benefit to posterity. It brought to America the finest horseflesh to be found in Europe. These horses were shipped to New Spain and in time sired the great-hearted mustang, the vaquero's horse. True, before the vaquero went out of existence he rode horses of many breeds and mixtures, but the mustang was the perfect horse for working cattle—sure-footed, utterly loyal, tireless, patient and brave. He was the welder of two continents, a worthy descendant of the Andalusian barb.

The vaquero while working cattle rode hard and was hard on horses, but he never abused them to make a spectacle. The way the vaquero went about taming a horse was not always gentle, but he was not deliberately cruel. He had applied his military riding to the herding of cattle and the roping of grizzly bears, Tule elk, and wild hogs. He never overestimated the intelligence of his mustang, and had studied the degree to which a horse could be taught. He had learned that patience and repetition were the only means to success in teaching the horse. He never asked the animal to do more than could be expected of it.

The blood of caballeros, bullfighters, Jews, Moors, Basques, and Indian heroes ran in the vaquero's veins. He was a strange mixture of races. He admired his Iberian father, but sided and sympathized with his raped Indian mother. If food was short he fed his horse before he fed his wife. Though often a strange contradiction, he was, without doubt, the most interesting man in the New World.

He was a descendant of the old conquerors, and retained the language of Spain. In living the free life of the nomad he imitated the Spaniard in the trappings of his horse, and the Indian in his abode. He spent his wealth on silver-mounted bits and spurs and often left his home destitute of necessities. He slept on the ground, but rode a silver-mounted saddle. He may not have combed his hair, but his horse's mane was trimmed, with one tuft for a colt and two for a bridle horse. He was named after the saint's day on which he was born; it was often Jesus who was the most proficient in stealing cattle.

The vaquero would lie on the ground with his saddle for a pillow even though the rain was falling, and sleep without a word of complaint, yet he would grumble when his saddle-blankets got wet. Wet saddle-blankets make a horse's back sore.

The vaquero's way of life gave him virtues which do not exist in this modern day, and at this distant time no man can judge a man of that era. His life was hard. He would stand shivering in the early morning cold, holding a cup of coffee in his shaking hand, then sit a horse all day in the driving sleet, chilled to the bone. He would ride from dawn to dusk in a cloud of alkali dust, his tongue parched and swollen, with rippling water in a mirage shimmering in the distance, with visions of all the water he had ever drunk or seen wasted haunting his memory, for memory plays queer, cruel tricks. The want of water was the vaquero's greatest hardship in the burning heat of a San Joaquin Valley summer. He often rode in a daze with visions of springs of cool water bubbling out of the pine-scented Sierra, of canals of water from which he had never bothered to drink. And when he came to drink it would more than likely be out of a reeking waterhole that contained the putrid remains of some animal.

But there was another side. A matchless sky overhead. An expanse of wild flowers that spread over the great valley like a purple carpet, so vast that a day's ride would take one only to the middle of it. The bold, brooding Sierra standing in grim outline that stretched away to the northern horizon. A wild chase down a mountainside in the fall when the air is like wine and life is good. The feel of a good horse between one's knees as he sweeps and wheels around a herd of restless cattle. The evening campfire when men broil *costillas*, ribs, on chamiso root coals, and gather around to tell tales of long ago, of Murrieta, Vasquez, and Garcia.

THE GOLD MINERS

by Francisco Salazar

The "discovery" of gold by Francisco Lopez on his *rancho* in the San Fernando hills near Los Angeles in 1841 began the "gold rush" of Sonoran miners, from northern Mexico. They were also among the first to reach the Sierra Nevada gold fields seven years later, when gold was re-"discovered" at Sutter's mill. And it was they who taught the Yankees how placer mining was done (*placero* was derived from the Spanish "to give pleasure," but came to mean "where gold is found"), and how to pan for gold (using a *beata* in the old Mexican-Indian way). In Hornitos, California, a gold-rush ghost town, the memory of the Sonoran "forty-oners" and "forty-niners" was preserved by Francisco Salazar, who died in 1962 at the age of 92. (*Hornitos*, by Francisco Salazar, as told to W. B. Secrest, Fresno, Cal., Saga West Publishing.)

Sometime in 1848 or 1849 a group of Mexican travelers stopped along what later became known as Burns Creek in the foothills of north central California. Who these people were is not known, but they were probably fresh from Mexico and heading into the gold country. They set up camp near the creek bed, and rested for a few days before pushing on into the gold country. Other Mexican families stopped here also, and gradually a tiny temporary tent and brush hut camp was established. No one stayed very long in the camp, but there were generally 20 or 30 Mexicans in the area for one reason or another. The ground was very hard and rocky in this vicinity, and whenever someone died they were buried in above ground tombs made of rock and adobe. To the unknowing, these graves resembled little, outdoor ovens, and even the Mexicans referred to them as "hornitos," the Spanish word for little ovens. By 1850, there were perhaps a dozen hornitos scattered along the hills by the creek.

About two miles east of this Mexican camp the town of Quartzburg was established early in 1850. The camp was rich in placer gold, and miners flocked to the area to pluck their share of the Mother Lode riches. As so often happened, a great many of the arrivals at Quartzburg were gamblers, thieves, outlaws and Mexican fandango hall girls. Consequently it was not long before the rough element was pretty much in control of things. The most prominent local citizen was Colonel Thorn, who had enacted some of the first mining laws of the region. He decided to act before things got out of control, and one night he led a local vigilance committee through the gambling dives and saloons and rounded up all of the camp's undesirables, mostly Mexicans. These early days were hard times, and men quickly learned that only stern measures would protect decent citizens from the riff-raff that inhabited a frontier community. There was no law at Quartzburg, and little more at neighboring Mariposa or Agua Fria. The undesirables were herded to the outskirts of the camp and given a simple ultimatum: "Leave town tonight or be hung." Needless to say, the outcasts lost no time in making themselves scarce.

The unwanted group made their way over the hills to the Mexican camp on Burns Creek, and decided to spend a few days there while pondering what to do next. They could have moved on to another town immediately, but the ever increasing gringos made them think twice. Within a few days something happened that resolved everything. One of the outcasts was walking along the creek, when something gleaming caught his eye. Upon examination it was discovered that the whole area was rich in surface, or placer, gold. No one had thought to prospect here before, and the inhabitants of the camp had been walking over fortunes every day. When some of the gold was traded for supplies at nearby Mariposa, there was a general rush to the area, and soon a tent camp of sizeable proportions had flowered into existence.

As the town grew it was always referred to as the place of the little ovens, because of the above ground graves that sprinkled the area, and so Hornitos was born.

The town grew rapidly, and since the earliest settlers there were Mexicans, the camp was fashioned after the Spanish motif with a central plaza, and narrow streets lined with predominantly adobe structures with 3 foot thick walls.

Hornitos was a rich town and it attracted people like a magnet. A man named John Studebaker stopped here in 1853 and worked as a blacksmith. When he had saved enough money, he moved on to Hangtown and went into the wheelbarrow business. Later he was to return to South Bend, Indiana, and become the largest of 5000 wagon makers in the country.

Soon there developed a great variety of establishments in Hornitos to suit the varying needs of the miners. Reeb's butcher shop was located on the plaza by 1852, as was the High Tone saloon. The first fraternal lodge was La Junta, a Mexican organization established in 1850. Rosie Martinez had built her two story adobe Fandango Hall by 1851, where any of the baser needs of man could be obtained. The Cassaretto store was also established in 1851. At the east end of town a growing Chinese neighborhood housed numerous opium dens and gambling halls.

In these earliest years, building materials were hard to come by as there was no good timber or sawmills in the vicinity. With the advent of mining to the area, the hard, rocky ground could be penetrated and some of the earliest saloons and fandango halls were built underground. My great-uncle, Zacharias Gonzales, built the first underground fandango hall in the early 1850's and also a blacksmith shop in nearby Indian Gulch. There were six of these underground fandango halls that lined the road leading to the plaza. They were all pretty much the same inside with tiles or hard packed earth for a floor and about 25 by 40 feet in size. The walls were plastered lime with wood paneling about 4 feet up from the floor. An orchestra pit was located generally in the corner, and two whale oil lamps hung from a stout beam in the ceiling. . . .

My mother, Mrs. Alice Virginia Meagher Salazar Glazier, at the time of her death, was the oldest resident who had been born in Hornitos. She passed away on May 31, 1962. It was from her that I learned so much first hand information of the old town and its colorful inhabitants; and it was she who patiently encouraged me in my quest for the story of old Hornitos. Her brothers were Dan Meagher, an early stage driver, Alex Meagher, a mine foreman and geologist, and Fred Meagher, a prominent cattleman and local butcher.

Hornitos was a fabulously wealthy town, and when the placers were worked out, shafts and mines were dug for the quartz gold riches below the surface. Wells Fargo opened their office here in 1853, and for a time $40,000.00 a day was shipped from this first express office in the county. There are records of nuggets weighing as much as 34 pounds being found in this locality.

But life wasn't all blood and gold in old Hornitos, and the Mexican origins of the town were manifested in numerous

sports and activities which kept alive the Spanish traditions
of the people. Bull and bear fights were exciting and spectacular as the chained animals fought to the death amid
cheering and betting crowds. Cock fights were also popular
as was the furious chicken race known as La Carrera del
Gallo. This time honored Mexican sport was liable to be the
feature attraction at any of the local festivities. The game
consisted of tying a ten dollar gold piece to the leg of a
chicken, then burying the hapless fowl, leaving just the head
exposed. Entry fees were then charged to anyone who
wanted to enter the contest, the object being to try and
snatch the chicken from the ground by the neck while gal-
loping past him on a horse. When one of the gaily garbed
Mexican miners or vaqueros succeeded in grabbing the
squalling chicken, the other riders then pursued him, trying
to snatch the rooster and the purse from his grasp. It was
great sport for everyone (except the chicken) and the crowd
indulged in a great deal of yelling and betting.

The women, in their quiet, civilizing way, contributed
much to the color and pioneer spirit of old Hornitos. . . .
Dona Calendaria was a very religious woman, and an
early settler in Hornitos. It was she who kept alive the
quaint Mexican customs through the years, but with her
death in 1903, some of the Spanish traditions of the town
died also. For many years she would place lighted candles
on the early settlers' graves on All Souls Day and similarly
celebrate other Mexican religious holidays. Being a devout
Catholic and very patriotic, she would always display her
large Mexican flag on the occasions of the death of Queen
Victoria, Lincoln and Garfield.

I remember taking part in some of these old Mexican customs when I was just a boy growing up among the crum-

bling ruins of Hornitos. One celebration I particularly remember was the "Burning of Judas" on the last day of Lent
each year. The night before the occasion, all of the children
of the town roamed through the streets picking up any personal property that could be found. The next day, "Judas," a
stuffed dummy, was placed astride a burro and paraded
through the town. The burro was led to the plaza where his
"will" was read, bequeathing all of the previously stolen
property to the original owners. Then, ceremoniously and
with squeals of delight from the children, the dummy
"Judas" was burned.

By the time Hornitos was incorporated as a city in 1870,
it was already beginning to show signs of fading as a principal town of the Mother Lode country. At its zenith in the
early 1860's, Hornitos had a population of nearly 15,000
people and boasted of 12 hotels and 36 saloons. But at last
the old days were gone and with the passing of the extensive
mining operations in the locality, the old town began the
slow process of depopulation and deterioration that was the
fate of so many of the gold rush communities. My mother
grew up here in the 1870's and '80's and often remarked to
me that there was little to hold people here, even then. A
comparison can be made in the fact that by 1896, only two
saloons were operating in the town.

THE SHEEPHERDERS

by Fabiola Cabeza de Baca

Sheepherders once ranged from the valley of the Rio
Grande, in Texas, to the deserts of California, to the
mountains of Montana. In the nineteenth century the
de Baca family, of New Mexico, alone had flocks of

one million sheep on the Llano Estacado (the Staked
Plains). Although the sheepherders lost out to the cat-
tlemen in such battles as the Lincoln County War,
their singular life contributed a resilience and strength
to the Raza character—as shown in the reminiscences
of Fabiola Cabeza de Baca, a descendant of the patrons of the Llano. (*We Fed Them Cactus* by Fabiola
Cabeza de Baca, Albuquerque, N. Mex., University of
New Mexico Press, 1954.)

In 1840, the sheep owners started sending herders with
their flocks into the *Ceja* and the *Llano*, and the Hispanos
continued to prosper in the sheep industry for more than
half a century.

In those days a man had to be courageous to face the
many dangers confronting lonely living far from the popu-
lated areas, yet there seems to have been no lack of men
who were willing to follow the herds for the employers, the
patrones. In feudal times, there were many poor people who
became indebted to the *ricos*, and the rich were never at a
loss to find men to be sent with flocks of sheep. Then, of
course, herding was one of the few kinds of employment
available in New Mexico. If a man became indebted to a
rico, he was in bond slavery to repay. Those in debt had a
deep feeling of honesty, and they did not bother to question
whether the system was right or wrong. Entire families
often served a *patron* for generations to meet their obligations.

If the flock of the *patron* ran into thousands, he employed
a *mayordomo*, or manager, and several overseers, called *caporales*. The *caporal* was in charge of the herders, and had
to see that the sheep were provided proper quarters in the
different seasons. He furnished the sheep camps with provisions, and it was his duty to make sure that water was available for the *partidas* under the care of each herder. A *par-

tida usually consisted of a thousand head of sheep. The *caporales* worked under the *mayordomo,* or directly under the *patron* if no manager were employed.

I can remember my paternal grandfather's sheep camps and the men who worked for him. They were loyal people, and as close to us as our own family. They were, every one of them, grandfather's *compadres,* for he and grandmother had stood as sponsors in baptism or marriage to many of their children.

Lambing season was a trying one, since the range was extensive. This happened in the early spring, and the weather on the Llano can be as changeable as the colors of the rainbow. If the season was rainy, it went hard with the sheep and many lambs were lost. If there had been a dry spell the year before, the ewes came out poorly and it was difficult for the mothers bringing in young lambs. Sheep raising was always a gamble until the day when feed became plentiful with the change in transportation facilities.

In order to save ewes and lambs during a cold spell, the herders built fires around the herds. The fires were kept burning day and night until better weather came to the rescue. Quite often the *patrones* and their sons, who might have just come back from Eastern colleges, helped during lambing.

Shearing the sheep was done in the summer and there were professional shearers who went from camp to camp each year. This was a bright spot in the life of the herders, for then they had a touch of the outside world. Among the shearers and herders there were always musicians and poets, and I heard Papa tell of pleasant evenings spent singing and storytelling, and of *corridos* composed to relate events which had taken place. These poets and singers were like the troubadours of old. The *corridos* dealt with the life of the people in the communities and ranches; they told of unrequited love, of death, of tragedies and events such as one reads about in the newspapers today.

The sheepherder watched his flock by day, traveling many miles while the sheep grazed on the range. As his flock pastured, he sat on a rock or on his coat; he whittled some object or composed songs or poetry until it was time to move the flock to water or better pasture. Many of the *corridos* are an inheritance from the unlettered sheepherder. At night he moved his flock to camp, a solitary tent where he prepared his food and where he slept. If there were several camps close to each other, the herders gathered at one tent for companionship.

In winter the sheepherder's life was dreary. Coming into his old tent at night, he had to prepare for possible storms. The wood for his fire might be wet, and with scarcely any matches, perhaps only a flint stone to light it, his hands would be numb before he had any warmth. He might not even have wood, for in many parts of the Llano there is no wood, and cowchips had to serve as fuel.

He went to sleep early to the sound of the coyote's plaintive cry, wondering how many lambs the wolves or coyotes might carry away during the night. The early call of the turtle dove and the bleating of lambs were his daily alarm clock, and he arose to face another day of snow, rain, or wind. Yet he always took care of his sheep, and I have never known any mishap due to the carelessness of the herder. The *caporales* traveled on horseback from camp to camp in all kinds of weather to make sure that all was well with the herders and the flocks.

I knew an old man who worked for my maternal grandmother for many years. Often I accompanied my grandmother to the sheep camp on the Salado, and I always came back with a feeling of loneliness. Yet, at camp, the old man always seemed happy. If he was not at camp when we arrived, we found him by listening for his whistle or singing in the distance. When I think about the herders on the endless Llano, I know that they are the unsung heroes of an industry which was our livelihood for generations.

THE CAMPESINOS

by Raymond Barrio

> In the beginning the men and women of La Raza were wedded to the earth by hunger and religion. "The last divine Aztec emperor Cuauhtemoc (Guatemotzin) was murdered and his descendants were put to work in the fields. We are still in the fields of America," writes Luis Valdez, director of El Teatro Campesino de Aztlan. Now the patron and the peon have been replaced by agri-business and the farm worker, but the ethos of their love and hate of the earth remains. Raymond Barrio, a California novelist, depicts the life of the contemporary *campesino*, and in doing so evokes ancient ties. (*The Plum, Plum Pickers* by Raymond Barrio, New York, Harper & Row, 1972.)

Dawn.
Outside, the coolest night.
Outside, the soft, plush, lingering sheen of nightlight.
Within his breezy air-conditioned shack Manuel lay half asleep in the middle of the biggest apricot orchard in the world, nothing but apricot trees all around, in one of a long double row of splintered boards nailed together and called a shack. A migrant's shack. He struggled to come awake. Everything seemed to be plugged up. A distant roar closed in steadily. He awoke in a cold sweat. He sat up abruptly in the cold darkness.

The roar grew louder and louder. He leaned forward, hunched in his worn, torn covers, and peered through the grimy window. A huge black monster was butting through trees, moving and pitching about, its headlights piercing the armor of night, then swinging away again as the roaring lessened. Manuel smiled. The roar of a tractor. He rubbed the sleep from his eyes. He stretched his aching arms and shoulders. He thought of Lupe and the kids back in Drawbridge.

On the very brink of the full onslaught of summer's punishing heat, with the plums and pears and apricots fattening madly on every vine, branch, bush, and limb in every section of every county in the country, pickers were needed right now immediately on every farm and orchard everywhere and all at once. The frantic demand for pickers increased rapidly as the hot days mounted. That sure looked good out there. What a cool job that was. Driving a tractor at night. Maybe he could get Ramiro to teach him to drive one.

Manuel well knew what his physical energy was.

His physical energy was his total worldly wealth.

No matter how anxious he was to work, he did have his limit. He had to rest his body. The finger joint he'd injured still hurt. He missed Lupe's chatter. He'd signed up with that shrewd contractor, Roberto Morales, that shrewd, fat, energetic contratista, manipulator of migrating farm workers, that smiling middleman who promised to deliver so many hands to the moon at such and such a time at such and such an orchard at such and such a price, for such a small commission. A tiny percentage. Such a little slice. Silvery slavery—modernized.

Roberto Morales, an organization man, was a built-in toll gate. A parasite. A collector of drops of human sweat. An efficiency expert. Had he had not been Mexican, he would have made a fantastic capitalist, like Turner. He was Turner upside down. Sucking blood from his own people. With the help and convenient connivance of Turner's insatiable greed.

The agricultural combine's imperative need to have its capital personally plucked when ripe so as to materialize its honest return on its critical investment in order to keep its executives relaxed in blue splendor in far-off desert pools, was coupled to the migrant workers' inexorable and uncompromising need to earn pennies to fend off stark starvation.

Good money.

Good dough.

Good hard work.

Pick fast.

Penny a bucket.

Check off.

Get the count right.

Cotsplumsprunespeachesbeanspeas.

Pods.

The seed of life.

And:—don't complain. . . .

Manuel lay back in the blackness. As the darkness receded and the light of day started creeping imperiously across its own land, he thought that these powerful orchard land owners were awfully generous to give him such a beautiful hostel to stop in overnight. The skylight hotel. There the land stood. A heaving, sleeping mother earth. A marvelous land. Ripening her fruit once again. Once more. Ripening it fatly and pregnantly for the thousandth time. It must be plucked said the wise man. For it cannot hang around on limbs a minute extra. At no man's convenience. As soon as the baby's ready. Lush and full of plump juices. Hugging its new seed around its own ripeness. The plum and the cot and the peach and the pear must plummet again to earth. Carrying the seed of its own delicate rebirth and redestruction back home to earth again. A clever mother earth who in her all-but-unbelievable generosity was capable of giving man fivefold, tenfold the quantity of fruit he could himself eat, five times fifty, and yet the pickers were never paid enough to satisfy their hunger beyond their actual working hours. And yet it was called a moral world. An ethical world. A good world. A happy world. A world full of golden opportunities. Manuel simply couldn't figure it out.

What was wrong with the figures?

Why was mother earth so generous? And men so greedy?

You got twenty-five cents a basket for tomatoes. A dollar a crate for some fruit. You had to work fast. That was the whole thing. A frantic lunatic to make your barely living wage. If you had no rent to pay, it was OK. You were ahead, amigo. Pay rent, however, stay in one place, and you couldn't migrate after other easy pickings. The joy of working was looking over your dreams locked to hunger.

Manuel studied the whorls in the woodwork whirling slowly, revealed in the faint crepuscular light penetrating his shack. His cot was a slab of half-inch plywood board twenty-two inches wide and eight feet long, the width of the shack, supported by two two-by-four beams butted up against the wall at both ends beneath the side window. The shack itself was eight by twelve by seven feet high. Its roof had a slight pitch. The rain stains in the ceiling planks revealed the ease with which the rain penetrated. Except for two small panes of glass exposed near the top, most of the window at the opposite end was boarded up. A single, old, paint-encrusted door was the only entry. No curtains. No interior paneling. Just a shack. A shack of misery. He found he was able to admire and appreciate the simplicity and the strength of the construction. He counted the upright studs, level, two feet apart, the double joists across the top supporting the roof. Cracks and knotholes aplenty, in the wall

siding, let in bright chinks of light during the day and welcome wisps of clear fresh air at night. The rough planking of
the siding was stained dark. The floor was only partly covered with odd sections of plywood. Some of the rough
planking below was exposed, revealing cracks leading down
to the cool black earth beneath. A small thick table was
firmly studded to a portion of the wall opposite the door. A
few small pieces of clear lumber stood bunched together,
unsung, unused, unhurried, in the far corner. An overhead
shelf, supported from the ceiling by a small extending per-
pendicular arm, containing some boxes of left-over chemi-
cals and fertilizers, completed the furnishings in his temporary abode.

It was habitable.

He could raise his family in it.

If they were rabbits.

The first rays of a brute new day clinked in through the
small rectangle of panes. The ray hovered, then peaked,
then rested on the covers pushed up by his knees. He recalled his mountain trips with his uncle to the great forbid-
ding barrancas near Durango in Central Mexico, and stopping to rest in the middle of the wild woods, and coming
unexpectedly upon a crumbling, splintered hulk of a shack
that was all falling apart. It barely gave them shelter from
the sudden pelting storm they were trying to escape, he as a
young frightened boy, but shelter it was—and how beautiful
that experience was, then, for they were free, daring, adventurers, out there in that wilderness, alone and daring, with
nothing between them and God's own overpowering nature,
alone. They belonged to nothing. To no one. But themselves. They were dignity purified. No one forced them to
go or stay there. They were delighted and grateful to the
shack. For the protection it afforded them. Though it was
hardly more than a ratty pile of splinters. Far worse than

this one he was now occupying . . . but also somehow far more beautiful in his memory.

And now. Here he was. Shut up in this miserable shack. So sturdily built. Thinking how it sickened him inside because it was more a jail cell than a shelter. He didn't care how comfortable and convenient the growers made the shacks for him. They were huts of slavery. What he wanted was an outlet for his pride. A sudden fierce wave of anger made him want to cross the shack with his fists. There had to be some way to cross the ungulfable bridge. Why was necessity always the bride of hunger? To be free . . . ah, and also to be able to eat all one wanted. My heart, mi corazon, why did work always have to blend with such misery? The welcome warmth of the sun's early rays, penetrating more, warmed his frame. But it was a false, false hope. He knew it. The work that lay ahead of him that day would drain and stupify and fatigue him once again to the point of senseless torpor, ready to fall over long before the work day was done. And that fatigue wasn't merely so bad to bear as the deadly repetitious monotony of never changing, never resting, doing the same plucking over and over and over again. But he had to do it. He had no choice. It was all he could do. It had to be done if he wanted the money. And he had to have the money, if he wanted to feed his family. The brain in his arms was his only capital. Not very much, true, but it was the only sacrifice he could offer the money gods, the only heart he could offer on the pyramid of gold.

His life. La gran vida.

Wide awake now, fully refreshed, his whole body lithe and toned, Manuel was ashamed to find himself eager to start in work, knowing that he would do well, but ashamed because he could think of nothing he would rather do more. The final step.

The final the final the final the final the final the final step.

To want to work oneself to death. A la muerte. It wasn't the work itself that bothered him. It was the total immersion, the endless, ceaseless, total use of all his energies and spirit and mind and being that tore him apart within. He didn't know what else he was good for or could do with his life. But there had to be something else. He had to be something more than a miserable plucking animal. Pluck pluck pluck. Feed feed feed. Glug glug glug. Dressing quickly, rolling up his blanket roll and stuffing it into a corner to use again that night, Manuel stepped coolly out into the morning sweetness and breathed the honeyscented humidity rinsing air rising from the honied soil, and joined the thickening throng of his fellow pluckers milling about the large open barn serving as a cookout. Feeding all the pickers was another of the fat man's unholy prerogatives, for he cheated and overpriced on meals too. Roberto Morales, the fat man, the shrewd contratista, was a bully man, busily darting his blob about, exhorting his priceless pickers to hurry, answering questions, giving advice, in the cool half-light, impatiently, pushing, giving orders. Manuel, in order to avoid having to greet him, scowled at his toes when Roberto came trouncing by, saying, "Apurense, compañeros, hurry, hurry, hurry, amigos." Sure. Amigos. Si. Si. Frens. They all gulped their food down hurriedly, standing. Just like home. Paper plates, plastic cups. Wooden spoons. And bits of garbage flying into large canisters. Then in the still cool nightlike morning air, like a flood of disturbed birds, they all picked up their pails and filed into the orchard.

The apricots were plump.

Smooth.

A golden syrupy orange.

Manuel popped two into his mouth, enjoying their cool natural sweetness after the bitter coffee. He knew he could not eat too many. His stomach muscles would cramp. Other pickers started pulling rapidly away from him. Let them. Calmly he calculated the struggle. Start the press sure, slow, and keep it going steady. Piecework. Fill the bucket, fill another, and still another. The competition was among a set of savages, as savage for money as himself, savages with machetes, hacking their way through the thickets of modern civilization back to the good old Aztec days, waiting to see who'd be first in line to wrench his heart out. Savage beasts, eager to fill as many buckets as possible in as short a time as possible, cleaning out an entire orchard, picking everything in sight clean, tons of fruit, delivering every bit of ripe fruit to the accountants in their cool air-conditioned orifices.

The competition was not between pickers and growers. It was between pickers—Jorge and Guillermo.

Between the poor and the hungry, the desperate, and the hunted, the slave and the slave, slob against slob, the depraved and himself. You were your own terrible boss. That was the cleverest part of the whole thing. The picker his own bone picker, his own willing built-in slave driver. God, that was good! That was where they reached into your scrotum and screwed you royally and drained your brain and directed your sinews and nerves and muscles with invisible fingers. To fatten their coffers. And drive you to your coffin. That sure was smart. Meant to be smart. Bookkeepers aren't dumb. You worked hard because you wanted to do that hard work above everything else. Pickfast pickhard pickfurious pick pick pick. They didn't need straw bosses studying your neck to see if you kept bobbing up and down to keep your picking pace up. Like the barn-stupid chicken, you drove yourself to do it. You were your own money monkey foreman, monkey on top of your own back.

You over-charged yourself.

With your own frenzy.

Neat.

You pushed your gut and your tired aching arms and your twitching legs pumping adrenalin until your tongue tasted like coarse sandpaper.

You didn't even stop to take a drink, let alone a piss, for fear you'd get fined, fired, or bawled out.

And then, after all that effort, you got your miserable pay.

Would the bobbing boss's sons stoop to that?

His fingers were loose and dexterous now. The plump orange balls plopped pitter patter like heavy drops of golden rain into his swaying, sweaty canvas bucket. His earnings depended entirely on how quickly he worked and how well he kept the pressure up. The morning sun was high. The sweet shade was fragrant and refreshing and comfortable under the leafy branches. The soil too was still cool and humid. It was going to be another hot one.

There.

Another row ended.

He swung around the end of the row and for a moment he was all alone, all by himself. He looked out far across the neighboring alfalfa field, dark green and rich and ripe. Then he looked at the long low Diablo Range close by, rising up into the misty pale blue air kept cool by the unseen bay nearby. This was all his. For a flowing, deceptive minute, all this rich, enormous terrain was all his. All this warm balmy baby air. All this healthful sunny breeze. All those hills, this rich fertile valley, these orchards, these tiled huertas, these magnificent farms all, all his . . . for his eyes to feast upon. It was a moment he wished he could capture forever and etch permanently on his memory, making it a part of living life for his heart to feast joyously on, forever. Why couldn't he stop? Why? Why couldn't he just put the bucket down and open his arms and walk into the hills and merge himself with the hills and just wander invisibly in the blue?

What Manuel couldn't really know was that he was completing yet another arc in the unending circle that had been started by one of his Mexican forebears exactly two hundred years before—for even the memory of history was also robbed from him—when Gaspar de Portola, hugging the coastline, nearing present-day San Francisco, climbed what is now Sweeney Ridge, and looked down upon San Francisco's magnificent land-locked Bay, overlooking what is now the International Airport.

Both don Gaspar and don Manuel were landlords and landless at precisely the same instant of viewing all this heady beauty. And both were equally dispossessed. Both were also possessed of a keen sense of pride and natural absorption with the ritual and mystery of all life. The living that looked mighty good in a flash to Manuel lasted a good deal longer for don Gaspar whose stumbling accident swept him into the honored and indelible pages of glorious history.

Manuel was now a mere straw among the enormous sludge of humanity flowing past, a creature of limb and his own driving appetites, a creature of heed and need. Swinging around another end run he placed his ladder on the next heavy limb of the next pregnant tree. He reached up. He plucked bunches of small golden fruit with both hands. He worked like a frenzied windmill in slow motion. He cleared away an arc as far as the circumference of his plucking fingers permitted. A living model for da Vinci's outstretched man. Adam heeding God's moving finger. He moved higher. He repeated another circle. Then down and around again to another side of the tree, until he cleared it, cleared it of all visible, viable, delectable, succulent fruit. It was sweet work. The biggest difference between him and the honey-gathering ant was that the ant had a home.

Several pickers were halfway down the next row, well in advance of him. He was satisfied he was pacing himself well. Most of the band was still behind him. The moving sun, vaulting the sky dome's crackling earth parting with its bronzing rays, pounded its fierce heat into every dead and living crevice. Perspiration poured down his sideburns, down his forehead, down his cheek, down his neck, into his ears, off his chin. He tasted its saltiness with the tip of his dry tongue. He wished he'd brought some salt tablets. Roberto Morales wasn't about to worry about the pickers, and Manuel wasn't worried either. Despite the heat, he felt some protection from the ocean and bay. It had been much, much worse in Texas, and much hotter in Delano in the San Joaquin valley and worst of all in Satan's own land, the Imperial Valley.

No matter which way he turned, he was trapped in an endless maze of apricot trees, as though forever, neat rows of them, neatly planted, row after row, just like the blackest bars on the jails of hell. There had to be an end. There had to be. There—trapped. There had to be a way out. Locked. There had to be a respite. Animal. The buckets and the crates kept piling up higher. Brute. He felt alone. Though surrounded by other pickers. Beast. Though he was perspiring heavily, his shirt was powder dry. Savage. The hot dry air. The hot dry air sucking every drop of living moisture from his brute body. Wreck. He stopped and walked to the farthest end of the first row for some water, raised the dented dipper from the brute tank, drank the holy water in great brute gulps so he wouldn't have to savor its tastelessness, letting it spill down his torn shirt to cool his exhausted body, to replenish his brute cells and animal pores and stinking follicles and pig gristle, a truly refined wreck of an animal, pleased to meetcha. Predator.

Lunch.

Almost too exhausted to eat, he munched his cheese with tortillas, smoked on ashes, then lay back on the cool ground for half an hour. That short rest in the hot shade replenished some of his humor and resolve. He felt his spirit swell out again like a thirsty sponge in water. Then up again. The trees. The branches again. The briarly branches. The scratching leaves. The twigs tearing at his shirt sleeves. The ladder. The rough bark. The endlessly unending piling up of bucket upon box upon crate upon stack upon rack upon mound upon mountain. He picked a mountain of cots automatically. An automaton. A beast. A ray of enemy sun penetrated the tree that was hiding him and split his forehead open. His mind whirred. He blacked out. Luckily he'd been leaning against a heavy branch. His feet hooked to the ladder's rung. His half-filled bucket slipped from his grasp and fell in slow motion, splattering the fruit he'd so laboriously picked. To the ground. Roberto happened by and shook his head. "Whatsamatter, can't you see straight, pendejo." Manuel was too tired even to curse. He should have had some salt pills.

Midafternoon.

The summer's fierce zenith passed overhead. It passed. Then dropped. It started to light the ocean behind him, back of the hills. Sandy dreams. Cool nights. Cold drinks. Soft guitar music with Lupe sitting beside him. All wafting through his feverish moments. Tiredness drained his spirit of will. Exhaustion drained his mind. His fingers burned. His arms flailed the innocent trees. He was slowing down. He could hardly fill his last bucket. Suddenly the whistle blew. The day's work was at last ended.

Ended!

The contratista Roberto Morales stood there.

His feet straddled. Mexican style. A real robber. A Mexican general. A gentlemanly, friendly, polite, grinning, vicious, thieving brute. The worst kind. To his own people. Despite his being a fellow Mexican, despite his torn, old clothing, everyone knew what kind of clever criminal he was. Despite his crude, ignorant manner, showing that he was one of them, that he'd started with them, that he grew up with them, that he'd suffered all the sordid deprivations with them, he was actually the shrewdest, smartest, richest cannibal in forty counties around. They sure couldn't blame the gueros for this miscarriage. He was a crew chief. How could anyone know what he did to his own people? And what did the gueros care? So the anglo growers and guero executives, smiling in their cool filtered offices, puffing their elegant thin cigars, washed their clean blond bloodless dirtless hands of the whole matter. All they did was hire Roberto Morales. Firm, fair, and square. For an agreed-upon price. Good. How he got his people down to the pickings was no concern of theirs. They were honest, those gueros. They could sleep at night. They fulfilled their end of the bargain, and cheated no one. Their only crime; their only soul crime indeed was that they just didn't give a shit how that migratory scum lived. It was no concern of theirs. Their religion said it was no concern of theirs. Their wives said it was no concern of theirs. Their aldermen said it was no concern of theirs. Their—

Whenever Roberto Morales spoke, Manuel had to force himself not to answer. He had to keep his temper from flaring.

"Now," announced Morales at last, in his friendliest tone. "Now. I must take two cents from every bucket. I am sorry. There was a miscalculation. Everybody understands. Everybody?" He slid his eyes around smiling, palms up.

The tired, exhausted pickers gasped as one.

Yes. Everyone understood. Freezing in place. After all that hard work.

"Any questions, men?"

Still grinning, knowing, everyone realizing that he had the upper hand, that that would mean a loss of two or three dollars out of each picker's pay that day, a huge windfall for Morales.

"You promised to take nothing!" Manuel heard himself saying. Everyone turned in astonishment to stare at Manuel.

"I said two cents, hombre. You got a problem or what?"

"You promised."

The two men, centered in a huge ring of red-ringed eyes, glared at each other. Reaching for each other's jugular. The other exhausted animals studied the tableau through widening eyes. It was so unequal. Morales remained calm, confident, studying Manuel. As though memorizing his features. He had the whole advantage. Then, with his last remaining energy, Manuel lifted his foot and clumsily tipped over his own last bucket of cots. They rolled away in all directions around everyone's feet.

Roberto Morales' eyes blazed. His fists clenched. "You pick them up, Gutierrez."

So. He knew his name. After all. For answer, Manuel kicked over another bucket, and again the fruit rolled away in all directions.

Then an astonishing thing happened.

All the other pickers moved toward their own buckets still standing beside them on the ground awaiting the truck gatherer, and took an ominous position over them, straddling their feet over them. Without looking around, without taking his eyes off Manuel, Roberto Morales said sharply, "All right. All right, men, I shall take nothing this time."

Manuel felt a thrill of power course through his nerves.

He had never won anything before. He would have to pay for this, for his defiance, somehow, again, later. But he had shown defiance. He had salvaged his money savagely and he had earned respect from his fellow slaves. The gringo hijos de la chingada would never know of this little incident, and would probably be surprised, and perhaps even a little mortified, for a few minutes. But they wouldn't give a damn. It was bread, pan y tortillas out of his children's mouths. But they still wouldn't give a single damn. Manuel had wrenched Morales' greedy fingers away and removed a fat slug of a purse from his sticky grasp. And in his slow way, in his stupid, accidental, dangerous way, Manuel had made an extravagant discovery, as Don Gaspar had also made two centuries before, in almost exactly the same spot. And that was—that a man counted for something. For men, Manuel dimly suspected, are built for something more important and less trifling than the mere gathering of prunes and apricots, hour upon hour, decade upon decade, insensibly, mechanically, antlike. Men are built to experience a certain sense of honor and pride.

Or else they are dead before they die.

THE BRACEROS: A MAN WHO HAS LOST HIS DOCUMENTS HAS LOST HIS RIGHTS. HE IS ABOLISHED.

by Ernesto Galarza

In the years before World War I there was hardly a border. Merely a line. The annual reports of the U.S. Commissioner of Immigration did not list Mexicans as "aliens," for the labor of these men was needed to lay the railroads, dig the mines, and build the cities of the Southwest. More recently the *Bracero* Program was established by the governments of Mexico and the United States (in the 1950's) for the legal importation of hundreds of thousands of farm workers, outside the quota, to work in the fields from Texas to California. Ernesto Galarza, who has organized farm workers and worked in the fields, sorrows for these "invisible men

and women" who have no rights beyond a slip of
paper—a "green card." (*Merchants of Labor: The
Mexican Bracero Story*, by Ernesto Galarza, Santa Barbara, Cal., McNally & Loftin, 1964.)

The line between complaining and agitation was a thin one.
Braceros feared to be called *"huelguistas"* (from *huelga*,
meaning strike). It was almost always a portent of trouble.
As a committee of Catholic bishops found in Texas, men
who complained were called communists and sent home.
Those who criticized administration or probed for information were likely to earn the title of tools of communism. Secretary of Labor James P. Mitchell, in a letter addressed to a
national magazine in 1958, lamented such criticism, holding
that it was nothing more than ready-made propaganda for
the use of communist countries.

An additional deterrent to discontent was the possibility
that a carping *bracero* could be picked up by the Immigration Service on complaint of the employer or the Department of Labor for agitating. In 1957 the Service requested
that the Department identify men who caused unrest
among their fellows. Department officials construed this to
mean behavior having internal security implications, and it
was understood that investigation of complaints did not ex-
clude the possibility of discovering subversive acts or intentions, and that these should be reported to the Department
of Justice. A worker who was cross-examined by an Employer Service Representative, an immigration officer and
an association field man could not help being impressed.

Constraint was also placed on the *bracero* by the practice
of many employers of collecting the passports and other
documents of the aliens on their arrival in camp. In exchange the employer issued an identification card which
could be presented to police officers as evidence of legal

entry into the United States. The card was valid only in the area of employment. On one worker's card was the typical notation: "He does not have his passport as it was picked up when his contract was renewed." Director Brockway of the Department of Labor submitted this matter for discussion with the RFLOAC in February 1957, expressing his concern over the deprivation of workers of their official papers. To the *bracero* this was a matter of great importance. In the briefing he received at El Centro it was strongly impressed on him that he was employed by a designated association in a limited area described in his contract, and that if he were found outside of that area without proper identification he could be arrested and deported. Deprived of his "papeles" he was like the immigrant described by Vaillant: "A man who has lost his documents has lost his rights. He has no legal existence. He is abolished."

The mental state of the *bracero* was not one that would buck him up in the face of these deliberately imposed handicaps. In four cases out of ten he was illiterate. His chief concern from the day he arrived on the job was to have his brief contract renewed, for it was quickly obvious to him that his earnings over so short a time would not be enough to meet his debts and leave him a surplus of dollars. His personal expenses in obtaining a contract included his living costs en route to the selection center, and probably payments to venal Mexican officials. More than likely he had borrowed at heavy rates of interest to finance his way. If he harbored any notion of skipping he was aware that his contract would not be renewed. As the peso fell in value from 4.5 to 12 to the dollar the possible loss to him in case of dismissal and repatriation was multiplied. In the life of the barracks and the field gang he was an individual, detachable unit. The circle of his trust and confidence was small. Only with some luck he might find himself in the same camp with fellow workers from his home district, his *rancheria, municipio* or *ejido.*

These were the subjective effects of isolation as the *bracero* experienced it. His fears were not born when he signed up as a managed migrant. They came from a lifetime experience of poverty and authoritarianism as a Mexican rural proletarian. This was his cultural inheritance, so deeply ingrained that it seemed almost a racial trait. Such fears were not allayed by anything he experienced when he became a ward of an association and an official bureaucracy too alien for him to understand, and too powerful to resist. . . .

The restraints placed on the Mexicans which set them apart from the national free labor market were defended by commercial farmers as necessary safeguards on behalf of domestic harvesters, and as a barrier to infiltration by aliens of industrial crafts and service trades. The progress of domination showed how ineffective those safeguards were, and infiltration of unauthorized occupations was not prevented. The insulation of the aliens served other purposes. It guaranteed that the *bracero* would be there when called. It prevented labor pirating. It was the remedy for the annoying habit of domestic seasonal laborers of moving from field to field as the picking became thinner in order to catch the peaks—"creaming the crops" as it was called.

One evening in the fall of 1958 a group of twenty Mexicans held a prayer meeting in their barracks near the town of Soledad. The cots had been cleared from one end of the bunk house. On an empty tomato box standing on end there was a figurine of the Virgin of Guadalupe, attended by a sputtering circle of candle stubs set in tin cans. There was no priest present. An elderly *bracero* clasping a rosary of brown beads led the service. Those who had not joined it sat quietly on the beds or stood along the walls of the room.

The responses of the kneeling worshippers rumbled softly in the air staled by warm bodies and soiled clothes. The stagnant gloom, spiced by the flicker of the candles, centered in the bright blue mantle, the pink face and the golden halo of the illumined Virgin. When the service ended and the lights were turned on, the leader explained that the men had been asking for divine intercession for more work than the three or four hours a day they were getting, for the removal of a harsh foreman and for the renewal of their contracts. Asked why they did not appoint a committee to deal with the employer on these matters, the *bracero* replied: "We did, last week, but our leader was taken to the association the next day and he has not returned."

WITH THE COMING OF THE BARBWIRE, CAME HUNGER: FOLK-LORE OF THE TEXAS-MEXICAN VAQUERO

by Jovita Gonzales

"Great cattle corporations" began buying up the ranges in the last half of the nineteenth century. Soon they would turn "Western cattle-raising into a monopoly," wrote Baron Ferdinand von Richtofen in his *Cattle Raising on the Plains of North America* (1885). With the coming of the cattle empires, came the barbed wire. And, "with the coming of the barbwire, came hunger," wrote Jovita Gonzales, a historian and folklorist of the *tejanos*. It meant the end of the trail for the wandering and independent vaquero, so lovingly eulogized by Mrs. Gonzales. ("Folk-Lore of the Texas-Mexican Vaquero" by Jovita Gonzales, from *Texas and Southwestern Lore*, edited by J. Frank Dobie, Austin, Tex., Texas Folklore Society.)

It is hardly conceivable that in this era of publicity and in this Texas, where every phase of ranching has been more or less popularized, there should exist unknown to the vast majority of Texans and other Americans an extraordinary type of range men. Such, nevertheless, is a fact. Moreover, this distinct and unfamiliar man of the range has been in Texas for nearly two centuries. Texas born and Texas bred, he is considered even by many of those who know him—superficially—as an undesirable alien. He is a product of the state, and loves Texas as his country; yet to Anglo-Americans of a few years' stay in the state he is an outcast. On one side, he descends from the first Americans, the Indians; on the other, his ancestry can be traced to the Spanish adventurer and conquistador. From the mingling of these two races a unique type has resulted, possessing not only salient racial characteristics of both but also certain peculiar traits created by the natural environment and surroundings in which he lives. This composite type is the vaquero of the Texas-Mexican frontier.[*]

First, his inherited traits will be considered. From his Indian ancestor he has inherited a love for freedom and the open prairie, a dislike for law and restraint, a plaintive melancholy that permeates all his actions, and a fatalistic tendency that makes him see the hand of fate guiding and mastering all his efforts. *"Suerte y Mortaja del cielo bajan"* ("Fortune and Death come from above") seems to be his motto in life. When misfortune assails him, the only answer to his problem is a shrug of the shoulder and a *"Si es mi suerte que le voy a hacer?"* ("It is fate: what can I do about it?")

[*] The vaquero is not the aristocratic, landed proprietor of the borderland, but the wandering cowboy whose only possessions are his horse, an unlimited store of legends and traditions, and the love for his *chata*, by which name the Spanish-American cowboy, whether Mexican vaquero or Argentinian gaucho, calls his sweetheart.

From the Spaniard comes a courteous attitude toward women (especially before he is married), a daring spirit of adventure, and a deep rooted love for beauty, particularly music and singing. From the same source he has also inherited a sincere religious feeling, which, mingled with pagan superstitions and beliefs, has added flavor and color to the legends and other forms of folk-lore of the borderland.

Living far from all contact with civilization, he is naturally suspicious of all innovations and newcomers. Every new invention introduced is a check to his freedom. An old vaquero told me once of what to him was paradise: the open prairies with no fences to hinder the roaming of the cattle and the wanderings of the cowboys. *"Cuando vino el alambre, vino el hambre."* ("With the coming of barbwire, came hunger.") In spite of his pessimism, the vaquero is a poet at heart. He sees the beauty of the sage-brush in bloom; the singing of the mocking bird on clear moonlight nights invites him to sing—not songs of joy and happiness but plaintive melodies of unrequited love and tragedies. Like all people who live in close touch with Nature, he understands all the creatures of the woods and interprets them in his fanciful way. . . .

As has already been stated, the vaquero is at heart a religious man; all the wonders of Nature he attributes to a super-natural power. All goodness and beauty come from the Virgin Mary and are part of her. A beautiful sunset is her smile; the blue sky is the blue of her mantle; the rainbow is formed by the tears that she sheds for sinners.

The folk-lore of the Mexican vaquero has the combined charm of the Andalusian lore as told by Fernan Caballero and the quaintness and simplicity of the Indian myth. To understand it is to understand the spirit and the soul of the Mexican people.

LOS CABALLEROS DE LABOR
Y LOS GORRAS BLANCAS

by Fabiola Cabeza de Baca

> By cutting fences and burning barns the Raza sheep-
> herders of New Mexico fought the advance of the cat-
> tlemen, as they had fought the invasion of the Texans
> in 1841 before the War against Mexico. In guerrilla
> warfare the villagers turned against the patrons. On
> the Llano Estacado the opponents organized into Los
> Caballeros de Labor (the Gentlemen of Labor) and the
> night-riding Gorras Blancas (the White Caps) in a
> bloody familial battle whose scars are still visible on
> the Raza body politic of the Southwest. The idyll of
> "the simple pastoral life" had ended. (*We Fed Them
> Cactus*, Cabeza de Baca.)

While I gathered material for this book, I made visits to men
and women who were living in some of the San Miguel
County communities at the time of Los Gorras Blancas.
Among them was Don Luciano Lopez, who is now past
eighty and lives as our neighbor at El Valle.

In 1890, Don Luciano was living at La Concepcion, about
twenty miles east and south of Las Vegas. He tells that the
citizens of the different communities who had sheep on the
Ceja and Llano had banded together for protection against
the building of fences on their grazing lands and to help
each other with crops and farming in the communities.
They called the organization Caballeros de Labor, Gentlemen of Labor.

The party served a good purpose, but as there is always
some bad element in all organizations, politicians saw where
they could gain prestige. In place of protection, this element
wanted common pastures and since the cutting of fences on

public domain had appealed to them, they carried the practice to the farming lands of the communities. These men called themselves El Partido del Pueblo, the People's Party. It became a secret society. They sent anonymous letters to those not in their party, threatening their lives and telling them that their fences would be cut down, their homes and farm buildings set on fire. They carried out their threats. Don Luciano tells how they tore down his father's gristmill and burned his barns and corrals. I remember my grandmother telling us about their fences being cut down at La Liendre. She heard the bandits when they came and she wanted to go out and fight, but Grandfather knew it would be suicide. Next morning miles and miles of their pasture and farmland fences were cut into fragments.

The respectable citizens could not go out at night without a bodyguard and heavily armed. They did not know who the members of the gang were—in many cases they were the same neighbors who had been Los Caballeros de Labor, as it was learned later.

These marauders wore white hoods over their heads when they were out pillaging and came to be known as Los Gorras Blancas, the White Caps.

For protection, the good citizens formed a new party which they called El Partido de la Union, the Union Party, composed of members of both major political parties. They held community meetings and for protection they used a password in order to keep out those from the bad element who might seek admittance. Don Luciano served as secretary to El Partido de la Union in 1891. He tells that there were men whom they never suspected as belonging to El Partido del Pueblo in the new organization and they served as spies for the corrupt politicians. The wife of one of these men once confided to a neighbor about her husband's work. She was found out and was given fifty lashes as punishment.

El Partido de la Union became strong, but in it were many from the other faction. Often they would get rid of the good citizens by breaking up the meetings with the pretense that it was late and proceed to their own haunts to plan their maraudings.

During this time the Republican Party was down. When it was built up again many who had been Republicans left El Partido de la Union and joined the Democratic Party.

In going over grandfather's papers, I found a printed notice which explains El Partido de la Union, and which I have translated:

BE ON THE WATCH
UNION PARTY OF SAN MIGUEL COUNTY!

"Being that a few days ago we have seen some leaflets signed by _____, as president of the Central Committee of the Union party, in which a call is made to the *Republican Unionists,* that they gather in convention on March 17, 1896, with the aim of dissolving the Union which now exists in our county; we wish to make public that said call is without the authority of the Central Committee of said party, which has neither been consulted nor has any Republican Unionist, being merely a wicked treason by means of which the president of the Central Committee of the Union Party desires to seek personal vengeance and for which end he wishes to use the people, who in our concept are not ready to lend themselves as instruments to satisfy personal vengeances for any person whoever he may be.

"Now, since it might happen that the Republican Unionists, who read the communication from said Senor _____, believe that the Union has dissolved and that the adherents of that party will have to follow whatever path they desire, we advise the people in general and our friends in particular that what the *President* exposes is only a trap built by others and signed by him with the aim of breaking up the Union Party, which has been of great service and to form, not a political party, which they boast as the Republican party, but the old Ring so that they may divide among themselves the political offices and to bring to the people displeasure, rivalry, enmity, quarrels and general misery as were prevalent during the rule of some of the officials of a past administration, whose records form a black page in the history of our county.

"Wherefore, those of us who are signed publish the present notice to inform the people in general and to the loyal adherents of the Union Party that today, more than ever, we are ready to remain with the party which we formed of our own free will and with the will of the people, not with the aim of renouncing our political affiliations, but in order to hold back the reins of government from the hands of those who defalcated it, the protectors of all evil and political usurpers and in order to place it in the hands of honest and upright men.

"The reasons which motivated this declaration from us are here exposed and in conclusion we appeal to the patriotism of all the San Miguel County citizens to cooperate with us in upholding the Union Party which has to this day given us enduring results and thereby establishing, as everyone knows, peace and harmony in our county.

Very respectfully,"

There are forty-nine signatures to this paper, among them those of two of my uncles and many of our relatives and friends from both major political parties.

From the Gorras Blancas grew up another menace to the citizens of San Miguel and the surrounding counties and that was Vicente Silva and his forty bandits.

IV. THE GODS OF WAR: DEATH TO THE GRINGOS!

THE INVASIONS OF THIS MODERN ROME

by Jose Maria Tornel y Mendivil

When the Republic of Mexico was founded in 1824, it looked to the United States Constitution and Jeffersonian democracy as its political idols. The new republic opened its Texas border and offered land grants to settlers from the United States, like Stephen Austin, who pledged allegiance to the Mexican government. But in 1835, the Easterners-cum-*tejanos*, angered by Mexican taxes and Catholicism, and wishing to extend slavery to Texas (which Mexico had abolished), revolted. The bitterness of Jose Maria Tornel y Mendivil's denunciation of the rebels, written in the name of Mexican President Miguel Barragan, reflected his feeling of betrayal ("To the Texas Colonists 'Mexican' Is an Execrable Word," *The Siege and Taking of the Alamo* by General Miguel A. Sanchez Lamego, translated by Consuelo Velasco, Sante Fe, N. Mex., Blue Feather Press, 1968), which was elaborated in his official report as Minister of War ("After We Took Them to Our Bosom, They Destroyed Us," *The Mexican Side of the Texas Revolution*, edited and translated by Carlos E. Castaneda, Dallas, Tex., P. L. Turner Company, 1956).

To the Texas Colonists
"Mexican" Is an Execrable Word

For a long time the ungrateful Texas colonists have made fun of the national laws of Mexico; disregarding the fact that Mexico gave them a generous welcome and kept them close to our bosom; dispensing to them the same—and even more—benefits than to our own sons.

Every time we have had internal agitation they have thought the Republic weak and impotent to control their (the Texan) excesses. These have multiplied intensely, producing insults again and again against the whole of our National Arms.

When order was finally established in the interior, they hypocritically pretended a bond they did not feel to the institutions of their Stepmother.

Given the slightest opportunity, they returned to their aggressions, throwing insults at our customs employees and even fighting the small detachments which protected them.

To the Texas colonists, the word MEXICAN is, and has been, an execrable word. There has been no insult or violation that our countrymen have not suffered, including being jailed as "foreigners" in their own country.

The Texas colonies have been considered, for a long time, as general quarters for the enemies of the Nation; where all the bums and adventurers from the whole world have been gathered to revolt against the generous nation which has tolerated their insolence.

All this has reached the point where the flag of rebellion has been raised; the Texans aspiring shamelessly to take over one of the most precious parts of our land. Accomplices to this wickedness are adventurers from the State of

Louisiana who foment disturbances and give necessary support to the rebels. The civilized world will not delay in pronouncing the judgment they deserve for this infamous and detestable conduct. The Supreme Government knows its duties and knows how to execute them.

But our brave soldiers, so many times victorious over outside and inside enemies, are already marching to maintain in Texas our flag and honor, to punish the traitors and to reward those who remain faithful to their oaths, duties and obligations. In this national war, so unjustly provoked, justice and power are on our side; on the rebel's side crime, usurpation and the torch of discord they intend to use against our Republic in order to humble and vilify it.

Their ideas will be frustrated; our Nation is and will be what it ought to be—a great and glorious country when our laws, property and rights are being violently attacked. Your Excellencies, make a call to the troops under your command that they will produce brilliant testaments of their invincibility in this foreign war as they were in Tepeaca, Cordoba, Azcapozalco, in the Huerta, in Veracruz and Tampico de Tamaulipas.

The Government believes that not one Mexican worthy of his country will favor the treason of foreign rebels, but that if such a misfortune exists, the power and duty of punishing him lies in your hands.

God and Liberty! Mexico, 31st of October 1835. (Signed) Tornel.

After We Took Them to Our Bosom, They Destroyed Us

For more than fifty years, that is, from the very period of their political infancy, the prevailing thought in the United

States of America has been the acquisition of the greater part of the territory that formerly belonged to Spain, particularly that part which today belongs to the Mexican nation. Democrats and Federalists, all their political parties, whatever their old or new designations, have been in perfect accord upon one point, their desire to extend the limits of the republic to the north, to the south, and to the west, using for the purpose all the means at their command, guided by cunning, deceit, and bad faith. It has been neither an Alexander nor a Napoleon, desirous of conquest in order to extend his dominions or add to his glory, who has inspired the proud Anglo-Saxon race in its desire, its frenzy to usurp and gain control of that which rightfully belongs to its neighbors; rather it has been the nation itself which, possessed of that roving spirit that moved the barbarous hordes of a former age in a far remote north, has swept away whatever has stood in the way of its aggrandizement. . . .

Our continuous revolts made that country conceive the hope that we would neglect or abandon our national and sacred charge, while the ill-advised colonization laws and our still more imprudent and scandalous mismanagement of the public lands, so coveted and yet so freely and generously distributed and given away, clearly showed that we knew neither how to appreciate nor how to keep the precious heritage of the Spaniards. Unfortunately they were not mistaken in their assumption, for at every step we have displayed that candor, weakness, and inexperience so characteristic of infant nations. Too late have we come to know the restless and enterprising neighbor who set himself up as our mentor, holding up his institutions for us to copy them, institutions which transplanted to our soil could not but produce constant anarchy, and which, by draining our resources, perverting our character, and weakening our vigor, have left us powerless against the attacks and the invasions of this modern Rome. The example of an *ever increasing* prosperity was treacherously pointed out to us, and, attributing to the written law the influence of habit and custom, we adopted the first without the steadying influence of the second. Thus we have chosen to live in perpetual contradiction, in an anomalous state. How costly have been to us the gifts of these new Greeks!

As a native of America I cannot regret the triumph of the Revolution of 1776, nor can I condemn the vast experiment in social welfare that has been undertaken upon our continent. But that same Revolution which bore such happy results for the American people,—even though they may not be as extensive, as perfect, and as complete as its partisans would have us believe—brought many misfortunes to the human race when considered from other points of view. . . .

The events of Madrid and Bayone in 1808, the subsequent uprising of the Spanish people against the hordes of Napoleon, the disordered state of the administration which naturally followed, the weakness of her revolutionary governments, barely able to maintain a precarious existence, all these circumstances united to favor the ambitious plans of the United States who now, ill-concealing their joy, threw off the hypocritical mask with which, for a time, they covered their true designs. The thinking men of the United States had clearly foreseen that their emancipation would be but the prelude to the emancipation of all the New World. They realized that sooner or later the important revelation that resistance to a remote and tyrannical power could be crowned with complete victory would not be disregarded by the Spanish colonies. Nor were they ignorant of the fact that their early independent existence, their progress in civilization, and the experience gained through their own administration would assure them a preeminent position of power and influence in determining the fate of the new nations when they became established. To cooperate in this great enterprise was to safeguard their own existence by the most effective means. In spite of the advantageous position of the United States, of their growing maritime power, of the war-like disposition of their inhabitants, of the determination displayed in their struggles, of the abundant resources of their soil and the bright prospects of their industry, they could not aspire to a superior rank among the nations of the world, as long as they had to compete with the old and powerful countries of Europe. The setting changed, however, with the appearance of other independent nations in the New World. It was, therefore, to the essential interest of the United States to encourage by their example, their counsel, and their material help the insurrection of Spanish America. Here they saw the realization of their ulterior motives enhanced by the sympathy created for themselves and the inherent weakness of the ephemeral governments of the new nations. Egoism is an inseparable vice of the genius of the Anglo-Saxon race. If they proclaim or sustain the august rights of liberty and independence, it is not because of the noble sympathy felt for a just and sacred cause; rather it is out of regard for their interests, it is their own improvement which they seek with indefatigable zeal. The time that has elapsed since our fortunate emancipation, a time so rich in disappointments, has removed the band that inexperience placed over our eyes. Who is ignorant today of the real cause, the prime motive behind the decision taken by the United States in favor of the independence of the Spanish colonies? . . . It cannot be denied that the immense majority of the American people participated in our melancholic tragedies for the purpose of weakening the power of Spain and out of a desire to exercise a direct

influence, inevitable as a result of the vigor of a people full
of life and dynamic activity, upon the fate of poorly educated peoples who would in the end destroy themselves by
their excesses and the horrors of continuous civil war. Nothing could withstand the popularity of the Anglo-American
system of government. The influence of Spain seemed to
end at the Pillars of Hercules. The newborn star of the nations that rose upon the ruins of a decrepit monarchy shined
fitfully and with a reddish glow.

The Americans decided to fan the spirit of insurrection in
the Spanish colonies during the darkest hour of the conflict
for their former ally and benefactor, taking advantage of the
critical situation, and aware of the ultimate success which
they foresaw. Companies which rendered direct services to
the rebels were organized in Baltimore, expeditions were
outfitted in New York; money, munitions, and armament
were liberally furnished in New Orleans to carry on the
struggle against Spain, to destroy and banish her commerce.
It was thus that the plans to weaken more and more the
power of a friendly nation were put into execution in order
to snatch from her, immediately after, her most valuable
possessions.

THE FALL OF THE ALAMO
by General Antonio Lopez de Santa Ana

The saga of the Alamo and the courage of its defenders
has been celebrated in literature and on film, but the
Mexican version of that battle, and the national celebration that followed the victory, are little known in
the United States. General Santa Ana, the ill-fated
"Napoleon of Mexico," voiced the exultation of his

troops and the euphoria of his victory in "The Fall of
the Alamo." (*The Siege and Taking of the Alamo*, by
Lamega.)

ARMY OF OPERATIONS.
Distinguished Gentlemen:

Victory accompanies the Mexican Army and at this very
moment, 8 o'clock in the morning, it has just gained the
most complete and glorious one in history.

As I informed you on the 27th of last month, when I announced the taking of this city, I expected the First Infantry
Brigade to act decisively against the fort, The Alamo; but,
unable to arrive at full strength, they regrouped by doubling
their marches. Among these were the Sappers, Aldama and
Toluca Battalions, plus the Matamoros, Jimenez and San
Luis Potosi. All but 1,400 young men of the Infantry were
chosen. I divided my men into four columns, plus one in reserve, as I indicated in yesterday's General Order (a copy of
which I include). The assault began at 5:00 o'clock in the
morning. The resistance was very obstinate so that in the
hour and a half the battle lasted, even the reserves had to be
used.

The picture this fight presented was extraordinary. The
men fought individually, each one aiming to perform a heroic act. They found 21 artillery pieces the enemy used with
great expertness. Firing was so active it seemed to illumi-
nate the interior of the fort. The foss and ramparts were not
obstacles for our intrepid Mexicans; they fulfilled their duty
bravely and deserve all kinds of consideration from the Supreme Government and the gratitude of their countrymen.

The fort, finally, fell into our power with its artillery, pa-
rade grounds, etc. Buried in its foss and trenches were more
than 600 corpses, all foreign; and in the vicinity are a great
number more we have not as yet been able to examine.

They, wanting to escape from the Infantry bayonets, fell under the sabres of the Cavalry, which I had placed on the spot for that very purpose.

I can well assure you now that very few would have escaped with the news of the event to their comrades.

Among the dead are the first and second enemy commanders, Bowie and Travis. Colonels they were. Of the same rank was Crockett. All the other commanders and officers holding commissions from the Convention are among them.

On our part, we have suffered about 70 dead and 300 wounded; among them are 2 commanders and 23 officers. Their loss is made less painful because of the just cause in which we are engaged. It is the duty of Mexican military men to die defending their country's rights, and for its glory. We are all ready to make such a dear sacrifice rather than allow foreigners, no matter where they came from, to insult our land and take our territory.

Opportunely, I will send all the details about this important victory; but now I will close this by congratulating the Nation and the Supreme Excellency, The Provisionally Appointed President.

The courier is carrying a flag taken today from one of the enemy's installations. From it will be seen the real intentions of the traitor colonists and their allies who came from several parts of the United States.

God and Liberty! Headquarters in Bejar, March 6, 1836.
          Antonio Lopez de Santa Ana,

    To the Most Excellent Minister of War and Navy,
        General D. Jose Maria Tornel

WHAT CHILD WILL NOT SHED ABUNDANT TEARS AT THE TOMB OF HIS PARENTS

by Governor Juan Bautista Vigil

It was the "most unjust [war] ever waged by a stronger against a weaker nation," General Ulysses S. Grant wrote, in his *Memoirs*, of the War against Mexico (1846–1848). The commander of the U.S. Army, General Winfield Scott, lamented that his troops had "committed atrocities to make heaven weep and every American of Christian morals blush for his country." Overwhelmed by the power and zeal of their foe, the inhabitants of the "Borderland" quickly succumbed. In conquering New Mexico, General Stephen Kearny sought to assure the citizenry, "We come as friends, to better your condition," but acting Governor Juan Bautista Vigil replied, in a rueful surrender speech, with a sly reference to "the condition of the Poles" under the Russian czar. (Archives of the State of New Mexico; translated by Stan Steiner.)

General (Stephen Kearny): The speech which you have just delivered, in which you announce that you have taken possession of this great country in the name of the United States of America, gives us some idea of the wonderful future that awaits us. It is not for us to determine the boundaries of nations. The cabinets of Mexico and Washington will arrange these differences. It is for us to obey and respect the established authorities, no matter what may be our private opinions.

The inhabitants of this territory humbly and honorably present their loyalty and allegiance to the government of North America. No one in this world can successfully resist the power of him who is stronger.

Do not find it strange if there is no manifestation of joy and enthusiasm in seeing this city (Santa Fe) occupied by your military forces. To us the power of the Mexican Republic is dead. No matter what the condition, she was our mother. What child will not shed abundant tears at the tomb of his parents? I might indicate some of the causes of her misfortunes, but family problems should not be made public. Let it suffice to say that civil war is the cursed source of the deadly poison that has stifled one of the noblest and greatest countries that was ever created. Today we belong to a great and wonderful nation; its flag, with its stars and stripes covers the horizon of New Mexico, and its brilliant light shall grow in our soil like good seed well cultivated. We recognize your kindness, your courtesy, and that of your accommodating officers, and the strict discipline of your troops; we know we belong to the Republic that owes its origins to the immortal Washington, whom all civilized nations admire and respect. How different would be our situation had we been invaded by European nations! We are aware of the unfortunate condition of the Poles.

In the name, then, of the entire land, I swear obedience to the Northern Republic, and I tender my respect to its laws and authority.

THE TREATY OF GUADALUPE HIDALGO

Article VIII: Rights of Mexicans Established in Territories Ceded to United States

The Treaty of Guadalupe Hidalgo was one of the most controversial ever signed by this country. It ended the War against Mexico by Mexico's ceding all the land from Texas to the Pacific, and north to Wyoming, to

the United States—roughly one fourth of this nation—
while the United States guaranteed the "equality" of
Mexicans in the territory and pledged that their
"property of every kind" would be "inviolably respected." In the Southwest to this day, La Raza groups
accuse the United States of having violated the treaty.
(*Guadalupe Hidalgo Treaty of Peace, 1848* . . . , Truchas, N. Mex., Tate Gallery, 1969.)

Mexicans now established in territories previously belonging
to Mexico, and which remain for the future within the limits
of the United States, as defined by the present treaty, shall
be free to continue where they now reside, or to remove at
any time to the Mexican republic retaining the property
which they possess in the said territories, or disposing
thereof, and removing the proceeds wherever they please,
without their being subjected, on this account, to any contribution, tax, or charge whatever.

Those who shall prefer to remain in the said territories,
may either retain the title and rights of Mexican citizens, or
acquire those of citizens of the United States. But they shall
be under obligation to make their election within one year
from the date of the exchange of ratifications of this treaty;
and those who shall remain in the said territories after the
expiration of that year, without having declared their intention to retain the character of Mexicans, shall be considered
to have elected to become citizens of the United States.

In the said territories, property of every kind, now belonging to Mexicans not established there, shall be inviolably respected. The present owners, the heirs of these, and
all Mexicans who may hereafter acquire said property by
contract, shall enjoy with respect to it guaranties equally
ample as if the same belonged to citizens of the United
States.

THE BETRAYAL

In California, as in New Mexico and Texas, the citizens of the "Borderland" had been in civil and armed rebellion against the Mexican government before the war. Some of *la gente razon* (people of reason), the provincial leaders, did not resist, even if they did not welcome, the invasion of the United States Army, hoping it might free them from Mexican tyranny and corruption. However, the years of occupation brought a *grito* (outcry) of doubt ("California Is Lost!" from *El Clamor Publico*, a Raza newspaper in California, 1855–59; reprinted from *The Decline of the Californios* by Leonard Pitt, Berkeley, Cal., University of California Press, 1966). Senator, and later Judge, Don Pablo de la Guerra, who helped write the constitution of California, voiced the despair of La Raza on the floor of the legislature in 1856 ("They Have No Voice," from *The Decline of the Californios*).

California Is Lost!

from El Clamor Publico

Oh! fatalidad! . . . Mexicans alone have been the victims of the people's insane fury! Mexicans alone have been sacrificed on the gibbet and launched into eternity! . . . This . . . is the *liberty* and *equality* of our adopted land! . . . *California is lost* to all Spanish-Americans.

We are Native California Americans born on the soil and we can exclaim with the Poet, this is OUR OWN, OUR NATIVE LAND. . . . (But) there is every probability that we shall remain (under the American flag) . . . for all time to come. . . . (Therefore) let us divest ourselves of all bygone traditions, and become Americanized all over—in language, in manners, in customs and habits . . . upon grounds of principle and expediency. . . .

Let us husband our resources; be careful of our means, and spend what we have to spare in *educating our children*, and bring them up in a thorough training of the English tongue. . . . We must learn them useful trades and professions, stimulate them to excel in the sciences and other utilitarian occupations.

Californios! . . . Let us give our sons the example of morality, virtue and patriotism which our fathers gave to us.

We say frankly: our own youths are more inclined than others to imitate blindly the bad customs of others. They do not have that ability to resist the temptation which for the most part had preserved our fathers during many spiritual dangers. . . . Go work on the ranchos—sow maize, wheat, etc.—find some useful occupation, instead of idling time in these detestable taverns and gambling houses. Work, work and thirst for independence . . . riches are not the greatest happiness (that) one may aspire to. . . .

They Have No Voice

by Don Pablo de la Guerra

(Californians) lay prostrate before the conqueror and ask for the protection of the few possessions which remain to them in the bad luck into which they had fallen . . . those who had been sold like sheep—those who were abandoned and sold by Mexico. They are unfamiliar with the prevalent language now spoken in their own country. They have no voice in this Senate, except such as I am now weakly speaking on their behalf. . . . I have seen old men of sixty and seventy years of age weeping because they have been cast out of their ancestral home. They have been humiliated and insulted. They have been refused the privilege of cutting their own firewood. And all those who have committed these outrages have come here looking for protection. . . . The Senate sympathizes with them, though it does not hear the complaints of *la clase espanol.* . . . After suffering all these injustices and enduring all kinds of injuries, now we find that the legislature is hungry to get from us our last penny, simply because the squatters are more numerous than we.

THE GUERRILLA WARS

Resistance to Yankee invaders of the "Borderland" did not become widespread until after Mexico's defeat in 1848. In 1853 the dons of the old families of California lent support to a rebellion by Sonoran miners who had been driven from their claims. Led by a young *vaquero* of "executive ability and genius," Joaquin Murieta (also spelled Murrieta), from Alamos, Sonora, the rebels launched what Major Horace Bell, of the California Rangers, termed "a revolution" in "bold defiance of the power of the government." Murieta, a taciturn man, left a rare statement of his aims ("I Will Not Submit," from *The Robin Hood of El Dorado* by Walter Noble Burns, New York, Coward McCann, 1932); he rode forth into defeat and history to become a folk hero ("Joaquin Murrieta," from *The Vaquero,* by Arnold R. Rojas). In the summer of 1969, a historian who was cleaning out the old gold-rush jail of Sonora, California, came upon an old newspaper clipping which confirmed Murieta's legendary fame ("Love Secrets of

Joaquin Murieta," from an undated and unidentified newspaper).

I Will Not Submit

by Joaquin Murieta

I was once a great admirer of Americans. I thought them the noblest, most honorable and high-minded people in the world. I had met many in my own country and all forms of tyranny seemed as hateful to them as the rule of the *Gachupines* (foreigners, or Spaniards) to the Mexicans. I was sick of the constant wars and insurrections in my native land and I came here thinking to end my days in California as an American citizen.

I located first near Stockton. But I was constantly annoyed and insulted by my neighbors and was not permitted to live in peace. I went then to the placers (gold mines) and was driven from my mining claim. I went into business and was cheated by everyone in whom I trusted. At every turn I was swindled and robbed by the very men for whom I had had the greatest friendship and admiration. I saw the Americans daily in acts of the most outrageous and lawless injustice, or of cunning and mean duplicity hateful to every honorable mind.

I then said to myself, I will revenge my wrongs and take the law into my own hands. The Americans who have injured me I will kill, and those who have not, I will rob because they are Americans. My trail shall be red with blood and those who seek me shall die or I shall lose my own life in the struggle! I will not submit tamely to outrage any longer.

I have killed many; I have robbed many; and many more will suffer in the same way. I will continue to the end of my life to take vengeance on the race that has wronged me so shamefully.

Joaquin Murrieta

by Arnold R. Rojas

The old stone church in Alamos, Sonora, faces the plaza and frowns down on the boys and girls who, serenely indifferent to its disapproval, walk round and round the brave little cluster of vegetation that serves as a park.

The girls chatter as they walk arm in arm. Each girl carries a flower. The girls walk counterclockwise, the boys walk clockwise to face the girls. Each boy also carries a flower.

When a boy meets a girl who pleases him, he offers her his flower, which the girl never refuses to accept. If the boy is to her liking, she will keep the flower and give him hers. On the other hand, if he does not please her, on the next turn around the plaza she will return his flower, and in this delicate way close the matter between them.

It was in the momentous year of 1849 in this oldest pueblo in northwestern New Spain that Joaquin Murrieta humbly offered his flower to Rosita, and was accepted. The records of the old church attest to their marriage before its altar.

Shortly after this important event in their lives Joaquin and Rosita set out to seek their fortune in the gold fields of California. They crossed the Devil's highroad, and after weeks of travel arrived in the gold fields. They found riches, nuggets of gold, but they also found disgrace and death.

Joaquin had gone to work on his placer claim, leaving his young bride alone. Thirteen gringos came to the cabin. The thirteen men found Rosita without a defender. They must have beaten her into submission before each one of the thirteen ravished the poor little-girl bride. Joaquin came on the scene in time to find them robbing his house and his wife breathing her last. He fought, but to no avail. The thirteen men beat him until he no longer moved. Then they left him there for dead.

But Murrieta did not die. While the desperadoes were beating him, he had kept his senses long enough to impress on his memory the features of every one of his wife's murderers. He would recognize each one again whenever he should meet him.

He lived from then on for revenge. When, after many days, he could ride again, he set out to do the task for which he thenceforth lived. For many weary, desperate years he hunted down his wife's ravishers. He searched from one mining camp to another until, one by one, he found them all, and the last of the thirteen died begging for mercy.

Murrieta, his work done, went back to Sonora to live out his broken life, not with gold, a wife, children, happiness, but with bitter memories.

How long he lived in Cucurpe after his return from California, we do not know. When he died the compassionate people of the town laid him to rest in the old cemetery with a prayer that this much abused man might now sleep in peace after a ruined life.

But it was not to be. The gringos who had never been sure whether they had actually killed the nemesis of California's gold rush days, or an innocent man, learned of his death and burial. Still in keeping with their earlier acts of barbarism, they denied him, to the very last, the right to human dignity. They committed the last indignity by an act of desecration of the dead. They dug up his bones to measure his cranium!

Murrieta, after a hundred years, still remains a legendary figure, and as long as the Spanish tongue remains in California, his tragedy will be remembered.

Love Secrets of Joaquin Murieta

from an old newspaper

LOVE SECRETS OF JOAQUIN MURIETA, PIONEER BANDIT CHIEF, REVEALED AT LAST. LONG SECRET ROMANTIC AFFAIRS OF WEST'S MOST COLORFUL LAWLESS CHARACTER ARE BROUGHT TO LIGHT BY DESCENDANT OF DARING CABALLERO.

THE STORY OF A WOMAN WHO LOVED JOAQUIN MURIETA, CALIFORNIA'S HISTORIC BANDIT, HAS BEEN UNCOVERED AFTER MANY YEARS.

History has a way of letting secrets slip, one by one. Joaquin Murieta died in 1853 and his head, in a bottle of alcohol, vanished in the fire of 1906. There has been no photograph of Joaquin discovered. Nor until this day a photograph of a woman he loved.

But he loved many.

Among them was the beautiful Pachita Soberanes, who lived in Monterey. She was his first cousin, and came to California from Mexico with his family aboard the Lexington in 1848.

Another cousin, Angelita Hipolito, came to California at the same time. Her son, Robert J. Richards of Daly City, owns the only photographs ever taken of the relatives of Joaquin.

"Joaquin was a mystery for 80 years," Richards explained. "We did not like his identity to be known. We did not tell his story.

"These two girl cousins adored Joaquin, as did his family.

To the Mexicans he was a great liberator, come out of Mexico to take California back from the hands of the gringos.

"They did not call his looting and killing banditry. They called it war.

"He kept his guitar at the home of his relatives in Monterey. He would come there, with a posse of a hundred men hunting him, and sing songs for his girl cousins.

"They knew there was a price on his head. They knew that at any moment the casa might be surrounded and Joaquin killed before their eyes. The Legislature had set a $10,000 reward on his head, and they knew no posse would want Joaquin alive.

"And yet, in the cool walls of their adobe, they managed to find contentment."

Pachita was the most beautiful of all Joaquin's cousins, and they were famous for their beauty. He himself was rated the handsomest man in California. When he was killed, legend has it, she cut off her luxuriant tresses and went into mourning and did not marry for many years, out of love for Joaquin.

Angelita was 17 when Joaquin was killed. She married a Rodriguez and died in San Jose in 1930, aged 94 years.

"The love affairs of Joaquin became as great a legend in California as his banditry," said Richards. "But I think his greatest love was for Rosita, his little wife, who was killed by Americans on the Stanislaus River. That was what made a bandit of Joaquin.

"But his two cousins who loved him spoke till the end of their days of his gentleness and his romantic ways."

SUFFER THE DEATH OF MARTYRS

Proclamation of Juan Nepomuceno Cortina

On September 28, 1859, a wealthy rancher in South Texas, Don Juan Nepomuceno Cortina, led his ranch *vaqueros* into Brownsville, occupied the city, and proclaimed the Republic of the Rio Grande. "Death to the Gringos!" the men shouted as they raised the Mexican flag. Until 1875 the raids of Cortina's men continued in a futile attempt to regain the lands and herds stolen from the *tejanos*. Major Heintzelman of the U.S. Army, sent to suppress the rebellion, likened Cortina to John Brown: "He was a champion of his race"; and President Juarez of Mexico appointed Cortina a general of the army. (*House Executive Documents*, 36th Congress, Session I, Vol. 8, No. 52, serial set no. 1050, 1859.)

County of Cameron
Camp in the Rancho del Carmen, November 23, 1859.

Compatriots: A sentiment of profound indignation, the love and esteem which I profess for you, the desire which you have for that tranquillity and those guarantees which are denied you, thus violating the most sacred laws, is that which moves me to address you these words, hoping that they may prove some consolation in the midst of your adversity, which heretofore has borne the appearance of predestination.

The history of great human actions teaches us that in certain instances the principal motive which gives them impulse is the natural right to resist and conquer our enemies with a firm spirit and lively will; to persist in and to reach the consummation of this object, opening a path through the obstacles which step by step are encountered, however imposing or terrible they may be.

In the series of such actions, events present themselves which public opinion, influenced by popular sentiment, calls for deliberation upon their effects, to form an exact and just conception of the interests which they promote; and this same public opinion should be considered as the best judge, which, with coolness and impartiality, does not fail to recognize some principle as the cause for the existence of open force and immutable firmness, which impart the noble desire of cooperating with true philanthropy to remedy the state of despair of him who, in his turn, becomes the victim of ambition, satisfied at the cost of justice.

There are, doubtless, persons so overcome by strange prejudices, men without confidence or courage to face danger in an undertaking in sisterhood with the love of liberty, who, examining, the merit of acts by a false light, and preferring that of the same opinion contrary to their own, prepare no other reward than that pronounced for the "bandit," for him who, with complete abnegation of self, dedicates himself to constant labor for the happiness of those who, suffering under the weight of misfortunes, eat their bread, mingled with tears, on the earth which they rated.

If, my dear compatriots, I am honored with that name, I am ready for combat.

The Mexicans who inhabit this wide region, some because they were born therein, others because since the treaty of Guadalupe Hidalgo, they have been attracted to its soil by the soft influence of wise laws and the advantages of a free government, paying little attention to the reasoning of politics, are honorably and exclusively dedicated to the exercise of industry, guided by that instinct which leads the good man to comprehend, as uncontradictory truth, that only in the reign of peace can he enjoy, without inquietude, the fruit of his labor. These, under an unjust imputation of selfishness and churlishness, which do not exist, are not devoid of those sincere and expressive evidences of such friendliness and tenderness as should gain for them that confidence with which they have inspired those who have met them in social intercourse. This genial affability seems as the foundation of that proverbial prudence which, as an oracle, is consulted in all their actions and undertakings. Their humility, simplicity, and docility, directed with dignity, it may be that with excess of goodness, can, if it be desired, lead them beyond the common class of men, but causes them to excel in an irresistible inclination towards ideas of equality, a proof of their simple manners, so well adapted to that which is styled the classic land of liberty. A man, a family, and a people, possessed of qualities so eminent, with their heart in their hand and purity on their lips, encounter every day renewed reasons to know that they are surrounded by malicious and crafty monsters, who rob them in the tranquil interior of home, or with open hatred and pursuit; it necessarily follows, however great may be their pain, if not abased by humiliation and ignominy, their groans suffocated and hushed by a pain which renders them insensible, they become resigned to suffering before an abyss of misfortunes.

Mexicans! When the State of Texas began to receive the new organization which its sovereignty required as an integrant part of the Union, flocks of vampires, in the guise of men, came and scattered themselves in the settlements, without any capital except the corrupt heart and the most perverse intentions. Some, brimful of laws, pledged to us their protection against the attacks of the rest; others assembled in shadowy councils, attempted and excited the robbery and burning of the houses of our relatives on the other side of the river Bravo; while others, to the abusing of our unlimited confidence, when we intrusted them with our titles, which secured the future of our families, refused to return them under false and frivolous pretexts; all, in short, with a smile on their faces, giving the lie to that which their black entrails were meditating. Many of you have been robbed of your property, incarcerated, chased, murdered, and hunted like wild beasts, because your labor was fruitful, and because your industry excited the vile avarice which led them. A voice infernal said, from the bottom of their soul, "kill them; the greater will be our gain!" Ah! this does not finish the sketch of your situation. It would appear that justice had fled from this world, leaving you to the caprice of your oppressors, who become each day more furious towards you; that, through witnesses and false charges, although the grounds may be insufficient, you may be interred in the penitentiaries, if you are not previously deprived of life by some keeper who covers himself from responsibility by the pretence of your flight. There are to be found criminals covered with frightful crimes, but they appear to have impunity until opportunity furnish them a victim; to these monsters indulgence is shown, because they are not of our race, which is unworthy, as they say, to belong to the human species. But this race, which the Anglo-American, so ostentatious of its own qualities, tries so much to blacken, depreciate, and load with insults, in a spirit of blindness, which goes to the full extent of such things so common on this frontier, does not fear, placed even in the midst of its very faults, those subtle inquisitions which are so frequently made as to its manners, habits, and sentiments; nor that its deeds should be put to the test of examination in the land of reason, of justice, and of honor. This race has never humbled itself before the conqueror, though the reverse has happened, and can be established; for he is not humbled who uses among his fellow-men those courtesies which humanity prescribes; charity being the root whence springs the rule of his actions. But this race, which you see filled with gentleness and inward sweetness, gives now the cry of alarm throughout the entire extent of the land which it occupies, against all the artifice interposed by those who have become chargeable with their division and discord. This race, adorned with the most lovely disposition towards all that is good and useful in the line of progress, omits no act of diligence which might correct its many imperfections, and lift its grand edifice among the ruins of the past, respecting the ancient traditions and the maxims bequeathed by their ancestors, without being dazzled by brilliant and false appearances, nor crawling to that exaggeration of institution which, like a sublime statue, is offered for their worship and adoration.

Mexicans! Is there no remedy for you? Inviolable laws, yet useless, serve, it is true, certain judges and hypocritical authorities, cemented in evil and injustice, to do whatever suits them, and to satisfy their vile avarice at the cost of your patience and suffering; rising in their frenzy, even to the taking of life, through the treacherous hands of their bailiffs. The wicked way in which many of you have been oftentimes involved in persecution, accompanied by circumstances making it the more bitter, is now well known; these crimes being hid from society under the shadow of a horrid night, those implacable people, with the haughty spirit which suggests impunity for a life of criminality, have pronounced, doubt ye not, your sentence, which is, with accustomed insensibility, as you have seen, on the point of execution.

Mexicans! My part is taken; the voice of revelation whispers to me that to me is entrusted the work of breaking the chains of your slavery, and that the Lord will enable me, with powerful arm, to fight against our enemies, in compliance with the requirements of that Sovereign Majesty, who, from this day forward, will hold us under His protection. On my part, I am ready to offer myself as a sacrifice for your happiness; and counting upon the means necessary for the discharge of my ministry, you may count upon my cooperation, should no cowardly attempt put an end to my days. This undertaking will be sustained on the following bases:

First. A society is organized in the State of Texas, which devotes itself sleeplessly until the work is crowned with success, to the improvement of the unhappy conditions of those Mexicans resident therein; exterminating their tyrants, to which end those which compose it are ready to shed their blood and suffer the death of martyrs.

Second. As this society contains within itself the elements necessary to accomplish the great end of its labors, the veil of impenetrable secrecy covers "The Great Book" in which the articles of its constitution are written while so delicate are the difficulties which must be overcome that no honorable man can have cause for alarm, if imperious exigencies require them to act without reserve.

Third. The Mexicans of Texas repose their lot under the good sentiments of the governor elect of the State, General Houston, and trust that upon his elevation to power he will begin with care to give us legal protection within the limits of his powers.

Mexicans! Peace be with you! Good inhabitants of the State of Texas, look on them as brothers, and keep in mind that which the Holy Spirit saith: "Thou shalt not be the friend of the passionate man; nor join thyself to the madman, lest thou learn his mode of work and scandalize thy soul."

REVOLUTIONARIES ARE ALSO SONS OF GOD

by General Francisco Villa

"Villa Awaits the Taking of Mexico City with His Thoughts Centered on God, Religion, and the Priests": this is the title of chapter 5 of General Villa's *Memoirs*. The revolutions of Mexico were revolutions of ideas, as well as of men. Although Francisco "Pancho" Villa has been stereotyped as a "bandido" and a "man of action," he too meditated upon and articulated the ideas of the revolution. His rough manner characteristic of those from the rugged regions of Chihuahua (south of New Mexico) where he was born, and the strenuous campaigns he waged, made the public image of this man whose inner thoughts were reluctantly expressed. (*The Memoirs of Pancho Villa*, edited by M. L. Guzman, translated by V. Turner, Austin, Tex., University of Texas Press, 1970.)

I made a trip to Santa Isabel, Bustillos, Guerreo, and other towns in the district where my sister Martina lived. She wanted me to be present for a baptism, and the priest who, as I said before, was performing the bishop's duties in Chihuahua, went with me. That priest was a man who had his own ideas, though he was also my friend. And knowing that I followed no religion, and was especially opposed to the ways of the Jesuits, he discussed the protective doctrines and teachings of the Church with the intention of influencing me.

(The priest) "Sr. General, as you have consented to contract the duties of godfather, you do recognize the laws of our Catholic Church, as God disposes; you live under the mantel of our Holy Religion, and you are therefore obligated to follow its decrees and practices and to obey it insofar as it commands us to live and die as its good sons.

(The general) "Senor, to contract the duties of godfather does not imply recognizing any laws in this world, or any other. Men are compadres by virtue of friendship and custom. That is, if a man consents to take on himself the tutelage of the child of another, in case the other man fails or dies, this is not because of religious doctrine, but because the duties that unite us as fellowmen require it, and this is true although the believers believe something else, seeing that the Church intervenes in these deeds to sanctify them. However, I do not deny belief in God. I affirm it and certify to it since it has comforted men and all men in many of life's crises. But I do not consider everything sacred that is covered by the name of religion. Most so-called religious men use religion to promote their own interests, not the things they preach, and so there are good priests and bad priests, and we must accept some and help them and prosecute and annihilate others. The bad priests, Senor, like the Jesuits, are the worst men in the world because it is their duty to teach what is good by means of sacrifice but instead they dedicate themselves to the fulfillment of their passions in ways that are evil. I think they deserve greater punishment than the worst bandits in the world, for the bandits do not deceive others in their conduct or pretend to be what they are not, while the Jesuits do, and by this deception they work great hardships on the people."

The priest said, "Sr. General, the bad priests will be punished in their time, but while they walk on earth they deserve our respect. God puts them here among us, and if He does, He knows why."

(The general) "No, Senor. If I, as a Revolutionary, arise to punish rulers who fail to fulfil their duty to the people, I must extend punishment to religious men who betray the cause of the poor. And our punishment is beneficial to the churches in warning the clergy to be charitable and useful, not greedy and destructive, just as the punishment of a bad soldier is beneficial to the military. I understand your reasons, Senor, for thinking God has good and bad priests in this world. He knows why, and He will reward them afterward, or punish them according to the conduct of each. But you can be sure, Sr. Priest, that God has many ways, as you religious men preach in your sermons, and that one of the punishments He can impose upon bad priests is the punishment we mete out. God has us too, the Revolutionaries, and if He permits us to struggle for our love of the people in the way we do, He knows why."

The priest replied, "Yes, Sr. General, Revolutionaries are also sons of God. For that I bless them, as I do all creatures. Those men who die or suffer for their fellowman are not untouched or abandoned by the hand of God. But He has His ministers here to prevent these men from exceeding the limits in their passionate impulses, and the law of God does not entitle the Revolution to deny sacred ministers and annoy and persecute them instead of listening to what they preach."

(The general) "Remember, Sr. Priest, that our Revolution is the struggle of the poor against the rich, who thrive on the poverty of the poor. And if in this struggle we discover that the so-called priests of religion, or most of them, are on the side of the rich and not of the poor, what faith, Senor, can the people have in their advice? In my opinion, our justice involves such holiness that the priests and the churches who deny us their help have forfeited their claim to be men of God."

On the trip we went to the Hacienda Bustillos, which belonged to one of the richest families in Chihuahua. The owner was a lady by the name of Dona Luz, who was married to an uncle of Sr. Madero's. As a friend of mine in former times, she welcomed us and treated us cordially. She asked us to stay in her house, which was grand and elegant as a palace. The meals prepared for us were excellent. She did her best to make us comfortable. And, in truth, we had a happy time there.

She too spoke of religion, giving me advice on my duties to God. She did it every time she spoke to me, and I consented because she was agreeable, and really very kind, and closely related to Sr. Madero, but principally because she was a woman of great beauty. I enjoyed looking at her while she was talking about God, and I said yes to everything or argued only to get her to say more, and did everything she recommended unless it conflicted with my sacred duty.

With a smile or a reproach she passed judgment on my conduct. Each time we saw each other, she said, "General Villa, you are a very sinful man; your hands are stained with much blood; in thought and act you have committed many other crimes. Put yourself in God's graces and He will pardon your sins."

I said, "Sra. Dona Luz, I have never killed anybody without reason."

She answered, "I believe you Sr. General. But God says 'Thou shalt not kill,' and He does not say with or without reason."

I said, "Senora, to kill is a cruel necessity for men who are at war. If we do not kill, how can we conquer? And if we do not want to conquer what future is there for the cause of the people? Death is an accident in the course of our struggle, and we all either kill or die."

She replied, "Not all your deaths have occurred in war, Sr. General."

I said, "Sra. Dona Luz, for me the war began the day I was born. I am a man whom God brought into the world to battle with I do not know how many enemies."

She answered, "Moreover you have committed many robberies, Sr. General Villa, and God says, 'Thou shalt not steal.'"

I replied, "I have never stolen, Sra. Dona Luz. I have taken from those who had much in order to give to those who had little, or nothing. For myself, I have never taken anything belonging to another except in a situation of utmost necessity. And he who takes food when he is hungry does not steal, Sra. Dona Luz. He only complies with his duty to sustain himself. It is the rich who steal because, having everything they need, they still deprive the poor of their miserable bread."

She answered, "That may be true, Senor, but why do you persecute the Church and its ministers? Some day you will need them for the salvation of your soul, and if you continue in your ways the tortures of hell will await you after your death."

I said, "I will do what you command. Since you are so good, your advice cannot be harmful to me. And I say this much more to you: while I listen to you, I am not bothered by the threats of hell, but only by the fact that I deserve your reproaches."

I said that to her knowing that she would suffer if she thought I was going to condemn myself, because she was so religious she wanted to save the souls of all who were near her, and she prayed to God for all of them in the chapel of the hacienda. That chapel was large, very fine and beautiful, and had cost much money. It was a replica, they say, of San Sulpicio, the church by that name in Paris.

VIVA LA REVOLUCION:
WE ARE HEADING TOWARD LIFE

by Ricardo Flores Magon

> In the Southwest the *gusto,* ideas, fears, and *corazon*
> (heart) of the Mexican Revolution had a dual effect. To
> some it was the signal to conceal their Mexican iden-
> tity; to others it revived *gritos* of pride and retribution.
> Ricardo Flores Magon was a newspaper editor and a
> crusader for La Causa, in the years before World War
> I, who brought the "revolutionary cosmos" to La Raza
> in California. He came to believe in anarchism and so-
> cialism, condemning the war as an "imperialist" ad-
> venture. For this he was jailed, and he died in Leaven-
> worth prison. In his writing, such as this editorial from
> his newspaper, *Revolucion* (July, 1907), Flores her-
> alded the contemporary Raza movement. (*Antologia
> Ricardo Flores Magon*, Universidad Nacional Auto-
> noma de Mexico, 1970; this selection translated by
> Luis Valdez.)

"Every man," says Carlos Malato, "is at once the REAC-
TIONARY of another man and the REVOLUTIONARY of still another."

To the reactionaries—"serious" men of today—we are
revolutionaries; for the revolutionaries of tomorrow our
deeds will have been those of "serious" men. The ideas of
humanity concerning progress are forever changing, and it
is absurd to pretend that they are immutable like plant and
animal fossils imbedded in geological strata.

But if God-fearing and "serious" men pale with fear and
are scandalized by our doctrine, the coming generations are
inspired. Faces made ugly by misery and pain are trans-
figured; down the sunburned cheeks, tears no longer run;

the faces are humanized; better yet, they are deified, animated by the sacred fire of rebellion.

What sculptor has ever sculpted an ugly hero? What painter has ever left the deformed figure of a hero on canvas? There is a mysterious light that surrounds heroes and makes them dazzling. Hidalgo, Juarez, Morelos, Zaragoza, dazzle like suns. The Greeks placed their heroes among their demigods.

We are heading toward life; that is why our heirs are inspired, that is why the giant has awakened, that is why the brave will not turn back. From his Olympus, built on the rocks of Chapultepec, a musical comedy Jupiter puts a price on the heads of those who struggle; his old hands sign bloodthirsty sentences; his dishonorable white hairs curl up like the hairs of a rabid dog. A dishonor to old age, this perverse old man grasps on to life with the desperation of a shipwrecked victim. He has taken the life of thousands of men, and he desperately resists death so as not to lose his.

It does not matter; we revolutionaries are moving onward. The abyss does not hold us back; water is more beautiful in a waterfall.

If we die, we shall die like suns: giving off light.

V. THE MIGRATIONS

THE ROOTS OF MIGRATION

by Ernesto Galarza

"Where is the border?" asks Eduardo Perez, former secretary of the Democratic State Committee of California. "There is no border in our hearts." The exodus from the deserts of northern Mexico to the deserts of the southwestern United States became heavier after the Mexican revolutions. It was not to flee the revolutions as much as to flee their aftermath of defeat and frustration, that the landless came, says Ernesto Galarza. In his analysis of the land system and social injustices that caused the migrations of millions, Dr. Galarza calls the exodus one of the great movements in history. (*Merchants of Labor*, by Ernesto Galarza, Santa Barbara, Cal., McNally & Loftin, 1964.)

Migration is the failure of roots. Displaced men are ecological victims. Between them and the sustaining earth a wedge has been driven. Eviction by drouths or dispossession by landlords, the impoverishment of the soil or conquest by arms—nature and man, separately or together, lay down the choice: move or die. Those who are able to break away do so, leaving a hostile world behind to face an uncertain one ahead.

The Mexicans who left their homeland in the six decades beginning in 1880 represented one of the major mass movements of people in the western hemisphere. During three-and-a-half centuries they had lived within a caste-bound, immobile society molded on Spanish colonial traditions. On the central plateau of the republic and its tropical fringes the bulk of the population vegetated, confined by desert, jungle, sea and medievalism. Out of these ancestral lands of the Indians the *haciendas* had been carved. The process had begun in the 16th century and was consolidated in the 17th with the royal confirmation of grants, the subjection of the *peones*, the seizure of the village lands and the autarchy of the landed estates. In these fiefs the *hacendado* ruled a subsistence economy which yielded him and his backwoods court enough surplus to maintain status and dominion.

The classic example was the domain of the Terrazas family, a northern *latifundio*. One of the Terrazas' *haciendas*, Encinillas, covered over 1,200,000 acres; another, more than 850,000 acres. In the South and East the holdings were smaller but their economic, social and political role was the same. Into the narrowing spaces between them the mass of agrarian population was squeezed. Ernest Gruening, surveying the scene in the early 1920's, found that in the state of Jalisco 96.2 per cent of the farm families owned no land. In the state of Veracruz 98.9 per cent were propertyless. In the state of Mexico monopoly nearly reached perfection: 99.8 per cent of the countryside belonged to less than one per cent of the rural families.

The permanent labor force of the *hacienda*, called the *peones ascasillados*, was held in bondage by such devices as the company store. The store was the only source of supply for the limited needs of the laboring community. It represented the local monopoly in commerce; outside tradesmen were excluded. In the store each peon had a line of credit against which he drew his allowances of cotton cloth and other necessities. Buying on credit was unavoidable since

his earnings were always inadequate for the current consumption of his family. To cover such needs the *hacienda*
customarily extended loans of a few pesos two or three
times a year. The loans were provided by the store, again as
credit, not in cash. They were a form of incentive wages or
bonus calculated to mount through the years into an obligation that the serf would never be able to pay. The *hacendado* could demand on the death of a peon that his sons
assume not only the tasks but also the debts of the insolvent
father.

In another class were the seasonal workers, known as the
peones de tarea, who were added to the regular labor force
at planting or harvest time. Their wages probably did not
exceed 100 to 150 pesos a year in 1913. Between seasons
these workers and their families subsisted on small plots of
ground, their economy eked out between the barter trade of
the village markets and the cash income from their toil on
the *hacienda.* Like the traditions of the markets, wages
changed but little over the years. In 1923 Gruening visited
haciendas on which wages had neither increased nor de-
creased within the memory of the oldest workers.

Custom and tradition, manifesting the power of the
landed gentry, regulated the economic relations of the *hacienda.* Since it possessed not only the best land but also controlled the water supply, some peasants exchanged a day's
work for their ration of drinking water. Unpaid labor was
exacted for the right to gather firewood or to pasture stock.
Seed corn could be bought only from the *hacienda.* The
culls of production—poultry, stock, grains—were set aside
for the use of local consumers who could pay only with their
depreciated labor.

The design and organization of the *hacienda* expressed
not only the historic role it had played throughout Spanish
colonialism, but also the self-containment and the inner

compression of Mexican feudalism. The headquarters of the *hacienda* was the *casa grande*, the manor of the *rancho grande*. It usually faced the plaza, around which were grouped the workshops, storehouses, stables, barns, the chapel and the jail. Surrounding the whole community was a masonry or adobe wall, often provided with battlements and towers. These fortresses, manned by armed retainers, served a double purpose. They protected the establishment from outside attack, and they held in check the discontents of the peasantry.

General Porfirio Diaz, who ruled Mexico for three decades, was the archetype of these local and regional absolutisms. Together they formed a pyramid of political privilege that rested on stagnant production, illiteracy, scarcity and iron military repression. The families and clans of the aristocracy were secure. A network of agents appointed by the governors who were in turn appointed by the dictator kept watch over municipal and provincial affairs.

What they saw, on the surface, was a placid countryside inhabited by a humble people. What they failed to sense was the ripening violence below. In 1910 a handful of intellectuals, themselves disappointed because the aristocracy made no room for them in public affairs, called upon the peons to "satisfy your needs with a hoe, if possible, and if not, with a gun." Under the leadership of fighters like Emiliano Zapata, the peasants had already risen, and by 1913 agrarian revolution was in possession of the country.

The land was seized and redistributed. On January 6, 1915, the national government nullified by decree all transactions in rural property during the previous 75 years by means of which the villages had been despoiled of their land, water and forest rights. A year later a National Agrarian Commission was created to carry out the reform. In December 1920 the fundamental *Ley de Ejidos* was enacted, restoring the communal form of land ownership and use to its ancestral rank. Between 1915 and 1934 more than a hundred agrarian laws, decrees and edicts were issued by the Federal government. The constitution itself, at Article 27, became the legal cornerstone of reform. "The necessary measures will be taken," it read, "for the breakdown of the *latifundia* and the encouragement of small landed property." One of these measures was the Agrarian Code of 1942 in which previous legislation was systematized.

The shifts in landholding brought about by the armed struggle were drastic. In the four decades following the decree of January, 1915, over 100,000,000 acres of land changed hands, the bulk of it wrested from the vanquished *haciendas* and restored to the ancient communal *ejidos*. Midway in this process it seemed to Eyler Simpson, the American scholar who gave it the most competent and sympathetic attention, that the *ejido* was truly Mexico's way out. "Mexico is already on the way," Simpson wrote in 1937, "and a new world beckons." He believed that the Mexicans had caught time by the forelock and were creating "a better way of life than has been achieved in any other part of the world."

But the day of the *ejido*, restored by revolution, had not yet arrived. In truth, several Mexicos—agrarian collectivism, rural yeomanry, incipient industrialism, foreign capital, the military caste, and the church—had taken part in the revolution openly or concealed in the wings, and a stalemate among them had set in. Zapata was assassinated in 1918. The survivors of the old regime had kept much of their liquid cash as well as the choicest of their land holdings. They moved into positions of vantage in the new revolutionary order from which a ceaseless delaying action was carried on. In the 1920's the nation was plunged into a struggle for power between rival generals and the fighting that ensued drained the revolutionary energies. In this state of affairs reaction appeared in the countryside. Villages were again attacked, buildings razed and crops burned to discourage the *ejido*. Collectivism fought back, and indeed continued to win victories on the statute books, but terror gripped many parts of the nation. It was still taking toll of the *campesinos* (peasants) forty years after the constitutional measures for the breakup of the *hacienda* had been adopted.

Twice in exactly one hundred years Mexico was shaken by uprisings of the dispossessed. In 1810 and again in 1910 the revolution was one of people wanting in, not out; they fought to regain possession of the ground they lived on. Migration came only after defeat, and its goal for many, was California.

CORRIDOS: THE SONGS OF EXODUS

"Wherever you go, you shall go singing," the War God of the Aztecs, Huitzilopochtli, commanded the people. With the *corridos* (ballads) of the Southwest La Raza has been singing its history ever since. "Out of poverty, poetry; out of suffering, song," says a modern Mexican proverb. On leaving his homeland the emigrant sang a lamentation ("An Emigrant's Farewell," from *Puro Mexicano*, edited by J. Frank Dobie, Austin, Tex., Texas Folklore Society, 1935) which he continued on his journey ("El Coyotito," translated by Alice Corbin, *Poetry* Vol. XVI, No. 5, August, 1920); he sang of the hardships of his labor ("Deported," from *Puro Mexicano*); and he sang of the strange customs of his new homeland, rewriting the hymn of the revolution ("La Cucaracha," from "Spanish Songs of New Mexico" by F. S. Curtis, Jr., *Happy Hunting Ground*, edited by J. Frank Dobie, Austin, Tex., Texas Folklore Society, 1925).

An Emigrant's Farewell

Goodbye, my beloved country,
Now I am going away;
I go to the United States,
where I intend to work.

Goodbye, my beloved mother,
the Virgin of Guadalupe;
goodbye, my beloved land,
my Mexican Republic.

At last I'm going,
I bear you in my heart;
my Mother Guadalupe,
give me your benediction.

I go sad and heavy-hearted
to suffer and endure;
my Mother Guadalupe,
grant my safe return.

Mexico is my home-land,
where I was born a Mexican;
give me the benediction
of your powerful hand.

I go to the United States
to seek to earn a living.
Goodbye, my beloved land;
I bear you in my heart.

For I am not to blame
that I leave my country thus;
the fault is that of poverty,
which keeps us all in want.

El Coyotito

When I left Hermosillo
  My tears fell like rain,
But the little red flower
  Consoled my pain.

I am like the coyote
  That rolls them, and goes
Trotting off side-ways,
  And nobody knows.

The green pine has fallen,
  Where the doves used to pair;
Now the black one may find on returning
  Little tow-heads with sandy hair!

The adobe is gone
  Where my sword hung suspended;
Why worry—when everything's
  At the last ended?

The adobe is gone
  Where my mirror was bright,
And the small cedar tree
  Is the rabbit's tonight.

The cactus is bare
  Where the tunas were sweet;
No longer need you be jealous
  Of the women I meet.

Friends, if you see her
  In the hills up above,
Don't tell her that I am in prison—
  For she is my love.

Deported

I shall sing you a song
of all who were deported,
who came back speaking English
from those wretches.

They are shoved around anywhere
and have to beg their way.
It's a pity to see them
with nothing to eat.

They set out for the north
with high hopes and eagerness,
but they work in the fields
like any field hand.

They go to pick cotton
and get on very badly;
they work on the track
or with shovel or with pick.

So they deserve that and more,
those poor countrymen,
for they knew that this land
is for the Mexicans.

They lop off their mustaches
and chew their tobacco;
it seems the thing to do
and they don't have a cent.

They cut their hair close
like a clipped donkey;
they go to second-hand stores
and buy worn-out clothes.

They're insulted, mistreated,
by those *gringo* wretches;
they have no shame,
they are always beaten there.

That is why I remain
in my beloved country:
Mexico is my country
and for it I give my life.

La Cucaracha

When a fellow loves a maiden
And that maiden doesn't love him,
It's the same as when a bald man
Finds a comb upon the highway.

CHORUS

The *cucaracha,* the *cucaracha,*
Doesn't want to travel on
Because she hasn't,
Oh no, she hasn't,
Marihuana for to smoke.

All the maidens are of pure gold;
All the married girls are silver;
All the widows are of copper,
And old women merely tin.

My neighbor across the highway
Used to be called Dona Clara,
And if she has not expired
Likely that's her name tomorrow.

All the girls up at Las Vegas
Are most awful tall and skinny,
But they're worse for plaintive
   pleading
Than the souls of Purgatory.

All the girls here in the city
Don't know how to give you kisses,
While the ones from Albuquerque
Stretch their necks to avoid misses.

All the girls from Mexico
Are as pretty as a flower
And they talk so very sweetly,
Fill your heart quite up with love.

One thing makes me laugh most hearty—
Pancho Villa with no shirt on.
Now the Carranzistas beat it
Because Villa's men are coming.

Fellow needs an automobile
If he undertakes the journey
To the place to which Zapata
Ordered the famous convention.

AS LOYAL CITIZENS OF THE UNITED STATES

> Often the emigrant faced hostility and prejudice. In
> Texas, after World War I, fear of the Mexican revolu-
> tions and the rise of the Ku Klux Klan forced the old
> *tejanos* and the newcomers to form civic and patriotic
> organizations for their own protection. The League of
> United Latin American Citizens (LULAC) was founded
> in Texas in 1929. Its constitution proclaimed loyalty to
> the "highest ideals of our American society." (Consti-
> tution of the League of United Latin American Cit-
> izens, reprinted in *Latin Americans in Texas* by Paul-
> ine R. Kibbe, Albuquerque, N. Mex., University of
> New Mexico Press, 1946.)

Section 1. As loyal citizens of the United States of America:

We believe in the democratic principle of individual political and religious freedom, in the right of equality of social
and economic opportunity, and in the duty of cooperative
endeavor towards the development of an American society
wherein the cultural resources and integrity of every individual and group constitute basic assets of the American
way of life. As citizens of Latin American descent, we assume our responsibilities and duties and claim our rights and
privileges in the pursuit of a fuller and richer civilization for
this, our native country.

We believe that education is the foundation for the cultural growth and development of this nation and that we are
obligated to protect and promote the education of our people in accordance with the best American principles and
standards. We deplore any infringement of this goal wherever it may occur and regardless of whom it may affect.

We accept that it is not only the privilege but also the obligation of every member of this organization to uphold and defend the rights and duties vested in every American citizen by the letter and the spirit of the law of the land.

Section 2. As members of a democratic society, we recognize our civic duties and responsibilities and we propose:

To use all the appropriate means at our disposal to implement with social action the principles set forth above.

To foster the acquisition and facile use of the official language of our country that we may thereby equip ourselves and our families for the fullest enjoyment of our rights and privileges and the efficient discharge of our duties and obligations to this, our country.

To establish cooperative relationships with other civic organizations and agencies in these fields of public service.

That the members of the League of United Latin American Citizens constitute themselves a service organization to actively promote suitable measures for the attainment of the highest ideals of our American society.

That, in the interests of the public welfare, we shall seek in every way possible to uphold the rights guaranteed to every individual by our state and national laws and to seek justice and equality of treatment in accordance with the law of the land. We shall courageously resist un-American tendencies that deprive citizens of these rights in educational institutions, in economic pursuits, and in social and civic activities.

EL ARRIMADO: THE GUEST IN THE LAND OF BUY NOW, PAY LATER

by Antonio Gomez

La Raza has been an "invisible minority." The emigrant wears not one mask, but several. He is an alien in the land of his ancestors; exile and native, newcomer and founding father, Spanish and Indian, Mexican and Anglo. In one of the first Chicano literary magazines barrio writer Antonio Gomez described the malaise of the emigrant whom he called el arrimado—the parasite, one who is a guest in his own house. ("El Arrimado," *Con Safos*, Vol. 1, No. 1.)

The great giant of America, the United States, casts a huge shadow over the entire hemisphere. Every poor Mexican is familiar with this powerful neighbor, and it is the dream of many to immigrate to the "land of opportunity"; however, the dream of many is the reality of few, for it is no easy task to enter the United States legally. The process of immigration is complicated, drawn out and humiliating. It becomes a process where a human is asking permission to enter the home of another. The latter thinks over this request very carefully. He asks for formal proof of his neighbor's character, and sends him for a medical examination, to rule out the possibility of contaminating his household.

Those Mexicans who pass the scrutiny of the "norte americano," cowed and thankful for the generosity bestowed upon them, enter the promised land of flush toilets, paved streets, electrical systems and a buy-now-pay-later economy. The technological level of the United States, and the relatively higher standard of living, impresses the immigrants and leaves them with a certain respect for the superior people responsible for this gimmickry.

The majority of immigrants obtain jobs that enable them to support themselves and their families in a manner that would be impossible in Mexico. It doesn't matter to them that they occupy the lower portion of the social and economic order. Nor does it matter to them that the white norte americano has a decidedly higher standard of living, and that he maintains all positions of authority. After all, isn't he, the Mexican immigrant, a guest, an "ensimado," and "arrimado," a parasite? Is it not unthinkable for a guest to complain about the lodgings and odd jobs that his host has given him?

The immigrant also finds it unthinkable that he take part in any civic activities, or school matters. What voice does a guest have in the operating of his host's household? What could a Mexican immigrant say or do that would be meaningful to the people responsible for this land of abundance?

It is above mentioned attitudes of the Mexican immigrant, together with the cooperation of the established community, that helps create the so called disinterested or apathetic Mexican American community. The established community has cooperated in the respect that it has never clarified what the status of an immigrant implies in terms of social functioning, nor how that social functioning differs from that of a citizen's. Is an immigrant to think of himself as a guest until he becomes a citizen? What about the thousands of Mexican immigrants who have been in this country for years and years, are they to continue thinking of themselves as guests? Are they to take no part in public affairs that directly involve them?

The above questions are not meant to be directed solely at the established Anglo community, but also at the Mexican American community which is a product of the "arrimado" mentality.

VI. IN THE BARRIOS

LIFE IN THE BARRIOS

The barrio is not a ghetto, though there are ghettos in the barrio. It is a microcosm of a Chicano city, a place of dualities: a liberated zone and a prison; a place of love and warmth, and a place of hatred and violence, where most of La Raza live out their lives. So it is a place of weddings, *bautismos, tardeadas, bailes, velorios,* and patriotic "enchilada dinners." It is a place of poverty and self-reliance, of beloved *ancianos* (the old ones), of *familias,* of *compadres.* To tell of life in the barrio we have selected five short stories by Chicano writers: "Pete Fonesca," the story of a wanderer from barrio to barrio, by Tomas Rivera, formerly of Sam Houston University in Texas, translated by Victoria Ortiz; "El Hoyo" and "Las Comadres" by Mario Suarez, once a migrant laborer, now professor of Romance languages at the University of Texas, whose stories evoke the humanity of a barrio in Tucson, Arizona (*Con Safos*); "Passing Time," by J. L. Navarro, which tells of growing to manhood in the barrios of East Los Angeles (*Con Safos*); and "The Sacred Spot," by Javier Alva, a story of the *pachucos* of Los Angeles (*Con Safos*).

On the Road to Texas: Pete Fonesca

by Tomas Rivera

He'd only just gotten there and he already wanted to leave. He arrived one Sunday afternoon walking from the little town where we bought our food Saturdays and where they didn't mind that we came in the afternoon all dirty from work. It was almost dark when we saw this shape crossing the field. We'd been fooling around in the trees and when we saw him we were almost scared, but then we remembered there was more of *us* so we weren't so scared. He spoke to us when he got near. He wanted to know if there was any work. We told him that there was and there wasn't. There was, but there wasn't till the weeds grew. It'd been pretty dry and the weeds didn't grow. It'd been pretty dry and the weeds didn't grow and all the fields were real clean. The boss was pretty happy about it since he didn't have to pay for weeding the onion fields. Our parents cursed the weather and prayed for rain so the weeds'd grow and we had to make like we cared too, but really we liked getting up late, wandering around in the trees and along the stream killing crows with our slingshots. That's why we said there was but there wasn't. There was work but not tomorrow.

"Aw, fuck it all."

We didn't mind him talking like that. I think we realized how good his words went with his body and clothes.

"There's no god damned work no fuckin' place. Hey, can you give me something to eat? I'm fuckin' hungry. Tomorrow I'm going to Illinois. There's work there for sure . . ."

He took off his baseball cap and we saw that his hair was combed good with a pretty neat wave. He wore those pointed shoes, a little dirty, but you could tell they were expensive ones. And his pants were almost pachuco pants. He

kept saying *chale* and also *nel* and *simón* and we finally decided that he was at least half pachuco. We went with him
to our chicken coop. That's what we called it because it
really was a turkey coop. The boss had bought ten little turkey coops from a guy who sold turkeys and brought them to
his farm. We lived in them, though they were pretty small
for two families, but pretty sturdy. They didn't leak when it
rained, but even though we cleaned them out pretty good
inside they never really lost that stink of chicken shit.

His name was Pete Fonesca and Dad knew a friend of his
pretty good. Dad said he was a big mouth since he was always talking about how he had fourteen gabardine shirts
and that's why they called him *El Catorce Camisas*. They
talked about fourteen shirts a while and when we went to
eat beans with slices of Spam and hot flour-tortillas, Dad invited him to eat with us. He washed his face good and his
hands too, and then he combed his hair real careful, asked
us for Brilliantine and combed his hair again. He liked the
supper a lot and we noticed that when Mom was there he
didn't use pachuco words. After supper he talked a little
more and then lay down on the grass, in the shadow where
the light from the house wouldn't hit him. A little while
later he got up and went to the outhouse and then he lay
down again and fell asleep. Before we went to sleep I heard
Mom say to Dad that she didn't trust that guy.

"Me neither. He's a real con man. Gotta be careful with
him. I've heard about him. *Catorce Camisas* is a big mouth,
but I think it's him who stabbed that wetback in Colorado
and they kicked him out of there or he got away from the
cops. I think it's him. He also likes to smoke marijuana. I
think it's him. I'm not too sure . . ."

Next morning it was raining and when we looked out the
window we saw that Pete had gotten in our car. He was sitting up but it looked like he was sleeping because he wasn't

moving at all. I guess the rain waked him up and that's how come he got in the car. Around nine it stopped raining so we went out and told him to come have breakfast. Mom made him some eggs and then he asked if there was any empty house or some place he could live. And when was work going to start? And how much did they pay? And how much could you get a day? And how many of us worked? Dad told him that we all worked, all five of us, and that sometimes we got almost seventy bucks a day if we could work about fourteen hours. After breakfast Dad and Pete went out and we heard him ask Dad if there was any broads on the farm. Dad answered laughing that there was only one and she was sort of a loser. La Chata, snub-nose. And they went on talking along the path that went round the huts and to the water pump.

They called her La Chata because when she was little she got sick with something like mange on her face and the nose bone had got infected. Then she got better but her nose stayed small. She was real pretty except for her nose and everyone spoke bad about her. They said that even when she was little she liked men a lot and everything about them. When she was fifteen she had her first kid. Everyone blamed one of her uncles but she never told who it was. Her Mom and Dad didn't even get angry. They were pretty nice. Still are. After that, she'd shack up with one guy and then another and each one left her at least one kid. She gave some away, her parents took care of others, but the two oldest stayed with her. They were big enough to work now. When Pete arrived, it was just two weeks after she'd lost again: her last husband had left, he didn't even get mad at her or anything. Just left. La Chata lived in one of the biggest chicken coops with her two sons. That's why Dad told Pete there was only one and she was sort of a loser. We figured Pete was pretty interested in what Dad said, and it seemed pretty funny since La Chata must've been about thirty-five and Pete, well he couldn't be more than twenty-five.

Anyhow, it turned out he *was* interested in what Dad said because later, when we were fooling around near the pump, he asked us about La Chata. Where did she live, how old was she, was she any good? We were just talking about that when La Chata came down to get water and we told him that was her. We said hello to her and she said hello to us, but we noticed that she kept on looking at Pete. Like the people say, she gave him the eye. And even more when he asked her her name.

"Chavela."

"Hey, that's my mother's name."

"No kidding."

"Honest, and my grandmother's, too."

"You son-of-a-bitch."

"You don't know me yet."

La Chata left the pump and when she was pretty far away, Pete sighed and said real loud:

"Hey, mamasita, mamasota linda!"

So she could hear, he told us after. Because according to him broads like to be called that. From then on we noticed that everytime La Chata was near Pete he would always call her *mi chavelona* real loud. He said it loud so she'd hear and I think La Chata liked it because when work started she always chose the rows nearest Pete and if he got ahead of her she'd try and catch up. And then when the boss brought us water Pete always let her drink first. Or he helped her get on and off the truck. The first Saturday they paid us after Pete got there, he bought some fritos for La Chata's kids. That's how it began.

I liked it best when he sang her songs. Pete was going to stay and work, he'd say, until everything was over. He went to live with two other guys in an old trailer they had there. We used to go after supper to talk to them, and sometimes we'd sing. He'd go outside, turn towards La Chata's house and would sing with all his might. In the fields too we'd just get close to her or she'd come along and Pete would let go with one of his songs. Sometimes he even sang in English: *sha bum sha bum* or *lemi go, lemi go lober,* and then in Spanish: *Ella quiso quedarse, cuando vió mi tristeza . . . Cuando te hablen de amor y de ilusiones.* Sometimes he'd even stop working and stand up in the row, if the boss wasn't there, and he'd sort of move his hands and his body. La Chata'd look out of the corner of her eye, like it bothered her, but she always went on taking the rows next to Pete, or meeting him, or catching up to him. About two weeks later they both started going to get water at the truck together, when the boss didn't bring it, and then they'd go behind the truck a while and then La Chata would come out fixing her blouse.

Pete would tell us everything afterwards. One day he told us that if we wanted to see something we should hide behind the trailer that night and he'd try and get her to go in the trailer.

"You know what for . . . to give her some candy. . . ."

Us and the guys who lived with him hid behind the trailer that night and then after a long time we saw La Chata coming towards the trailer. Pete was waiting for her and she'd just got there and he took her hand and pulled her towards him. He put his hand up under her skirt and started kissing her. La Chata didn't say nothing. Then he leaned her up against the trailer, but she got away and told him you son-of-a-bitch, not so fast. Pete was inviting her to come into the trailer but she didn't want to and so they stayed outside. Do you love me, will you marry me, yes I will, when, right now, what about that other cat. Finally she left. We came out of

the dark and he told us all about it. Then he started telling
us all about other broads he'd made. Even white ones. He'd
brought one from Chicago and set up his business in Austin.
There, according to him, the bastards would line up at five
bucks a throw. But he said that the broad he'd really loved
was the first one he married the right way, in the Church.
But she'd died with the first kid.

"I sure cried for that woman, and since then nothing.
This fuckin' life . . . now with this *chavelona,* I'm beginning to feel something for her . . . she's a good person, if
you know what I mean. . . ."

And sometimes he'd start thinking. Then he'd say real sincere like:

"Ay, mi chavelona . . . man, she's a hot one . . . but she
won't let me . . . until I marry her, she says."

Three days after we'd hid, Pete decided to get married.
That's why all that week that's all he talked about. He had
nothing to lose. Why, him and La Chata and the two boys
could save a lot. He'd also have someone to cook his gordi-
tas for him and his nice hot coffee, and someone to wash his
clothes and, according to Pete, she could handle at least one
John a night. He'd start calculating: at four dollars a throw
at least, times seven nights, that was twenty-eight dollars a
week. Even if *he* couldn't work things'd be pretty good. He
also said he liked La Chata's boys. They could buy a jalopy
and then Sundays they could take rides, go to a show, go
fishing or to the dump and collect copper wire to sell. In
fact, he said, him marrying La Chavelona was good for all of
them. And the sooner the better.

A little while later he came to talk to Dad one night. They
went out on the road where no one could hear them and
they talked a pretty long time. That night we heard what
Dad and Mom were saying in the dark:

"Get this: he wants to marry La Chata! He wanted to

elope with her, but what in? So it's better to get married for real. But—get this—he's got some sickness in his blood so he doesn't want to go into town and get the papers. So what he wants is for me to go and ask La Chata's father, Don Chon, for her hand. He wants me to go right away, tomorrow. . . . Don Chon, I've come today commissioned to ask you for the hand of your daughter, Isabel, in matrimony with young Pedro Fonesca . . . How's that, eh? . . . How's it sound, old lady? . . . Tomorrow after work, right before supper. . . ."

Next day all you heard about was how they were going to ask for La Chata's hand. That day Pete and Chavela didn't even talk to each other. Pete went around all day real quiet and sort of glum, like he wanted to show us how serious he was. He didn't even tell us any jokes like he always did. And La Chata also looked real serious. She didn't laugh any all day and every now and then she'd yell at her kids to work faster. Finally the work day finished and before supper Dad washed up, parted his hair four or five times, and went straight to Don Chon's house. Pete met him in the front yard and they both knocked at the door. They went in. *It was okay—they'd asked them to come in.* About half an hour later they all came out of the house laughing. *They'd agreed.* Pete was hugging La Chata real tight. Pretty soon they went into Chavela's house and when it got dark they closed the doors and pulled down the rags on the windows too. That night Dad told us about ten times what happened when he went to ask for her hand.

"Man, I just spoke real diplomatic and he couldn't say no . . ."

Next day it rained. It was Saturday and that was when we really celebrated the wedding. Almost everyone got drunk. There was a little dancing. Some guys got into fights but pretty soon everything calmed down.

They were real happy. There started to be more and more work. Pete, La Chata and the boys always had work. They bought a car. Sundays they'd go driving a lot. They went to Mason City to visit some of La Chata's relatives. She was sort of strutting around real proud. The boys were cleaner now than ever. Pete bought a lot of clothes and was also pretty clean. They worked together, they helped each other, they took real good care of each other, they even sang together in the fields. We all really liked to see them because sometimes they'd even kiss in the fields. They'd go up and down the rows holding hands . . . *Here come the young lovers*. Saturdays they'd go shopping, and go into some little bar and have a couple after buying the groceries. They'd come back to the farm and sometimes even go to a show at night. They really had it good.

"Who would of said that that son-of-a-gun would marry La Chata and do her so right? It looks like he really loves her a lot. Always calling her *mi chavelona*. And can you beat how much he loves those kids? I tell you he's got a good heart. But who was to say that he did. Boy, he looks like a real pachuco. He really loves her, and he doesn't act at all high and mighty. And she sure takes better care of him than that other guy she had before, don't you think? And the kids, all he does is play with them. They like him a lot too. And you gotta say this about him, he's a real hard worker. And La Chata too, she works just as hard. Boy, they're gonna pick up a pretty penny, no? . . . La Chata finally has it pretty good . . . Man, I don't know why you're so mistrusting, old lady. . . ."

Six weeks after the wedding the potato picking ended. There was only a couple of days more work. We figured Tuesday everything would be over and so we fixed up the car that weekend since our heads were already in Texas. Monday I remember we got up early and Dad like always beat us to the outhouse. But I don't even think he got there because he came right back with the news that Pete had left the farm.

"But what do you mean, old man?"

"Yeah, he left. He took the car and all the money they'd saved between him and La Chata and the boys. He left her without a cent. He took everything they'd made . . . What did I tell you? . . . He left . . . What did I tell you?"

La Chata didn't go to work that day. In the fields that's all people talked about. They told the boss about it but he just shook his head, they said. La Chata's folks were good and mad, but I guess we weren't too much. I guess because nothing had happened to us.

Next day work ended. We didn't see La Chata again that year. We came to Texas and a couple of months later, during Christmas, Dad talked to Don Chon who'd just come from Iowa. Dad asked about Pete and he said he didn't know, that he heard he'd been cut up in a bar in Minnesota and was going around saying the cops had taken all his money and the car, and that the boss had told the cops and they'd caught him in Albert Lea. Anyhow, no one had given any money to Don Chon or La Chata. All we remembered was how he'd only just gotten there and he already wanted to leave. Anyhow, Pete sure made his pile. But, like they say, no one knows who his boss is. That all happened around '48. I think La Chata must be dead by now, but her kids must be grown men.

Tucson, Arizona: El Hoyo
by Mario Suarez

From the center of downtown Tucson the ground slopes gently away to Main Street, drops a few feet, and then rolls to the banks of the Santa Cruz River. Here lies the section of the city known as El Hoyo. Why it is called El Hoyo is not very clear. In no sense is it a hole as its name would imply; it is simply the river's immediate valley. Its inhabitants are chicanos who raise hell on Saturday night and listen to Padre Estanislao on Sunday morning. While the term chicano is the short way of saying Mexicano, it is not restricted to the paisanos who came from old Mexico with the territory or the last famine to work for the railroad, labor, sing, and go on relief. Chicano is the easy way of referring to everybody. Pablo Gutierrez married the Chinese grocer's daughter and now runs a meat department; his sons of Killer Jones who threw a fight in Harlem and fled to El Hoyo to marry Cristina Mendez. And so are all of them. However, it is doubtful that all these spiritual sons of Mexico live in El Hoyo because of its scenic beauty—it is everything but beautiful. Its houses are simple affairs of unplastered adobe, wood, and abandoned car parts. Its narrow streets are mostly clearings which have, in time, acquired names. Except for some tall trees which nobody has ever cared to identify, nurse, or destroy, the main things known to grow in the general area are weeds, garbage piles, dark-eyed chavalos, and dogs. And it is doubtful that the chicanos live in El Hoyo because it is safe—many times the Santa Cruz has risen and inundated the area.

In other respects living in El Hoyo has its advantages. If one is born with a weakness for acquiring bills, El Hoyo is where the collectors are less likely to find you. If one has acquired the habit of listening to Octavio Perea's Mexican Hour in the wee hours of the morning with the radio on at full blast, El Hoyo is where you are less likely to be reported to the authorities. Besides, Perea is very popular and sooner or later to everybody "Smoke In The Eyes" is dedicated between the pinto beans and white flour commercials. If one, for any reason whatever, comes on an extended period of hard times, where, if not in El Hoyo are the neighbors more willing to offer solace? When Teofila Malacara's house burned to the ground with all her belongings and two children, a benevolent gentleman carried through the gesture that made tolerable her burden. He made a list of five hundred names and solicited from each a dollar. At the end of a month he turned over to the tearful but grateful senora one hundred dollars in cold cash and then accompanied her on a short vacation. When the new manager of a local store decided that no more chicanas were to work behind the counters, it was the chicanos of El Hoyo who, on taking their individually small but collectively great buying power elsewhere, drove the manager out and the girls returned to their jobs. When the Mexican Army was enroute to Baja California and the chicanos found out that the enlisted men ate only at infrequent intervals, it was El Hoyo's chicanos who crusaded across town with pots of beans and trays of tortillas to meet the train. When someone gets married, celebrating is not restricted to the immediate friends of the couple. Everybody is invited. Anything calls for a celebration and a celebration calls for anything. On Armistice Day there are no less than half a dozen good fights at the Riverside Dance Hall. On Mexican Independence Day more than one flag is sworn allegiance to amid cheers for the queen.

And El Hoyo is something more. It is this something more which brought Felipe Sanchez back from the wars after having killed a score of Germans with his body resembling a patch-work quilt to marry Julia Armijo. It brought Joe Zepeda, a gunner flying B-24's over Germany, back to compose boleros. He has a metal plate for a skull. Perhaps El Hoyo is proof that those people exist, and perhaps exist best, who have as yet failed to observe the more popular modes of human conduct. Perhaps the humble appearance of El Hoyo justifies the indifferent shrug of those made aware of its existence. Perhaps El Hoyo's simplicity motivates an occasional chicano to move away from its narrow streets, babbling comadres and shrieking children to deny the blood-well from which he springs and to claim the blood of a conquistador while his hair is straight and his face beardless. Yet El Hoyo is not an outpost of a few families against the world. It fights for no causes except those which soothe its immediate angers. It laughs and cries with the same amount of passion in times of plenty and of want.

Perhaps El Hoyo, its inhabitants, and its essence can best be explained by telling a bit about a dish called capirotada. Its origin is uncertain. But, according to the time and the circumstance, it is made of old, new or hard bread. It is softened with water and then cooked with peanuts, raisins, onions, cheese, and panocha. It is fired with sherry wine. Then it is served hot, cold, or just "on the weather" as they say in El Hoyo. The Sermenos like it one way, the Garcias another, and the Ortegas still another. While it might differ greatly from one home to another, nevertheless it is still capirotada. And so it is with El Hoyo's chicanos. While being divided from within and from without, like the capirotada, they remain chicanos.

Tucson, Arizona: Las Comadres

by Mario Suarez

Whenever two chicanos find that they have many things in common they often end up baptizing each other's children and becoming compadres. If they work together, one compadre will often say to the other for all to hear, "Compadre, you are the best boilermaker in Arizona. Tell them who is number two." If they drink together it means they constantly seek each other's company, share the most intimate of secrets, and even cry over their beers, at least until they become cosigners. All of this automatically makes their wives comadres. When two comadres meet, no matter how much they criticize one another behind each others back, they hug one another as though they had not seen each other for years. Then they sit down somewhere and talk over the latest mitote, gossip, flying over El Hoyo's back fences.

In the late 20's two comadres, escaping the crowded tenements on Alvarado Street, bought adjoining lots in El Hoyo and in time moved into half-finished adobe structures. One of these, Anastacia Elizondo, was a stout comadre with four daughters and a husband named Lazarillo who worked for the railroad and who, it was known to everybody, beat her up now and then for being a lousy housekeeper. The other, Lola Lopez, was a comadre who, to escape the city laundry, had converted her front room into a store where she eked out a living by selling the five cents of yellow cheese, the ten cents of beans, and the chango coffee. She had two young sons, Tino and Kiko, as well as a husband named Nacho who constantly complained of the ailments he had incurred in a fall while building the house and therefore could not work but always came home drunk to serenade his Lola, as well as the neighbors, at daybreak.

Whenever Anastacia got one of her beatings she immediately ran next door to her comadre Lola with tears welling from her eyes to bubble, "Me p . . pego. He . . He b . . beat me, c . . comadre. Wh . . what am I t . . do?

"Oh, he will change, Anastacia. He will change," comforted Lola. "I am sure of it."

Wh . . what a m . . miserable cr . . creature I am," sobbed Anastacia. "I wish I were d . . dead."

In the ensuing years, though the rest of the world was to experience such far reaching events as the stock market crash, the end of prohibition, a cruel depression and the rise of Schicklgruber, the human condition of El Hoyo and its inhabitants remained very much the same. True, a decade and a half had given Anastacia a slight down over her upper lip along with a few more pounds. However, her bad house-keeping habits continued, along with her usual beatings. Lola, in turn, had enlarged her store and ran it with the help of her two sons. She was still serenaded by her ever ailing Nacho at daybreak. Meanwhile, Anastacia's oldest daughter Maria Luisa and Lola's son Tino, who had scratched, bit, and kicked one another in the days when Anastacia came over after one of her beatings and who saw one another through the years with the familiarity of brother and sister, came to fall in love, an event which, once realized, was obvious and final.

Hitler's march, however, could not but have repercussions felt all the way to El Hoyo. And, Pearl Harbor, the ensuing trickle, then river, of money which found its way to El Hoyo via the air base, increased railroad activity, an aircraft plant and ultimately allotment checks, was such that even the spirit of comadreada underwent a change. Soon comadres who had known each for years, on installing inside plumbing, suddenly turned their faces and put their noses in the air when they chanced on one another in the street. Other comadres, buying chenille bed spreads and venetian blinds for the first time, soon said of other comadres not yet as fortunate, "Ai, those peoples. Esa gente. They do not know how to live." And still other comadres, moving out of El Hoyo, thanks to their husbands' steady encounter with the time clock, went as far as to say, "El Hoyo. Where is that?" The sickness even afflicted a few compadres.

Through all of this Anastacia, considering herself a very

level headed person, merely said to her comadre Lola, "Ai comadre. What liars some women are. They have much more tongue than sense. As for me, you know how my Lazarillo has always earned his good checks, especially now that he often works double shifts. Yet never have I given to bragging."

Lola merely nodded and said nothing.

One night Lazarillo's rage was so great on finding that his food was not ready when he came home from a long shift that he blackened one of Anastacia's eyes. Immediately Anastacia ran next door to her comadre Lola with tears welling from her eyes. "He has tr . . tried t . . to k . . kill me," she cried. "Ai comadre. What am I t . . to do?"

Lola, often tempted to tell Anastacia to correct her housekeeping habits, merely said, "Oh, he will change."

However, the following beatings Anastacia received were so violent that she decided on a separation. She cashed in a few war bonds and, with her daughters in tow, moved far away from El Hoyo and her tormenting husband Lazarillo. For a long time nobody saw or heard much of Anastacia. Mitote had it, however, that she was now working at the air base and had dyed her hair. And, mitote had it that one day she was overheard saying to another comadre who had also moved out of El Hoyo, "Ai, how good it feels to live away from El Hoyo, away from so many low class people. I am so glad my daughters now live away from there and will never marry beneath their class." As to her comadre Lola, Anastacia had been known to answer when asked about her, "I am sorry, pero yo . . I do not know any Lola Lopez."

Anastacia's daughter Maria Luisa, however, kept on seeing Lola's Tino in spite of her mother's advice until the day Uncle Sam greeted him and gave him travel orders. Anastacia, overjoyed, sighed with relief and said, "Thank God he is gone. I am sure any daughter of mine can do better than to keep company with the son of an ex-laundry worker." But Maria Luisa, having given her beloved Tino the greatest proof of her love to take with him . . .

Months later . . . when it was obvious, Anastacia became indignant. She cried. She cursed. She threatened to kill herself. "But what will your father say? What of our neighbors? What of . . ."

"I don't care about the neighbors, mama," replied Maria Luisa. "As for my father, I already told him."

"You what?" asked Anastacia, shocked.

"I phoned him and told him," said Maria Luisa, matter of factly. "All he asks is that I be a good wife."

Once again Anastacia cried, cursed, threatened to kill herself. But, realizing it was to no avail, the embossed invitations went out the minute Tino phoned informing Maria Luisa the dates of his leave.

On the morning the young couple emerged from the cathedral as man and wife, Anastacia, in white satin, white gloves, and a gigantic hat, excitedly went about her new friends, among them many Smiths and Hendersons, assuring them that her new son-in-law was of the most excellent family, scarcely noticing the presence of her comadre Lola and her compadre Nacho, both of these awed by the magnificence of the affair. At the reception, held at Anastacia's fashionable apartment rather than at Lola's house in El Hoyo as tradition dictated, it happened that Maria Luisa's corsets did their job so well that, to the surprise of the select guests, the bride's labor pangs began and even before she could be helped to the bedroom, nature relieved the bride of a screaming, kicking chicano. In the excitement the young priest who had arrived at the house for his chocolate and cake could do no more than to start to make a half hearted effort to preach about sin. But with Anastacia crying, then fainting, the guests in a state of exhilaration and disbelief, and the affair in a general state of confusion, he smiled inwardly and poured himself some whiskey from a nearby bottle. To have been heard above all the commotion he would have needed a bigger set of lungs.

Late that afternoon, the petals of Maria Luisa's bridal bouquet still fragrant, found Anastacia in El Hoyo, crying inconsolably on her comadre Lola's shoulder. "What a miserable creature I am, comadre. Today has been the most tragic day of my life. How I wish I were dead."

"Tragic? On the contrary," said Lola. "I think this day has been a very memorable one for both of us. We are both now mother-in-laws, grandmothers as well as comadres. And, because we are now more than comadres, I must tell you it would be best if you moved back to your house. Lazarillo is still there. I am sure he misses you even though it is said you have forgotten him."

"Bad tongues, comadre. Bad tongues. I have never forgotten my beloved Lazarillo. Ai comadre. What would I ever do without you?"

That very night, under cover of darkness, Anastacia and her daughters were back in El Hoyo. But if Lazarillo had once rained blows on her, more to Anastacia's dismay, he was now indifferent. Everyday Lazarillo got up, ate in silence, and went to work. Even though he often came home past midnight, Anastacia now had his food ready, not to mention the great care she took to wash his clothes, clean the house. Still Lazarillo remained indifferent.

"Que hare?" asked Anastacia, crying on her comadre's shoulder. "What shall I do?"

"All you can do is cook his food, prepare his clothes and clean the house as you are doing," said Lola. "He will change."

"Alas, comadre," sighed Anastacia, the tears running

down her cheeks. "I fear I have lost his love. How I wish I were dead."

A few weeks later, however, most of El Hoyo was awakened one night by wails, cries, and crashing furniture. For a while it seemed as though somebody was being murdered. A few comadres maliciously even thought of phoning the police because a good scandal would provide mitote for weeks. But nobody did and in a few hours all was peaceful again.

Our comadre Anastacia, lying in bed with a pair of black eyes and her hair dishevelled, bubbled on her pillow. As she heard her comadre Lola's Nacho start her serenade a few windows away, Anastacia breathed deeply of El Hoyo's cool summer air and sighed dreamily. Then she gently scratched her own Lazarillo's shoulder and asked, "Are you awake, my love?"

East Los Angeles: Passing Time

by J. L. Navarro

Midnoon. The sun was out, shining modest heat over the city, bathing the Valley in the light of the sun. All the bright and rich colors of summer flowed to the eyes with the sight of cracked streets and walks, loose houses, hills with jade grass and trees and brush; and people walked and cars passed and dogs ran about, and the odors of these things mingled with the gentle currents of the wind.

Denny walked the paved length of Humbolt Street, tripping leisurely as he smoked his last J. At the moment he was on his way to pick up some more weed at Bear's place. All the components of this day were just right he thought. The houses on either side of this narrow street seemed right for this street; the children that played with worn toys were the children that belonged here. The old ladies and old men, the relics of the neighborhood were well in their place here; the girls, young, pretty and shy looking girls, rowdy Cholas, and the little girls playing with little boys were still indefinite about themselves, where they will be, how they will fit into the neighborhood in later years; the guys, the schoolbook-types that were seldom seen on the streets after dark, and the lowriders riding low over the streets, standing on corners ready to intimidate whom they choose, taking dope, digging sounds, pinning down female ass on the streets, ogling bouncing tits and curving legs. Yes, he thought, everything seemed to be in its place.

He came to Isabelle Street and, heading away from the Rose Hill housing projects, began to walk its incline. He passed Juan's store and Oscar's store, and then Manuel's store. They were all small establishments that grossly lacked the glamor of the supermarkets. They were all dingy looking and, yet, in contradiction, there was a genuine wholesomeness about them. On their walls they had the Happy Valley gang writings that were prevalent throughout the neighborhood. There wasn't a store in the Valley that didn't have the Valley's art on its walls.

Denny walked up Isabelle Street enjoying the sights and the pleasant weather, and thinking of the neighborhood. It was, and it said of itself, in silent pride, a poor people's neighborhood. Happy Valley wasn't a fairyland type village, or a Westwood, or a Beverly Hills. It was harsh and antiquated with a petrified charm that touched everything from the rotting pads to the last blade of grass on the earth. Bel Air and Brentwood and Beverly Hills and Westwood shove their manicured lawns up their ass, and every other paddy neighborhood in between could go fuck itself with a hot iron. They could have their paddy ground with sweat off his balls. And he knew only too well that the people of those places would tell him the same thing. He couldn't understand the Negro, with his want, not for a better life, but for a better pad, better rags, a better car, better everything the whites had. Whatever better things the blacks got they wouldn't be able to show them off in a paddy neighborhood, and that was for sure. Yeah, maybe a handful could. But shit, by thousands? That's the way it is, the way it's got to be. The sick thing called prejudice that infected damn near everyone on earth would not allow it to be any other way.

The Mexicans had problems too, just like the blacks had problems; they were similar problems, because they all related to the same things. But as far as Denny was concerned, both groups were where they were, and there was nothing that could be done about it. But, he wondered, is this really the way to think? Isn't there something better? For everyone? . . . Yeah. Sure. There had to be. There was a solution somewhere. But he would not live long enough to see it, of this he was convinced. Everybody's always looking for something better, and most of the time they don't know what the fuck they're really looking for. And if, by chance, they do know, they don't know how to attain it. The answers that have been given, the bills that have been passed, as far as he was concerned, have been one put-on after another to keep everyone cool, on ice . . . The hell with it.

A car was coming down Isabelle, lowriding and coasting over the cracked asphalt. It was Peanuts' car. As the '53 Chevy approached Denny it slowed down, pulling over to the curb.

Little Man sat on the passenger side of the front seat. He said, "Where you going, Denny?"

"Up to Bear's place."

"To get some weed?"

"Yeah."

"Get in, man. We'll give you a ride. You turn us on?"

"Yeah, I'll turn you on with a pinch."

Denny got in the back. The seats were diamond-tuck

black leather. The car itself was a luminous green, augmented by new whitewalls and mag rims. Peanuts was one
for keeping his cars looking clean. His car was typical low-
rider in style: low seats allowed for only the heads of the
passengers to peer over the windows, and the frame of the
car was lowered all around to about six or seven inches off
the ground. The panelboard was spotless and the chrome
gleamed, and Denny noticed that Peanuts had had an F.M.
radio installed. He wondered where Peanuts had stolen it.

"Where'd you get the radio, Peanuts?"

"In the Avenues. Some chump left his car open. He was
in a party, you know. Hell, I saw it, I took it."

Little Man said, "What happened to your car, Denny?"

"Nothing. I just thought I'd walk."

"Man, if I had a car I'd never walk. I'd cruise and pick up
broads and just plain ball."

"You punk," Peanuts said. "You don't even know how to
drive. What are you going to do with a car?"

"Drive it up your ass!" said Little Man, laughing and
snapping his fingers.

Peanuts smiled and ignored him. "Ey, Denny," he said.
"Know what we did to this guy." He indicated Little Man
with a shake of his head. "We got him so fucked up on reds
and wine one night we had him with his pants off. Yeah, we
pantsed him and took him on like a regular punk. No shit."

"You fuckin' liar!" yelled Little Man.

Peanuts smiled and continued. "And Marco, you know
what he did? He got a needle and some ink and then tat-
tooed a spider on Little Man's ass. A hairy black widow on
his left bun, big as life."

"You're a fuckin' liar, you prick."

"Yeah? Take down your pants and show him the spider."

"Fuck you!"

"See, you know I ain't lyin'. You don't want to take your

pants down 'cause you know there's a spider plastered there on your bun. He's just waiting for the scab to fall off so it'll look pretty for you, Denny."

"Later with you," said Little Man. "You're crazy."

"If I'm lyin', then prove you ain't got no spider on your ass."

"Fuck you!" said Little Man. "I don't have to do nothing."

"Look, man, I swear to God, if you don't have a spider on your ass I'll take back everything I said. But you know and I know that you got one big black widow on your left bun."

"I'm going to shine it on," said Little Man. "You're crazy."

Peanuts took his eyes off the road to look back at Denny. "See," he said. "I told you."

Denny just smiled at the trip. He didn't want to get in on it. It was between them. Peanuts and Little Man were hardcore lowriders and they would always be. That's how their lives had shaped them. Perhaps they would have been different altogether if they had lived in a different part of town, or had fallen in with a different group of boys. There was no way of telling, because so many things had made them what they were. Peanuts was the product of a family that had breeded a string of hypes, from the youngest sister to the oldest brother. Peanuts himself wasn't strung out, and perhaps this was because he was the youngest of the clan. Lately though, both him and Little Man had fallen into the habit of sharing a bag whenever one of them had the coin. Denny didn't care for hypes and he hoped they wouldn't get hooked. But this wasn't his business. Everyone had his own hang ups.

Little Man said, "Denny, want to score some stuff? Nardo says he gots two dollars. I got one. If you put in two more we can get a bag and all of us goez."

"I don't go for that shit, man."

"No? Well then loan me the two bills."

"I ain't got it, man. I just got enough for the grass."

"Listen to him. Orale, Denny, don't be like that."

"I tell you what, Little Man. You show me the spider on your ass and I'll give you the bread."

"Fuck you, too!"

Peanuts laughed. "Go on, man, show it to him. It's an easy two bones."

Again, Little Man said, "Fuck you!"

Peanuts drove the car to the top of the northern hill and turned the car onto a dead-end street. Denny got out and walked over to Bear who was standing with some of the younger guys from the Cobras. The much practiced tough looks came to their faces as Denny approached them, and they pinned him down in a group. He knew Bear well enough, but the younger dudes from the Valley were those whom he saw every now and again. He greeted a few of them. Some of them continued staring.

Bear and Denny walked away from the group to an unpainted fence that was decorated with gang signs and symbols: H V, 13, (Swastika), C/S, crosses, names, Por Vida, Tu Mama, Rifa, Peggy de la Valley. Over the fence was Bear's back yard. It was spacious and shaded by two wide spreading avocado trees. A husky German Shepherd was leashed to a pole of the back porch with a long extending cord. Dry turds were scattered over the ground and flies were buzzing over them.

"What can I do for you," said Bear.

He was short, a heavyset Mexican with a piggish face, and there was a mechanical animation about the way he moved. It may have been how the arms hung down over the squat, seemingly inert, body. Bear wore his wool "beanie" cap and

his thick woolen tanker jacket. He was a lowrider that pre-
ferred khaki pants to the later styles, and he was the kind of
pusher everyone liked to have around.

"I'll take a half pound," Denny said, feeling very much
the customer in an underground market. He took out three
tens and a five, and gave the bills to Bear who nodded silently and went to get the grass somewhere from his back
yard, behind the house.

As of late, Bear had taken to dealing in the afternoons because the heat was getting strong on the block. A few weeks
back the narcs had thrown a raid. No one was busted and
nothing was found. Business was still happening, in the afternoon, of course, when the law could be seen behind the
bushes, or coming up the hills. Bear was around when business hours were on, from Monday to Saturday, except Sunday, which was his day off. During his working days, if he
was holding, he would faithfully be there to fill the needs of
the many heads in the neighborhood. He dealt in pills (reds
& whites) and grass, from a lik to a pound, and if you
wanted he could get you bricks. He was a heavy retail
pusher. A smart one, Denny thought. He wondered if jive
would ever become legal. If it did, it would put a lot of guys
like Bear out of business. Moonlighting pushers and full
time pushers took pride in what they were doing; filling the
needs of the ever increasing number of heads in L.A. The
only dealers Denny stayed away from were the hypes, and
those who pushed stuff on the side but who didn't take it
themselves. Of the latter there were few in the Valley. Most
hypes in the neighborhood pushed to maintain their own
habits. Those who pushed weed were the ones that separated the good guys from the bad. But, again, everyone had
his own trip. No matter how weird it may appear to others,
everyone had his own private trip.

Bear came back and on the sly handed Denny the bag of grass. "Take it easy," Denny said.

"Yeah," said Bear. "Take it easy."

Los Angeles: The Sacred Spot

by Javier Alva

A copy of that morning's Herald Express was spread out on the floor beneath Felipe's feet; it was open at the center exposing Mr. Hearst's editorial to the dim light.

"Last night's zoot suit riot may be only the beginning of a long overdue cleansing of our community of the Mexican criminal gangs that the citizens of Los Angeles have come to recognize because of their flamboyant and indecent attire and duck tail haircuts. Last night the Navy's taxicab brigade visited the North Broadway area. According to our latest reports fifteen zoot suiters were "cleansed" and divested of their ridiculous garb by a disciplined group of our sea-going fighting men. . ."

Felipe's left foot rested on the editorial, the sole of his shoe slightly soiling the crisp white paper while the heavy wooden stock of the 30-06 weighted against his cheek; shifting with the movement of his facial muscles, the weapon moved in a miniscule dance across the splintered windowsill where the barrel lay—waiting.

Across the narrow street Felipe could barely discern the hands of the old clock above don Ramon's grocery store. It was seven sixteen and not yet completely dark on this summer night of June 6, 1943. Tiring of holding up the rifle, Felipe glanced about the bare room looking for a chair with which to prop up the weapon so that it would remain in a firing position—sighting down into the empty street. There were no chairs, but across the room there was an empty

milk box that Felipe placed in position beneath the weapon
so that it held the stock with the barrel resting on the windowsill.

After peering out into the street, assuring himself that
there were no headlights approaching from either direction,
Felipe, satisfied that he could relax for a few seconds, pulled
a half-filled pack of Lucky Strikes out of his pocket and
shook out a cigarette. After inhaling deeply and expelling
the smoke slowly through his nostrils, he sat on the floor
with his back propped against the plaster wall. Holding the
smoking cigarette between his thumb and index finger, Felipe's eyes moved from the burning tip, to the long white
cylinder, to his hands: brown, wet with perspiration, and almost invisible in the darkness of the room; these hands—belonged in this room, in this barrio. They were born two
blocks away and had never left the barrio except for the one
summer when all the family had traveled north to pick lettuce near Salinas. The fingers were long, straight, and
strong; they were fingers of the barrio. These same hands,
that now held a cigarette, fashioned toy swords not too long
ago, and they shot slingshots, and they switched the blades
that were the instruments for defending Chicano honor in
the barrio. And within the skin of these same brown hands
there flowed the blood of the Aztec and the Spaniard, of the
Moor and the Toltec, the Iberian Christian and the Sephar-
dic Jew. These hands were Felipe and his history; Felipe as
a plumed serpent, and Felipe in his drapes that the gabachos called zoot-suits. It was because he wore a zoot-suit
that the sailors in the taxi cabs would find him and beat him,
would leave him lying bloodied and naked in the street.

Yesterday they had gotten his cousin Bobby and him having just come home from New Guinea, still sick from the
malaria. Felipe's mother had cried when she heard of it, she

couldn't understand why Bobby had been beaten. He was still in the Army! Next week he would go back, but yesterday when he took his girl to the show, he made the mistake, se le durmio el gallo. He wore his drapes instead of his uniform. When the gabacho sailors saw him walking down Broadway with his arm around Carmen's waist, he wasn't a paratrooper with two bronze stars recuperating from malaria; he was just a zoot-suiter, a pachuco, a dirty greaser.

The sound of approaching car engines startled Felipe; he quickly put out the cigarette against the sole of his shoe, and after flipping the butt on the floor, he turned toward the window. The first taxi was already half way around the corner. The laughter of the sailors floated up from the street and lapped bitterly at Felipe's ears. He pressed the stock of the rifle well against the crook of his shoulder, while sighting along the barrel; at the same time his finger tightened on the trigger. As the second taxi passed beneath the street lamp, Felipe squeezed the trigger. The rifle jumped in his arms, as the force of the exploding bullet drove the stock back, hard against his shoulder. Felipe saw the sailor's head burst like a small white hat flying out into the street; but the taxi did not stop! Others behind it were blowing their horns now, gaining speed, trying desperately—all of them like yellow bugs—to get out of the barrio. Before he could shoot a second time the last of them had turned the corner.

Felipe heard the first highpitched whine of police sirens while he was cleaning the rifle, wiping off all the fingerprints. After picking up the cigarette butt and used matches, he wiped off the windowsill, and kicking the door open, hurried down the stairs. Once outside, he climbed a tall chain-link fence, ran across Mrs. Olvera's yard, climbed a second shorter wooden fence, and opened the back door of his grandmother's house.

He sat on the edge of the small cot where he slept, and breathed heavily. He was safe. And this feeling of safety calmed his lungs, and eased the heaving of his chest. Then with steady fingers, he reached down into his pants cuff to extract the thin, half-smoked leno he had saved that day. He placed it in his lips, and set a match to it. Then drawing deeply, he felt the blue marijuana smoke fill him, then lift him, and then set his brain dancing around a bloody sailor hat in the street, around a bloody sacred spot, around another one of the many sacred spots in Felipe's barrio.

THE VATOS

The barrio is a place of death: not just biological death—the *pelona, calaca y dientuda*—that La Raza has known more intimately than the *gabacho* (foreigner), but also spiritual death and intellectual death. *Ya nos chingaron.* The youth of La Raza have immolated their flesh and hopes on the teeth of the Great *Chingada* (Whore)! In gang fights, street brawls, wife beatings, knifings, alcoholism, and heroin addiction they pay homage to *La Chiva.* "The Story of a Vato" (*La Raza Yearbook*, September, 1968), by an anonymous member of a street gang in San Fernando, California, tells of the camaraderie and fear that bind the *vatos* (gang members) together, while in "You Are Lower Than Animals," a Superior Court judge in San Jose voices the hatred of the *vatos* that pulls their knot tighter (*Carta Editorial*, Vol. 6, No. 9, October, 1969).

The Story of a Vato

This is the story of life in a Mexican barrio, the barrio is called "San Fer." The kids, so called Pachuco's, run this barrio; life in this barrio is rough, harsh. The boys learned early to carry can openers and knives. As soon as they got a little older they graduated to switchblades, lengths of chain and guns, if they could get hold of them.

The boys jointed together, to form street gangs and some of them sported the Pachuco's brand between the thumbs and forefingers of their left hands. They formed a closely knit group that regarded the Anglos as their natural enemies. You find these Pachuco's mostly in the barrio—Kalisher Street—in streets, corners, alleys, and inside dark streets; it is the largest barrio in San Fernando Valley, compared to other barrios.

This gang is the stuff of life as the Pachuco knows it. For it he will undertake the most fantastic stunts to prove a great deal, he will risk life and freedom to maintain his growing reputation as a tough fighter, a rugged guy, at the young age they enter the "front of life." They find conflicts so perplexing and so full of both cultures—that of their parents and that of America—and create their own world of Pachuquismo; the Vatos have created their own language, Pachucano; their own style of dress; their own folklore, and behavior patterns.

The Vatos have developed a barrio group spirit that has resulted in the establishment of a few-score areas and territories. One of these territories is "Borrego Valley." The Vatos in this territory are from O'Melveny St. to Laurel Canyon Blvd. These Vatos hang out in the center of Acala Ave., a dark street, and in the alleys around that area. These Vatos in this area are better organized and a little tighter due to the fact that it is a smaller group, and therefore, all the Vatos participate in the activities planned by them. Everybody shows and brings anything that will be enjoyed by the group; for instance, one boy will bring beer or wine while others will bring "rifa," still others bring money for the use of activities or gas for a member's car.

This is a thing that goes on every night with usually something different every night that can be called a "dead kick." This is a neighborhood that never looks for any trouble but is always full of excitement.

You Are Lower Than Animals

"We ought to send you out of the country—send you back to Mexico . . . You ought to commit suicide. You are lower than animals and haven't the right to live in organized society—just miserable, lousy, rotten people. Maybe Hitler was right. The animals in our society probably ought to be destroyed because they have no right to live among human beings."

Were these the mouthings of a lynch mob or the taunts of a racist sheriff?

No. They were uttered by the Honorable Gerald S. Chargin, a judge of the Superior Court of the State of California, presiding at a juvenile hearing in San Jose.

The outrageously intemperate language used by Judge Chargin clearly requires that he be removed from the bench.

Before the judge on Sept. 2 was a 17-year-old Mexican-American youth accused of incest involving his 15-year-old sister. He had originally pleaded innocent but reportedly changed his plea.

In his diatribe against the young defendant, Judge Chargin broadened his remarks including this gratuitous reference to the sister: "Well, probably she will have half a dozen children and three or four marriages before she is 18."

The judge's indictment of "miserable, lousy, rotten people" led Dep. Public Defender Fred Lucero to object that "the court is indicting the whole Mexican group . . . What appals me is that the court is saying that Hitler was right in genocide."

To which Judge Chargin replied: "What are we going to do with the mad dogs of our society?

"Either we have to kill them or send them to an institution or place them out of the hands of good people because that's the theory—one of the theories of punishment is if they get to the position that they want to act like mad dogs, then we have to separate them from society."

Although the judge told the defendant "You will probably end up in state prison before you are 25, and that's where you belong anyhow," he finally ordered the youth released on probation.

Chargin excused his behavior by saying that "it is an accepted fact that these lectures are stated in harsh terms to impress upon the minds of the youth the seriousness of the situation in which they find themselves."

Nothing, however, can excuse language so harsh and so intemperate as to arouse an entire community to anger over such racial slurs.

The transcript of the Sept. 2 hearing has now been forwarded by the Attorney General's office to the Commission on Judicial Qualifications with a formal request to "expedite" an investigation.

There can be no other conclusion than that Judge Chargin is not qualified to sit on the bench. He stands convicted by his own words.

JUSTICE IN THE SOUTHWEST

Report of the United States Commission on Civil Rights

In the barrio, according to a contemporary folk saying, "There are only two kinds of Anglos who are interested in us—the sociologists and the police." Eliezer Risco, a community leader in Los Angeles and Fresno, has likened the police to an "Army of Occupation." In the report of the United States Commission on Civil Rights, the activities of the police are emphasized as the most obvious example of *gabacho* regulation and control of barrio life; also described are the biases and disadvantages Chicanos face on juries and in the courts. (Mexican Americans and the Administration of Justice in the Southwest, Wash., D.C., U.S. Government Printing Office, March, 1970.)

FINDINGS

1. *Police misconduct*

There is evidence of widespread patterns of police misconduct against Mexican Americans in the Southwest. Such patterns include:

(a) incidents of excessive police violence against Mexican Americans;

(b) discriminatory treatment of juveniles by law enforcement officers;

(c) discourtesy toward Mexican Americans;

(d) discriminatory enforcement of motor vehicle ordinances;

(e) excessive use of arrests for "investigation" and of "stop and frisk";

(f) interference with attempts to rehabilitate narcotics addicts

2. *Inadequate protection*

Complaints also were heard that police protection in Mexican American neighborhoods was inadequate in comparison to that in other neighborhoods.

3. *Interference with Mexican American organizational efforts*

In several instances law enforcement officers interfered with Mexican American organizational efforts aimed at improving the conditions of Mexican Americans in the Southwest.

4. *Inadequacy of local remedies for police malpractice*

Remedies for police malpractice in the Southwest were inadequate:

(a) in most Southwestern cities the only places where individuals can file complaints against the police are the police departments themselves. Internal grievance procedures did not result in adequate remedies for police malpractice;

(b) some cities in the Southwest have established independent or quasi-independent police review boards but these have not provided effective relief to complainants;

(c) civil litigation by Mexican Americans against police officers accused of civil rights violations is infrequent;

(d) there are few instances of successful local prosecutions of police officers for unlawful acts toward Mexican Americans;

(e) there have been instances of retaliation against Mexican Americans who complain about law enforcement officers to the local police department or to the FBI.

5. *Federal remedies*

(a) Agents of the Federal Bureau of Investigation have often failed to interview important witnesses in cases of alleged violation of 18 U.S.C. 242 or interviewed such witnesses in a perfunctory and hostile manner.

(b) More aggressive efforts to implement 18 U.S.C. 242 by the Department of Justice are needed.

6. *Underrepresentation of Mexican Americans on juries*

There is a serious and widespread underrepresentation of Mexican Americans on grand and petit State juries in the Southwest:

(a) neither lack of knowledge of the English language nor low-incomes of Mexican Americans can explain the wide disparities between the Mexican American percentage of the population and their representation on juries;

(b) judges or jury commissioners frequently do not make affirmative efforts to obtain a representative cross section of the community for jury service;

(c) the peremptory challenge is used frequently both by prosecutors and defendants' lawyers to remove Mexican Americans from petit jury venires.

The underrepresentation of Mexican Americans on grand and petit juries results in distrust by Mexican Americans of the impartiality of verdicts.

7. *Bail*

Local officials in the Southwest abuse their discretion:

(a) in setting excessive bail to punish Mexican Americans rather than to guarantee their appearance for trial;

(b) in failing to give Mexican American defendants an opportunity to be released until long after they were taken into custody;

(c) by applying unduly rigid standards for release of Mexican Americans on their own recognizance where such release is authorized.

In many parts of the Southwest, Mexican American defendants are hindered in their attempts to gain release from custody before trial because they cannot afford the cost of bail under the traditional bail system.

8. *Counsel*

There are serious gaps in legal representation for Mexican Americans in the Southwest:

(a) the lack of appointed counsel in misdemeanor cases results in serious injustices to indigent Mexican American defendants;

(b) even in felony cases, where counsel must be provided for indigent defendants, there were many complaints that appointed counsel often was inadequate;

(c) where public defender's offices are available to indigent criminal defendants, they frequently did not have enough lawyers or other staff members to adequately represent all their clients, many of whom are Mexican Americans;

(d) in parts of the Southwest there are not enough attorneys to provide legal assistance to indigent Mexican Americans involved in civil matters;

(e) many lawyers in the Southwest will not handle cases for Mexican American plaintiffs or defendants because they are "controversial" or not sufficiently rewarding financially;

(f) despite the enormous need for lawyers fluent in Spanish and willing to handle cases for Mexican American clients, there are very few Mexican American lawyers in the Southwest.

9. *Attitudes toward the courts*

Mexican Americans in the Southwest distrust the courts and think they are insensitive to their background, culture, and language. The alienation of Mexican Americans from the courts and the traditional Anglo-American legal system is particularly pronounced in northern New Mexico.

10. *Language disability*

Many Mexican Americans in the Southwest have a language disability that seriously interferes with their relations with agencies and individuals responsible for the administration of justice:

(a) there are instances where the inability to communicate with police officers has resulted in the unnecessary aggravation of routine situations and has created serious law enforcement problems;

(b) Mexican Americans are disadvantaged in criminal cases because they cannot understand the charges against them nor the proceedings in the courtroom;

(c) in many cases Mexican American plaintiffs or defendants have difficulty communicating with their lawyers, which hampers preparation of their cases;

(d) language disability also adversely affects the relations of some Mexican Americans with probation and parole officers.

11. *Interpreters*

Interpreters are not readily available in many Southwestern courtrooms:

(a) in the lower courts, when interpreters were made available, they are often untrained and unqualified;

(b) in the higher courts, where qualified interpreters were more readily available, there has been criticism of the standards of their selection and training and skills.

12. *Employment by law enforcement agencies*

Employment of Mexican Americans by law enforcement agencies throughout the five Southwestern States does not reflect the population patterns of these areas:

(a) neither police departments, sheriffs' offices, nor State law enforcement agencies employ Mexican Americans in significant numbers;

(b) State and local law enforcement agencies in the Southwest do not have programs of affirmative recruitment which would attract more Mexican American employees;

(c) failure to employ more Mexican Americans creates problems in law enforcement, including problems in police-community relations.

13. *Courts and prosecutors*

Other agencies in charge of the administration of justice—courts, district attorneys' offices, and the Department of Justice—also have significantly fewer Mexican American employees than the proportion of Mexican Americans in the general population.

CONCLUSION

This report paints a bleak picture of the relationship between Mexican Americans in the Southwest and the agencies which administer justice in those States. The attitude of Mexican Americans toward the institutions responsible for the administration of justice—the police, the courts, and related agencies—is distrustful, fearful, and hostile. Police departments, courts, the law itself are viewed as Anglo institutions in which Mexican Americans have no stake and from which they do not expect fair treatment.

The Commission found that the attitudes of Mexican Americans are based, at least in part, on the actual experience of injustice. Contacts with police represent the most common encounters with the law for the average citizen. There is evidence of police misconduct against Mexican Americans. In the Southwest, as throughout the Nation, remedies for police misconduct are inadequate.

Acts of police misconduct result in mounting suspicion and incite incidents of resistance to officers. These are followed by police retaliation, which results in escalating hostilities.

The jury system is also not free from bias against Mexican Americans. At times, bail is set discriminatorily and inequalities in the availability of counsel lead to other injustices in trial and sentencing. Skilled interpreters, sensitive to the culture and background of Mexican Americans, are not in areas of the Southwest where Mexican Americans predominate. Finally, Mexican Americans have been excluded from full participation in many of the institutions which administer justice in the Southwest. Mexican Americans are underrepresented in employment in police departments, State prosecutor's offices, courts, and other official agencies. Consequently, these agencies tend to show a lack of knowledge about and understanding of the cultural background of Mexican Americans.

The Commission recognizes that individual law enforcement officers and court officers have made positive efforts to improve the administration of justice in their communities. The fact however, that Mexican Americans see justice being administered unevenly throughout the Southwest tends to weaken their confidence in an otherwise fair system. In addition, the absence of impartial tribunals in which claims of mistreatment can be litigated to a conclusion accepted by all sides tends to breed further distrust and cynicism.

This report is not intended to burden the agencies of justice with responsibilities which lie with society as a whole.

The police and the courts cannot resolve the problems of poverty and of alienation which play a large part in the incidence of crime which they attempt to control; and the police and the courts often treat legitimate demands for reform with hostility because society as a whole refuses to see them as justified. The Commission recognizes that the job of law enforcement is extremely difficult. Nevertheless, it finds no justification for illegal or unconstitutional action by the very persons who are responsible for the enforcement of the law.

This report shows that Mexican Americans believe that they are subjected to such treatment again and again because of their ethnic background. Moreover, their complaints bear striking similarities to those of other minority groups which have been documented in earlier Commission studies of the administration of justice. The inequalities suffered by black Americans and Indians described in the Commission's 1961 "Justice" report and its 1965 "Law Enforcement" report, are of a similar nature. Consequently, the Commission's recommendations in this report are designed to be sufficiently broad to be applicable to all minority groups.

The essence of this situation is summed up in the words of a Mexican American participant in the California State Advisory Committee meeting, who said: "I think that my race has contributed to this country with pride, honor, dignity, and we deserve to be treated as citizens, today, tomorrow, and every day of our lives. I think it is the duty of our Government to guarantee the equality that we have earned."

THE CASTE SYSTEM OF EMPLOYMENT

*Report of the Equal Employment
Opportunity Commission*

In Mexico the barrio is simply the cemented-grass roots of urban society. In the United States, however, *el barrio Chicano* is not the urban grass roots of Anglo society; it is its victim. Although an estimated eighty to eighty-five per cent of Chicanos live in urban areas, many of which their ancestors founded, they, like their *barrios*, exist on the periphery of metropolitan life. The "Summary of Findings" of the *Spanish Surnamed American Employment in the Southwest* details the job discrimination and inequality of status that faces Chicanos. (Report prepared by Fred H. Schmidt for the Colorado Civil Rights Commission under the auspices of the Equal Employment Opportunity Commission, Wash., D.C., U.S. Government Printing Office, 1970.)

Despite their being the Nation's second largest minority, Spanish Surnamed Americans have received scant attention in national affairs and are regarded as a regional phenomenon, rather than a national one. This comes partly from the one-sided treatment given the Southwest by U.S. historians.

Throughout the Southwest, among companies reporting to the Equal Employment Opportunity Commission, a general stairstep employment pattern for minority workers shows that their portion of the available jobs in an occupation descends as the occupational hierarchy ascends. They have a share of service, laborer, and operative jobs that is far in excess of their share in the labor force. In craftsmen jobs they approximate parity with the percentage they have in the labor force, but in all the other occupations they fall far below that level.

Their share of available jobs descends steeply once the line separating white-collar from blue-collar jobs is crossed. There is evidence of a job caste that walls off white-collar jobs from minority workers, and this wall is stouter against Spanish Surnameds in areas where their numbers in the population are proportionately greater, as it is for Negroes in those areas where they are a more prominent part of the population.

The presence of large minority groups in a local population does not appear as a factor that facilitates minority workers gaining white-collar positions. This holds true in even the lowest-skilled white-collar jobs for clerical and sales work, and is even true in the consumer-oriented industries.

The pattern of minority employment appears to be better for each minority group among employers who do not do contract work for the government than it is among prime contractors who have agreed to nondiscrimination clauses in their contracts with the Federal Government.

Spanish Surnameds are greatly underrepresented in on-the-job training programs for white-collar jobs while being overrepresented in those for blue-collar jobs, indicating that they may become even more characterized as a blue-collar work force in the future.

The pattern of minority employment is better among employers who have arrangements with labor unions that affect to some extent whom they may hire than it is among those who do not have such arrangements.

There is some indication that the advancement of Spanish Surnameds into occupations and industries heretofore reserved for the employment of Anglos seems to facilitate the entry of other minorities into those occupations and industries.

Spanish Surnameds, as are other Southwestern minorities,

are an immensely diverse group, but there are certain common features about the patterns of their employment throughout the region. In areas where they are a sizable part of local populations, they long have been regarded as casual, incidental workers, or as factory hands available for the laborer, service, and operative jobs in the generally lower paying industries that arose in those areas. Today, they do better than other minority workers in gaining skilled craftsmen jobs.

The place of Spanish Surnameds in the Southwest cannot be understood without a knowledge of how that region came to be joined to the Nation and the colonial attitudes that prevailed there toward all racial and ethnic minorities thereafter.

The Southwest has the most cosmopolitan population in the United States, over one-fifth of which belongs to easily identified minorities. All of these minority groups have experienced the segregation, discrimination, restriction of civil rights, and limited opportunities that are commonly known to be the lot of Negroes in this region and elsewhere.

These experiences provide further insight into the significance of racism, showing that racist attitudes cannot be dismissed as a consequence of a long-dead institution of slavery.

The shadows from past events in the lives of Indians, Spanish Surnameds, Orientals, and Negroes extend into the present and can be seen in the socio-economic characteristics of these groups today.

The 3½ million Spanish Surnameds in the Southwest are its largest minority, many of whom have extraordinary rates of birth and death, poverty, subemployment, poor health, poor education, poor housing, and limited employment opportunities. Notwithstanding, they have shown the same desire as others to be participants in the region's labor force.

The economic problems of Spanish Surnameds are exacerbated by the policies of the U.S. Government with respect to immigration and the contracting and commuting of workers from Mexico. No other region contends with these problems on a similar scale. No other group in the population is placed in the same continuing competition with the poverty of another nation.

MANANA IS TOO LATE—LABOR STANDARDS

by Maclovio R. Barraza

Quietly, slowly, inevitably, the barrio has become a place of rebirth. Chicano rebirth. Who is to say exactly when it began? In the early 1900's when the men of La Raza were working in the mines and building the railroads? In the 1920's when they entered the steel mills of Chicago and the tire factories of Los Angeles? In the 1940's when the restless *pachucos* exploded into national headlines? In the 1950's and 1960's when the *veteranos* of Korea and Vietnam came home to the barrios determined to be accepted as "first class citizens"? "*Simon, carnal!* (right, man!) It sprang from all these things," says a Chicano writer. "The *venditos* [sell-outs], the *pintos* [cons], the *veteranos,* the *chucos* [street boys], the *obreros* [laborers], and a million other *movidas* in the barrio. And because of them, through them, the barrio has been born anew." In his speech to the Cabinet Committee Hearings on Mexican American Affairs in El Paso, Texas (October 26–8, 1967), Maclovio R. Barraza, a regional vice-president of the United Steelworkers, AFL-CIO, and a veteran leader of the copper miners, caught the spirit of "the new barrio."

At the risk of being labeled a *malinchista*, which is the Mexican equivalent of what the American Negroes call "Uncle Tom," I, nevertheless, accept this invitation even if I may face the scorn and possible ostracism of my many dear friends in these organizations. Long ago I vowed that I would seek every available forum to tell the plight of my people who have for so long been neglected by our society and allowed to exist only in its shadows.

Whatever other reasons many may have for distrusting the intentions of this conference, perhaps the most central is that we Mexicans are very disappointed with the performance of all levels of government. In spite of the many studies and voluminous reports, the many conferences and the big promises, we have yet to see any significant evidence of the kind of action needed at all levels of government to correct the legitimate grievances of our people.

Neglected for years, the Mexican Americans, nevertheless, have not turned their backs on this country and have, in fact, displayed a steadfast loyalty to it. Their record of valor on the battlefields, for instance, is a shining example of their faith in the national ideals for which they are willing to sacrifice. Proudly I say that they have been and are among the best citizens and have assumed a responsible role every time they were called on. . . .

We are aware of some progress. We understand the difficulties and crises government faces. Along with all other minority groups, we saw hope in the passage of the important Civil Rights measures. The war on poverty programs advanced by this administration offered us a promise. The enactment of Medicare for our older citizens is a sign of new direction in social legislation. We in the hard-rock mining unions appreciate the Mine Safety Bill, which can be a start of a positive program to spare the life, limb and agony of the miners—a large percentage of whom are Mexican Americans in the Southwest.

We are most thankful for these and others. We regard them with favor. They speak loudly of the accomplishments of President Johnson and his administration.

But what the Mexican American is saying is: It's not enough and it barely touches the many problems that beg attention. Our people are saying that before we shout Viva Johnson, there better be a Viva la gente Mexicana program. There must be a bridge built immediately between the well-intentioned promises and some real positive action.

Along with the other disadvantaged people, the Mexican American is growing more and more restless. He's patient but it's running out. He may soon be forced to seek dramatic alternatives to his patience—alternatives that seem to bring more generous responses from government than obedient restraint in face of adversity and injustice.

I don't like to believe what is being said by a prominent sociologist at a leading Western university that the poverty conditions in the Mexican ghettoes of El Paso are far worse than any found in the grimmest sections of Lima, Peru. He is convinced that a powder keg exists here in El Paso and other cities of the Southwest which could at any moment explode into violent riots far more intense than those of Watts, Detroit, or other cities which experienced poverty outbursts. Significantly, when such should happen, there will not be a single Negro involved.

The common denominator is there—the same in Watts, Detroit or El Paso. It's poverty amid plenty. It's poverty brought about by the dominant segments of our society who callously ignore reality and are not permitting all the people to share in the abundance of this nation. And, I need not remind any person who cares to study the problem that it cannot be avoided by placing more Mexican Americans in the

National Guard of Texas or any other Southwestern state.

I wish to devote attention to some—by no means all—of the problems facing the Mexican Americans. While these are in many ways the same as those of other minority groups, there are significant differences which, in my opinion, make the plight of the Mexican more difficult.

Allow me to mention but a few. To the Mexican American in the Southwest this is his land and his roots are sunk deep in it. Unlike that of the American Negro, his history is not one of economic slavery by force and chains. In many if not most cases, he preceded those who have and are exploiting him. The Mexican American has a culture with which he is able to and does identify. It's one he cherishes dearly.

His country of origin and its culture is not some vague place in a distant continent. It's Mexico. It's near. It's a country today much alive in growth, industrial expansion and cultural development. He knows it and understands it. He feels its winds of progress across the nearby border.

Strong in his allegiance to the United States, he fiercely resists any and all attempts to erode his culture, his language or his life style just to satisfy the whim of a marketplace morality. He is industrious—not lazy. He is proud—not humble. He wants to believe that the United States is a land of promise where he can preserve his values and to share equally with others an opportunity to be recognized and to be allowed to contribute to it.

His ancestry links him with the most advanced cultures and civilizations in the world. Yet his life in this country has been and is in too many ways inhuman degradation imposed on him by interests who distort the national ideals and who discriminate against him for their selfish economic ends.

These are very serious indictments of those who degrade the Mexican Americans. But they can be substantiated by readily available facts. It requires no depth study, no special commissions, to learn that it was not until World War II that in the Southwest the Mexican American miner was paid a very special rate of wages. Regardless of his classification or his skill, he received only 60% or less of the rate paid to his Anglo counterpart. Imagine, doing the very same work but getting but a fraction of the pay that the non-Mexican received for doing no more!

Were it not for the trade unions that were born through the New Deal, this practice would likely be continued to this date. Efforts of unions like the Mine, Mill and other CIO unions put an end to this fraud. It was union combat and not the benign employers or politicians in their hip pocket that erased this discriminatory differential.

But this did not end all of the problem or did it relax the persistence of the exploiters. Employers as well as state and other governmental agencies still use the Mexican worker in their not too subtle design to depress and keep depressed the wages of all the working people. This practice is prevalent today not only in the agricultural industry, which still craves economic slavery, but by other segments of the economy. The Mexican is sick and tired—and getting more so with each day—of being made a scapegoat for the employers and other chiselers to use in order to avoid their obligation to pay a decent living wage to the workers. . . .

It is far from the truth to say that it is the Mexican American alone who is the victim of social and economic injustice in the Southwest. The whole section of the country suffers from the discrimination being practiced. The Anglo—cannot make real progress so long as the Mexican is used to keep down wages. The Federal laws are being winked at every day and the brand new Civil Rights legislation is without teeth, has no investigatory power of its own that we can notice, and it is not being enforced.

A specific example: At Magma Copper Company in San

Manuel, Arizona, a copper operation which was put in business by the U.S. Government during the Korean War, there are many Mexican Americans working in the underground mines. But I stand and watch as some 60 or 70 employees from the offices and technical departments pass through the gates. I see maybe one or two Mexican Americans in that group even though there are certainly many qualified to perform those jobs. Many of our people are high school graduates but somehow there is no place for them outside the bull gangs of the mines. Yet, this company can prominently display the certificate that it is a Fair Employment and Equal Opportunity Employer—a title given it by an agency of the federal government. Apparently, there is not enough concern by the federal government to investigate the company's claim before a certification is issued.

Many companies maintain an employment policy requiring a high school education for employment. Many of the jobs to be filled require no such level of education.

A high school diploma—as desirable as it is—is not needed to muck the ore, to rustle timber or work on the track gang. Requiring a higher level of education than necessary for a job is interpreted as another form of denial—a definite discrimination against the Mexican American, who forced by circumstances often lacks a high school education. . . .

We have but to look at the plight of the Mexican American beyond the workplace to recognize even more startling examples of cruel discrimination. In housing, he is limited where he can live and his income will permit only the less desirable shelter. In education he is regarded as some special problem. He doesn't conform too easily to the ways of the Anglo, therefore he is assumed by some to be inferior. He clings to his Spanish language, therefore, he must not be trusted because those who are not bi-lingual can't understand his speech. He refuses to relinquish his mother tongue and he should be encouraged in his efforts.

While I suggest no programs that require even a fraction of what is spent to study the dark side of the moon, some money is needed to raise the nation's poor to a level of decency. It's needed in the area of public health education, welfare, training, and job or income protection. Most of the current programs in these areas have not yet significantly touched the Mexican American problems. Money must be made available and the investment of it in developing the human resources will be returned many times in the building of a better society.

Permit me to point out a geography lesson. South of us lie great nations of Spanish-speaking Americans. They are viewing our nation as a model—an example setter—after whom they may wish to pattern their development. They know we too came from a revolutionary movement that cast off the yoke of oppression. Abraham Lincoln's America is what they want to believe in. If we cannot meet the problems of our Mexican Americans, can we honestly hope to impress the other Latin countries? Our government and our institutions are confronted with a challenge to meet the crises in our own country. The Mexican American is eager to make this nation faithful to its democratic tenets.

If we accept this challenge as an opportunity to perfect our way of life, we will succeed in making this nation and the world a better place for all people. If we continue to be blinded by prejudice and selfishness of a few, do we deserve the place of world leadership that destiny has thrust upon us? We must start now towards our avowed national goals. *Manana is too late.*

VII. LA CAUSA: IN THE BEGINNING

THE PLAN OF DELANO

"The movement begins with the beat of one man's heart," writes Luis Valdez, director of El Teatro Campesino de Aztlan. In Delano, California, the headquarters of the United Farm Workers Organizing Committee (UFWOC), they say: When the first man got off his knees in the fields, and stood on his feet and shouted *Huelga!* (Strike!), La Causa began. If historians were to date the birth of La Causa, it would be September 16, 1965. On that day, in the Guadalupe Church hall, the *campesinos* of Cesar Chavez's National Farm Workers Association (NFWA) voted to join the Filipino grape pickers who were on strike. One of their earliest proclamations to the world, issued on their 250-mile pilgrimage to Sacramento, the state capital, was "The Plan of Delano" that declared "We want a new social order."

We, the undersigned, gathered in Pilgrimage to the capital of the State in Sacramento in penance for all the failings of Farm Workers as free and sovereign men, do solemnly declare before the civilized world which judges our actions, and before the nation to which we belong, the propositions we have formulated to end the injustice that oppresses us.

We are conscious of the historical significance of our Pilgrimage. It is clearly evident that our path travels through a valley well known to all Mexican farm workers. We know all of these towns of Delano, Madera, Fresno, Modesto, Stockton and Sacramento, because along this very same road, in this very same valley, the Mexican race has sacrificed itself for the last hundred years. Our sweat and our blood have fallen on this land to make other men rich. This Pilgrimage is a witness to the suffering we have seen for generations.

The Penance we accept symbolizes the suffering we shall have in order to bring justice to these same towns, to this same valley. The Pilgrimage we make symbolizes the long historical road we have travelled in this valley alone, and the long road we have yet to travel, with much penance, in order to bring about the Revolution we need, and for which we present the propositions in the following PLAN:

1. This is the beginning of a social movement in fact and not in pronouncements. We seek our basic, God-given rights as human beings. Because we have suffered—and are not afraid to suffer—in order to survive, we are ready to give up everything, even our lives, in our fight for social justice. We shall do it without violence because that is our destiny. To the ranchers, and to all those who oppose us, we say, in the words of Benito Juarez, "EL RESPETO AL DERECHO AJENO ES LA PAZ."

2. We seek the support of all political groups and protection of the government, which is also our government, in our struggle. For too many years we have been treated like the lowest of the low. Our wages and working conditions have been determined from above, because irresponsible legislators who could have helped us, have supported the rancher's argument that the plight of the Farm Worker was a "special case." They saw the obvious effects of an unjust system, starvation wages, contractors, day hauls, forced mi-

gration, sickness, illiteracy, camps and sub-human living conditions, and acted as if they were irremediable causes. The farm worker has been abandoned to his own fate— without representation, without power—subject to mercy and caprice of the rancher. We are tired of words, of betrayals, of indifference. To the politicians we say that the years are gone when the farm worker said nothing and did nothing to help himself. From this movement shall spring leaders who shall understand us, lead us, be faithful to us, and we shall elect them to represent us. WE SHALL BE HEARD.

3. We seek, and have, the support of the Church in what we do. At the head of the Pilgrimage we carry LA VIRGEN DE LA GUADALUPE because she is ours, all ours, Patroness of the Mexican people. We also carry the Sacred Cross and the Star of David because we are not sectarians, and because we ask the help and prayers of all religions. All men are brothers, sons of the same God; that is why we say to all men of good will, in the words of Pope Leo XII, "Everyone's first duty is to protect the workers from the greed of speculators who use human beings as instruments to provide themselves with money. It is neither just nor human to oppress men with excessive work to the point where their minds become enfeebled and their bodies worn out." GOD SHALL NOT ABANDON US.

4. We are suffering. We have suffered, and we are not afraid to suffer in order to win our cause. We have suffered unnumbered ills and crimes in the name of the Law of the Land. Our men, women, and children have suffered not only the basic brutality of stoop labor, and the most obvious injustices of the system; they have also suffered the desperation of knowing that that system caters to the greed of callous men and not to our needs. Now we will suffer for the purpose of ending the poverty, the misery, and the injustice,

with the hope that our children will not be exploited as we have been. They have imposed hungers on us, and now we hunger for justice. We draw our strength from the very despair in which we have been forced to live. WE SHALL ENDURE.

5. We shall unite. We have learned the meaning of UNITY. We know why these United States are just that—united. The strength of the poor is also in union. We know that the poverty of the Mexican or Filipino worker in California is the same as that of all farm workers across the country, the Negroes and poor whites, the Puerto Ricans, Japanese, and Arabians; in short, all of the races that comprise the oppressed minorities of the United States. The majority of the people on our Pilgrimage are of Mexican descent, but the triumph of our race depends on a national association of all farm workers. The ranchers want to keep us divided in order to keep us weak. Many of us have signed individual "work contracts" with the ranchers or contractors, contracts in which they had all the power. These contracts were farces, one more cynical joke at our impotence. That is why we must get together and bargain collectively. We must use the only strength we have, the force of our numbers. The ranchers are few; we are many. UNITED WE SHALL STAND.

6. We shall Strike. We shall pursue the REVOLUTION we have proposed. We are sons of the Mexican Revolution, a revolution of the poor seeking bread and justice. Our revolution will not be armed, but we want the existing social order to dissolve; we want a new social order. We are poor, we are humble, and our only choice is to Strike in those ranches where we are not treated with the respect we deserve as working men, where our rights as free and sovereign men are not recognized. We do not want the paternalism of the rancher; we do not want the contractor; we do

not want charity at the price of our dignity. We want to be equal with all the working men in the nation; we want a just wage, better working conditions, a decent future for our children. To those who oppose us, be they ranchers, police, politicians, or speculators, we say that we are going to continue fighting until we die, or we win. WE SHALL OVERCOME.

Across the San Joaquin Valley, across California, across the entire Southwest of the United States, wherever there are Mexican people, wherever there are farm workers, our movement is spreading like flames across a dry plain. Our PILGRIMAGE is the MATCH that will light our cause for all farm workers to see what is happening here, so that they may do as we have done. The time has come for the liberation of the poor farm worker.

History is on our side.

MAY THE STRIKE GO ON! VIVA LA CAUSA!

HUELGA!: THE HISTORY OF THE NATIONAL FARM WORKERS ASSOCIATION

Huelga!—it began with the word. Ironically, the word originally meant a time of rest and repose, a relaxation from work. The metamorphosis of the *campesinos* changed the word into a social movement. And the symbol and organizer of that metamorphosis is Cesar Estrada Chavez. He was a migrant (*estrada* means highway), as was his father, having lost their family farm near Yuma, Arizona, during the depression. A quiet man, thoughtful and intensely religious, Chavez has been the urbane political pragmatist and mystic, pacifist and militant, humble *campesino* and hard-headed union leader, grammar school drop-out (of thirty schools) and self-taught organizer of Chicanismo. "Cesar does not ask for freedom, he is freedom," writes a Chicano organizer. In "Why Delano?" (UFWOC, mimeographed, undated), he tells how the organization of the Huelga began, and in "Nothing Has Changed" (UFWOC, mimeographed, undated, reprinted from *The Movement*, newspaper of SNCC) he comments on his principles of organization and his political view of America.

Why Delano?

by Cesar Chavez

In community organizing you need a continuous program that meets the needs of the people in the organization. I have seen many groups attempt community organization and many have failed. The biggest reason for this is that there is a big emphasis on meetings and discussion and writing up programs and not on working with the people. Many organizers get lost in the shuffle of going to meetings, and somehow those who are being organized are lost. Too often we see as a remedy to this, people suggesting that you should have a survey or a study made.

Anyone who has done any community organizing would agree with me that you can't have a program until you have the people organized. I don't mean you have to wait until you're fully organized, but how can you write a program without the participation of those you are trying to organize? . . .

Another problem is respectability. If a minority group does "nice" things, like taking a petition to the Mayor, or having tea parties with the PTA, it's going to become respectable. And once you become a respectable group, you're not going to fight anymore. I've had a lot of experience in that. So if your group is going to City Hall or the Police Department and fight with the Police Chief, and someone on your Executive Board is friends with him, you're going to think twice before attacking him.

If an organizer comes looking for appreciation he might as well stay home. He's not going to get any, especially out of a group that's never been organized or had any power before. . . .

A lot of people have asked me—why Delano, and the answer is simple. I had no money. My wife's family lived there, and I have a brother. And I thought if things go very bad we can always go and have a meal there. Any place in the Valley would have made no difference.

I had some ideas on what should be done. No great plans; just that it would take an awful lot of work and also that it was a gamble. If I can't organize them to a point where they can carry on their own group then I'm finished, I can't do it, I'd move on and do something else.

I went around for about 11 months, and I went to about 87 communities and labor camps and in each place I'd find a few people who were committed to doing something; something had happened in their lives and they were ready for it. So we went around to the town, played the percentages, and came off with a group.

We had a convention here in Fresno, the first membership meeting, to set up a union—about 230 people from as many as 65 places. We knew the hardest thing would be to put across a program that would make them want to pay the $3.50 (monthly dues), because we were dependent on that. I felt that organizing couldn't be done on outside money.

We had signed up about 1100 people. The first month 211 payed. At the end of three months we had 10 people paying. Talk about being scared! But we went back and kept at it. By this time Dolores (Huerta) was helping me up in the Northern part of the Valley, and I was getting help from Gilbert Pedilla, both of whom are Vice-Presidents now. Gradually the membership was increasing. At the end of six months we were up to about 200 members. Instead of going all over the Valley as I did at first, I started staying in one place long enough for them to get in touch with me if they wanted to. We put a lot of emphasis on the people getting members.

We had hundreds of house meetings. Sometimes 2 or 3 would come, sometimes none. Sometimes even the family that called the house meeting would not be there.

I wasn't trying to prove anything to anyone who had given money. If I'd been under a board or a grant I don't think it would have worked. In the first place, I had to get the dues in order to eat. I suspect some of the members were paying dues because they felt sorry for me. . . .

At the beginning of the strike we had $85 in the treasury.

Nothing Has Changed

An Interview with Cesar Chavez

MOVEMENT: Last year you said that NFWA was half-way between a movement and a union. Now there seems to have been a change in the NFWA from a year ago as it moved from agitation to organization.

CHAVEZ: I don't agree with you. It's a case of carrying on 40 different strikes. We haven't changed. I think the outside world has changed, 'cause we're not a new thing. It's happened to civil rights. It happens to everybody. Our help is not coming from the same place it was coming from before.

MOVEMENT: One of the reasons people give—students especially—as an argument for not working with the strike anymore is the merger of the union with the AFL-CIO. People felt that the union would go bureaucratic and control would slip from Delano into the hands of George Meany. Would you speak to this issue?

CHAVEZ: We were as much pained as they were. We were pained for different reasons. We were pained that all of these forces—I'm talking about the students and others who felt this way—had such little faith in people . . . (and) these same people are guilty of idolizing the poor. This is not right because it is not the truth. I remember some of the fellows that helped us in the beginning had a very strange picture of poor people, in this case the farm workers. Like farm workers are all saints, you know.

MOVEMENT: What effects does that have?

CHAVEZ: It has a very bad effect on people. You can't help people if you feel sorry for them. You have to be practical. This type of feeling doesn't carry you for more than what it carried those people who were helping us. After a little while it becomes old, and there is no real basis for doing things that you're doing. There's got to be more than that.

But I think that what has really happened is that these forces that have been so helpful to the civil rights movement and to us have moved on. The movement doesn't stay still. It's like a cyclone: it swoops, you know?

MOVEMENT: So you're talking about something that would be a political force, not a political party?

CHAVEZ: Now a political force, yes, but not a party, the discipline wouldn't be there. There has to be discipline in a party.

See, it's not bad what the two parties do, because they are the pros. They are in power and the only criticism we can make is of ourselves for not being able to get that much power to counteract what they are doing. But to criticize them is, well, like . . .

MOVEMENT: It's like criticizing them for being what they are.

CHAVEZ: But that's not going to change anything. If we criticize ourselves, then that begins to change things.

See, I think groups that deal in power become impatient with groups who are strangers to power. I think even in individuals you can see this. A good example is Malcolm X. (I am reading his autobiography right now.)

When he talks about Uncle Toms, he puts it very clearly. He's saying that these guys will go to work for the devil white man. Really he is saying a lot more (he doesn't make it clear but I'm sure this is his thinking)—that the Negro thinks that if HE gets ahead he is going to be getting his people ahead. Malcolm really knew about power although he didn't put it in those words, he knew that you can't do it that way.

MOVEMENT: Malcolm has had a tremendous effect on black organizers.

CHAVEZ: He knew what he was doing. They understood him, and they didn't understand the others. But he had a very good base; he came right from the gutter so he wasn't compromised. The guys who don't come from the gutter have to compromise because they're going to school, they're getting a job, they're working for the government. All these little compromises which, by the time you get to be leader, have got your hands tied up. . . .

You organize for power so that you can get something. You organize so that you can build power to do something with it, and so, when you look back, you've got to see some people out there doing something. What I'm trying to say is you can't organize by just speaking. The civil rights movement's biggest drawback is that they don't have a group that pays its own way. They don't have a membership group. This is the kind of power that is needed.

So I would agree that Malcolm X was an organizer, but Stokely (Carmichael), well, it's an entirely different thing. I don't see any BUILDING. Maybe there is and I don't know, but I don't see any building of any power—like people, like money, like things that they themselves get so they can make their own determinations. Maybe there is lately. I know there wasn't before.

Now the approach that Malcolm X used was the house meeting—what we use, you know?—he was doing those things that we know pay: being patient and just accumulating, committing people and so forth. And he's gone, but the movement continues.

Now over on the other side . . . well, Martin Luther King in Chicago—nothing, you know? It's organizing, but not . . .

MOVEMENT: What do you feel is missing?

CHAVEZ: People. You don't have people working on it. I mean, who are you organizing? You have to have involvement, you know. It's not a one man show. There's got to be people involved. Once you have people then there's power to do things. But money won't do it alone—all these groups have had a lot of money. That's the other thing, you see, that is why they don't continue; the moment the money is taken away from them they fall.

MOVEMENT: Because they're depending on money from the outside . . .

CHAVEZ: As long as you have people, you'll have money, and if the money stops, that means you've lost the people so there's no reason to continue anyway.

MOVEMENT: Do you see organizing of farm workers into one big union?

CHAVEZ: It will be a miracle if there comes to be one big union of farm workers.

EL MALCRIADO:
THE VOICE OF THE FARM WORKER

"Our union is not just another union," says Cesar Chavez; it is "a movement more than a union" that seeks "to change the conditions of human life." For that reason "we resist giving our members numbers. Once we do that we are frightened that we will become one mass. Our people are human! They are not numbers!" The fierce individualism of the *campesino* is reflected in "The Dignity of the Farm Worker" (*El Malcriado*, newspaper of the UFWOC, English edition, No. 18) which proclaims the resistance of "the man [who has been] insulted." "What Is a Movement?" (*El Malcriado*, English edition, No. 19) shows the humanism of the Chicano movement and defines it as "the idea that someday he [the farm worker] will be respected" as a man.

The Dignity of the Farm Worker

For nearly all people there is a thing that is more important than money. It is a thing called dignity or self-respect or honor, and it shows itself in many ways. Sometimes it is shown by the man who will fight when he is insulted.

We who are farm workers have all been insulted. We have seen ourselves treated like cattle, we have seen how they have taken the work of our hands and bodies and made themselves rich, while we are left with empty hands between the earth and the sky.

We have seen our children treated as inferiors in the schools. We have seen in the face of the cop our inequality before the law. We have known what it is like to be less respected, to be unwanted, to live in a world which did not belong to us.

Our color or our language or our job have kept us apart. And the people who are profiting from our separateness are determined to keep it that way. It is a fact that in San Francisco the growers associations keep an office full of people busy writing propaganda about how farm workers are all winos, bums, incompetents. There is money in the advancement of these lies.

We who are picking the grapes and the peaches and the tomatoes which are the life-blood of California are soon going to share in the richness we have made. The little fights against the little grower and contractor that you read about today are only the beginning. The dignity of the farm worker shows itself in many ways.

This year and in the years to come, it will be shown by the man who will fight when he is insulted.

What Is a Movement?

What is a movement? It is when there are enough people with one idea so that their actions are together like a huge wave of water which nothing can stop. It is when a group of people begin to care enough so that they are willing to make sacrifices.

The movement of the Negro began in the hot summer of Alabama ten years ago when a Negro woman refused to be pushed to the back of the bus. Thus began a gigantic wave of protest throughout the South. The Negro is willing to fight for what is his: an equal place under the sun.

Sometime in the future they will say that in the hot summer of California in 1965 the movement of the farm workers began. It began with a small series of strikes. It started so slowly that at first it was only one man, then five, then one hundred.

This is how a movement begins. This is why the farm workers association is a "movement" more than a "union." Once a movement begins it is impossible to stop. It will sweep through California and it will not be over until the farm worker has the equality of a living wage and decent treatment. And the only way it will be done is through organization. The farm worker must organize to fight for what is his.

What is a movement? It is the idea that someday the farm worker will be respected. It is the idea that someday he will earn a living wage.

It is when the silent hopes of many people begin to become a real part of life.

WALKOUT IN ALBUQUERQUE: THE CHICANO MOVEMENT BECOMES NATIONWIDE

> The struggle of the *campesinos* in the little town of Delano was a "cultural volcano spewing out still glowing memories of the Mexican revolution." "We are the sons of the Mexican revolution," declared "The Plan of Delano." It had a startling effect on the Mexican Americans in the cities: they began to rethink their self-definition as second-class citizens and to redefine themselves as Chicanos. The Huelga of Cesar Chavez suddenly had millions of adherents in the urban barrios, far from the fields, and the once quiescent leaders of Mexican-American officialdom responded with demands for equality. During President Johnson's term the first Committee on Mexican-American Affairs in the history of the United States was established by the government. ("Walkout in Albuquerque," *Carta Editorial*, Vol. 3, No. 12, April 8, 1966.)

All 50 Mexican-American delegates representing six Southwestern states walked out on a federal Equal Employment Opportunity Commission conference here today, after charging that the Commission is indifferent to Mexican-American needs and guilty of discrimination in its own hiring practices.

The walkout took place less than an hour after the scheduled all-day conference began.

Before leaving, spokesmen for the group stood up and directed several specific charges at the Commission, which is headed by Franklin D. Roosevelt, Jr.

Alfred J. Hernandez, national president of the League of United Latin American Citizens (LULAC), stated that while Mexican-Americans comprise the nation's No. 2 minority in size, with approximately six million persons, none of the present EEOC commissioners is of Mexican descent.

Hernandez, from Houston, Texas, added: "Our employment problems are severe and complex. Yet we have no one on the Commission with any insight into them."

Dr. Miguel Montes, from San Fernando, California, president of the Latin American Civic Association (LACA), complained of inequities in the employment practices of the EEOC itself.

"The EEOC has only one Mexican-American compliance officer on its Washington staff," Montes said. "Based on its present staffing and budget appropriations, that figure should be at least 20."

Commissioner Albert Pena, of San Antonio, Texas, past president of Political Association of Spanish-Speaking Organizations (PASSO), cited the fact that the commission now has a list of some 800 major Southwestern companies which employ more than 600,000 persons, but have no Mexican-Americans on their payrolls. He demanded to know when the Commission was going to take action against these companies.

Augustin Flores, of Riverside, California, national president of the American G. I. Forum charged that the Commission has made no visible effort to reach the Mexican-American community and that its services and staff are not geared to meet the needs of this distinct bilingual, bicultural group.

"When EEOC regional offices are needed in Los Angeles, the Commission puts them in San Francisco," he stated. "An office is vitally needed in South Texas—San Antonio or Corpus Christi. So the Commission places it in Dallas."

The group was also critical of the fact that only one commissioner, Richard A. Graham, attended the long-publicized conference—and that he came without any background in Mexican-American employment problems.

He was presented with eight resolutions drawn up by the delegates expressing their dissatisfaction. The resolutions were directed to President Johnson who, according to Pena, was wired a copy. The resolution statement read:

We, the delegates representing Mexican-American organizations from throughout the six Pacific Southwestern states, realize that further participation in this conference—under conditions imposed upon us by the federal Equal Employment Opportunity Commission—will be valueless.

Through its actions both here and in Washington, D.C. the Commission has shown a total lack of interest and understanding of the problems facing our nation's six million Mexican-Americans.

We feel that the Commission has been insincere in its relations with the Mexican-American community.

Rather than continuing to deal with this body, as it is presently constituted, we are making the following appeal to the President of the United States, Lyndon B. Johnson, so that our community may share in the prosperity which should be part of our American heritage.

To President Johnson, we submit the following resolutions (all delegates were urged to wire President Johnson asking him to name a Mexican-American to the Commission):

1. That at least one Mexican-American, with full understanding of the unique employment problems of America's second-largest minority, be appointed to the five-member Equal Employment Opportunity Commission.

2. That staff hiring practices of the EEOC—an organization which should serve as a model for all of our nation's employers, be investigated and changed to eliminate current ethnic imbalances which work against the Mexican-American.

3. That the commission send knowledgeable representatives to

any future conferences involving federal agencies and the Mexican-American community.

4. That regional offices of the EEOC be relocated into areas where employment discrimination is most severe.

5. That the entire program of the EEOC be reoriented, and new procedures be established to reach the Mexican-American community.

6. That the Mexican-American be allowed full participation in the upcoming June White House Conference on Civil Rights, and in all other civil rights programs and activities engaged in or sponsored by the federal government.

7. That the EEOC take immediate steps against some 800 major national companies in the Pacific Southwest which have more than 600,000 employees on their payrolls, yet hire no Mexican-Americans.

8. That the hiring practices of all governmental agencies be reviewed and that affirmative action be taken to rectify present imbalances against Mexican-Americans and all other ethnic minorities.

The delegates added that if a Mexican-American commissioner were hired, they would be willing to meet with the EEOC again, only if all of the commissioners attended such a conference.

VENCEREMOS!: MEXICAN-AMERICAN STATEMENT ON TRAVEL TO CUBA

by Luis Valdez and Roberto Rubalcava

As always it was the youth—the veterans and students—who were among the most outspoken supporters of La Causa. In the summer of 1964 two young Chicanos from Delano took advantage of a visit to Cuba to use their experiences as a platform from

which to voice some of the concepts that were to herald the Chicano student movement. ("Mexican-American Statement on Travel to Cuba" by Luis Valdez and
Roberto Rubalcava, mimeographed, undated.)

The Mexican in the United States has been, and continues
to be, no less a victim of American imperialism than his im-
poverished brothers in Latin America.

In the words of the Second Declaration of Havana, tell
him of "misery, feudal exploitation, illiteracy, starvation
wages," and he will tell you that you speak of Texas; tell
him of "unemployment, the policy of repression against the
workers, discrimination . . . oppression by the obligar-
chies," and he will tell you that you speak of California; tell
him of U.S. domination in Latin America, and he will tell
you that he knows that Shark and what he devours, because
he has lived in its very entrails.

The history of the American Southwest provides a brutal
panorama of nascent imperialism. The uninformed need
only look to Fidel Castro's address of July 26, 1964 in Santi-
ago de Cuba, which we had the honor to witness and in
which he said, "Mexico is the country robbed of half of its
territory by the United States; Mexico is the country that
has suffered in its flesh and in its blood from the claws of imperialism."

Between 1838 and 1853, to be more exact, the North
Americans stole 949,808 square miles of land unimaginably
rich in agriculture, oil and mineral resources, and gave the
Mexican government, which had no choice in the matter, a
mere 25 million dollars. This territory is now occupied by
the states of Texas, Nevada, Utah, California, New Mexico,
Arizona and Colorado.

This same territory has spawned Barry Goldwater and
Lyndon B. Johnson, who are representative of the white

population that squatted on the land and usurped it acre by acre, with the full support of their government.

In addition to the land, the native population of Mexicans and Indians also passed into Yankee hands. Saved from actual slavery by one of the provisions of the Treaty of Guadalupe Hidalgo, these natives nonetheless became the facile victims of merciless exploitation and, in the case of the Indians, of utter annihilation.

It was in the Southwest that the systematic genocide of the American Indian reached its ultimate stage, with the deliberate campaign of the U.S. cavalry. There, emaciated and exhausted, wasted by war, starvation and flight, the last warriors made their final desperate stand in the 1870's, only to have their survivors herded into reservations like animals. A few, as in the case of New Mexico, escaped total extinction by mixing with the Mexicans. But even that was not much of an escape. The Mexicans, or rather, the "Mexican-Americans" were now citizens of the United States and thus immediately accessible for legal exploitation.

Betrayed by the upper classes, who married off their daughters to as many gringos as they could find, the Mexican-American peasants became subject to new masters. As the hard-knuckled Yankee farmer divided up the old latifundias, the peasants were stripped of the comparative protection of feudalism, without escaping the evils of peonage. Utilizing these peasants as a perfect source for cheap "stoop labor," Yankee farmers became agricultural industrialists and instituted the monopolies that today exist throughout the Southwest.

The Mexican, by contrast, was left to his own fate, without a government, without representation, without hope. Squalor, poverty, starvation, abysmal illiteracy, discrimination and migrant labor are his wages in America. During the last hundred years since the Mexican-American War, his Spanish-speaking leaders are not leaders at all; Americanized beyond recall, they neither understand or care about the basic Mexican-American population, which has an identity of its own.

As sons of Mexican manual laborers in California, we have travelled to Revolutionary Cuba, in defiance of the travel ban, in order to emphasize the historical and cultural unanimity of all Latin American peoples, north or south of the border. Having no real leaders of our own, we accept Fidel Castro. We believe the example of Cuba will inevitably bring socialist revolution to the whole of Latin America.

After a two month visit to Cuba, we can now see why the U.S. government has put a travel ban on the island. It is because the social problems characteristic of Latin America are being solved there. This is the first Latin American country to provide free education for its mass population. This is the first Latin American country that is feeding all of its people and providing work for them. This is the first Latin American country whose leadership is solely dedicated to solving the social crimes committed by imperialism upon an underdeveloped country and at the same time, not interested in personal wealth.

We two members of the Mexican-American population present the following points in the form of a declaration:

(1) That Cuba is an example of social revolution for all Latin America.
(2) That we support the position of Mexico in maintaining relations with Cuba, in spite of U.S. intimidation via the O.A.S.
(3) That the international position of Cuba and the voice of Fidel Castro are making clear to the entire world the so-

cial crimes committed in Latin America by U.S. imperialism, as well as the prime solution to these crimes: social revolution.

(4) That we support Fidel Castro as the real voice of Latin America, declaring to the world with dignity that social justice must be given to Latin America.

As Mexican-American citizens of the United States, we petition the U.S. government to stop immediately its aggressive policy on Cuba and to allow our brothers in Latin America to choose their own course of solving their social problems.

QUE VIVA AMERICA LATINA!

QUE VIVA CUBA REVOLUCIONARIA!!

QUE VIVA FIDEL CASTRO RUZ!!!

WE DEMAND:
STATEMENT OF CHICANOS OF THE SOUTHWEST IN THE POOR PEOPLE'S CAMPAIGN

by Rodolfo "Corky" Gonzales

Several hundred Chicanos journeyed to Washington, D.C., in the spring of 1968 to participate in the Poor People's Campaign. The caravans from the Southwest brought together Raza from the isolated villages and urban barrios. Under the leadership of Reies Lopez Tijerina, of New Mexico, and Rodolfo "Corky" Gonzales, of Colorado, they issued a national policy statement—"We Demand." It was Gonzales, a former Democratic party leader in Denver, businessman, poet, and national and international amateur boxing champion, who was largely responsible for the formulation of the statement that was to become a focal point of the annual Chicano Youth Liberation Conferences sponsored by his organization, Crusada por Justicia—Crusade for Justice. ("We Demand," *La Raza Yearbook*, Sept., 1968.)

Education

We demand that our schools be built in the same communal fashion as our neighborhoods . . . that they be warm and inviting facilities and not jails. That the teachers and other personnel live in the neighborhoods of the schools they work in. We demand a completely free education from kindergarten to college with no fees, no lunch charges, no supplies charges, no tuition, no dues . . . this in compensation for decades of poor education given our raza. . . .

That from kindergarten through college, Spanish be the first language and English the second language and that the textbooks be rewritten to emphasize the heritage and contributions of the Mexican-Americans in the building of the Southwest. We also demand the teaching of the contributions and history of other minorities which have also helped build this country.

We also feel that each neighborhood school complex should have its own school board made up of members who live in the community the school serves.

Housing

The necessary resources to plan our living accomodations so that it is possible for extended family homes to be situated in a communal style . . . around plazas or parks with plenty of space for the children. We want our living areas to fit the needs of the family and not the needs of the city pork barrel, the building corporations or architects.

Agricultural Reforms

We demand that not only the land which is our ancestral right be given back to those pueblos with restitution given for mineral, natural resources, grazing and timber used.

We demand compensation for taxes, legal costs, etc., which pueblos and heirs spent trying to save their land. We demand the suspension of taxation by the acre and institute instead the previous taxation system of our ancestors; that is the products of the land are taxed, not the land itself.

Job Development

We demand training and placement programs which would develop the vast human resources available in the Southwest. For those of our people who want further choices in employment and professions we wish training programs which would be implemented and administered by our own people.

In job placement, we demand that first of all, racist placement tests be dropped and in their place tests be used which relate only to the qualifications necessary for that job. Further, we demand non-discrimination by all private and public agencies.

We demand seed money to organize the necessary trade, labor, welfare, housing, etc., unions to represent those groups. We further demand that existing labor, trade and white collar unions non-discriminatory membership practices be enforced by a national labor relations act.

Law Enforcement

We demand an immediate investigation of the records of all prisoners to correct the legal errors, or detect the prejudice which operated in those court proceedings, causing their convictions or extra heavy sentencing. As these cases are found, we demand that the federal government reimburse those prisoners for loss of time and money.

We demand immediate suspension of officers suspected of police brutality until a full hearing is held in the neighborhood of the event.

We demand suspension of the city-wide juvenile court system and the creation of a neighborhood community court to deal with allegations of crime. In addition, instead of prowl-car, precinct system, we want to gradually install a neighborhood protection system, where residents are hired every few families to assist and safeguard in matters of community safety or possible crime.

Economic Opportunities

We demand that the businesses serving our community be owned by that community. Seed money is required to start cooperative grocery stores, gas stations, furniture stores, etc. Instead of our people working in big factories across the city, we want training and low interest loans to set up small industries in our own communities. These industries would be co-ops with the profits staying in the community.

LA RAZA UNIDA

by Jorge Lara-Braud

"Our father, the Spaniard, left us. We decided to stay with our mother, the Indian, here in New Mexico," said Reies Lopez Tijerina, the land grant leader. ". . . we were born as the consequence of a conflict of races and cultures, when the Spanish discovered, explored and christianized this continent. Out of that conflict came a New Breed, a new people. Sometimes we are known as *La Raza*, which is The Race, The People. But the name we are known by does not matter. We are a New Breed." In the many attempts to define the New Breed, one of the earliest was this analysis of *La Raza Unida* ("What Is La Raza," by Jorge Lara-Braud, *La Raza Yearbook*, September, 1968).

1. What is LA RAZA UNIDA? It is a ground swell movement of Mexican-American solidarity throughout the Southwest comprising a loose fellowship of some two or three hundred civic, social, cultural, religious, and political groups.

2. What has brought it about? The need deeply felt among Mexican-Americans to dramatize their plight as a disadvantaged minority, to assert their rights as first-rate citizens, and to assume their rightful share of the social, economic, educational, and political opportunities guaranteed by the American democratic system.

3. Are Mexican-Americans a disadvantaged minority? The most recent study, the Mexican-American Study Project conducted at UCLA and funded by the Ford Foundation, has disclosed that in the Southwest, as compared to the Negro, the Mexican-American is on generally the same level economically, but substantially below educationally. As for dilapidated housing and unemployment, the Mexican-American is not too much better off than the Negro.

4. Why this sudden awakening? Actually, it is not as sudden as it looks. Its first manifestations begin in the period following the Second World War. Mexican-Americans emerged from that conflict with a new determination to

make their sacrifice count. No ethnic group has received a larger proportion of decorations, and few had sustained as large a share of casualties. These veterans challenged in and out of court the blatant legacy of discrimination still prevailing in the Southwest, often displayed by the glaring signs or the brutal words "No Mexicans allowed." The G.I. Bill made it possible for quite a few to obtain college degrees, better jobs, and positions of leadership. For some the new status proved an irresistible temptation to overidentify with the Anglo way of life, to the distress of thoughtful Mexican-Americans and Anglos alike. Fortunately, a much larger number of those who "arrived" saw in their hard-fought-for success a call to advance the cause of their ethnic brethren without supine surrender, or excessive glorification of their cultural uniqueness.

Since then Latin America has been rediscovered south and north of the Rio Grande, following the tremors set off by the Cuban revolution. Spanish is once again a prestige language, and being bilingual somehow is no longer un-American. Then came the radiation fall-out of the Negro civil rights struggle which made even the most disillusioned Mexican-American begin to dream large dreams again. But if anyone thought the new vision borrowed from this struggle would give way to violence, there emerged in 1965 the most inspirational of all, Cesar Chavez. It is he, more than anyone else, who has contributed to LA RAZA UNIDA the mystique of the pursuit of justice through non-violent means. His recent 24-day penitential fast was undertaken to signify the Christian determination of himself and his followers not to be driven into acts of violence by the obdurate grape-growing firms near Delano, California, which refuse to enter into contract negotiations with his fledgling union, while using every conceivable means to discredit it.

5. Are all members of LA RAZA UNIDA non-violent? The vast majority abhor violence. Indeed, one of their most persistent criticisms is that they have been the victims of too much violence, and they are sick of it. From painful experience they know the animal-like quality of him who has perpetrated it against them, whether by legal or illegal means. Some have begun to use excessively militant language and symbols, something many of us genuinely regret. But even then we see them resorting to the only language that apparently present-day society is able to understand. The rare instances of actual violence are to be seen more as a last-ditch attempt at survival, than as a premeditated strategy. Their profound disenchantment with things as they are today in this nation has made them turn their eyes to the land of their ancestors. There, many have found symbols of redress in the events and figures of the Mexican Revolution. The result is a commitment to nothing less than revolution, but with a difference—through non-violent means, if possible. An unbiased look at this vigorous awakening of the Mexican-American will make us realize it is a tremendous affirmation of faith in the American dream. They actually believe, unlike many other sectors, that this society is still capable of undergoing a reformation of "freedom and justice for all."

6. Isn't the term "la raza" a racist term? No, quite the opposite. It has been borrowed from the countries south of the Rio Grande, where it connotes a blending of a new family of man composed of the original inhabitants of the Americas, the Indians, and all other immigrants from throughout the earth, who, since the time of Columbus, have come to the New World in search of a new creation. Hence, it is not surprising that October 12, south of the Rio Grande is not so much Columbus Day as "el Dia de la Raza."

VVVVVVVVVVVVVVVVVVV

VIII. LA CAUSA:
LA TIERRA
(THE EARTH)

MOTHER OF ALL LIFE—THE EARTH

by Cleofas Vigil

In the village of San Cristobal, high in the Sangre de
Cristo (Blood of Christ) mountains of northern New
Mexico, there is a poet by the name of Cleofas Vigil.
He is a farmer and herdsman whose fame as a singer of
the old *alabados* and *corridos* has spread throughout
the Southwest. When Cleofas Vigil writes of the earth
—"Mother of All Life"—the simplicity of his *hispano*
love of the land is so pure, it reaches back through the
centuries to the ancient *indigena* memories of *La
Tierra*. Though he does not name her, he is speaking of
the *indio* goddess of fertility, Tonantzin, who became
the Virgen de Guadalupe, *Nuestra madre*, the Earth
. . . ("Mother of All Life," *La Raza*, by Steiner.)

Ah, you who do not have false pride
Ah, brave companions,
Though we have no money
We travel hand in hand;
Though barefoot we are happy
With our belly heavy
Full of green beans
And gray Verdolagas.
   The poor man's heart rejoices
   When the fields are green

With the delicious food
That never wearies the hungry;
The rounded tortillas
Prepared in every style,
Ah, what a tasty mouthful
The fields provide for us.
The sublime aroma
Of green chilis in the hot embers,
Cooked with gusto,
Ready to be plucked;
How it stirs the appetite
Of a tired chicano.
In the morning he awakes
And goes into his garden;
He quickly works up a sweat
When he sees his crops
Grow before his eyes;
It delights his heart,
He comes alive, knowing
The earth, his mother
Is going to feed him.
My brother this is your mother,
Mother, fertile and fruitful;
If anyone takes her from you
You will be an orphan;
And from whose breasts
Will you drink sweet milk,
Be it of goat,
Or be it of cow?
The earth is your food, and your mother:
I tell you once again.

THE LAND GRANTS

by Clark S. Knowlton

A prophetic voice and political alchemist by the name of Reies Lopez Tijerina appeared in New Mexico in the early 1960's. He founded the Alianza Federal de Mercedes (Federal Alliance of Grants), which sought the return of the lost, sold, and stolen land grants that once belonged to the *Hispano* (Spanish American) farmers and villagers. In evoking old laws Tijerina was accused and tried by the new rulers for acts of "civil disobedience" and "insurrection." At one of his many trials an expert witness for the defense was the distinguished Dr. Clark S. Knowlton, director of the Center for the Study of Social Problems, at the University of Utah, whose prophetic study *Land-Grant Problems Among the State's Spanish-Americans* (Bureau of Business Research, University of New Mexico, *New Mexico Business*, June, 1967) had predicted history.

Although the government of the United States committed itself through the Treaty of Guadalupe Hidalgo at the conclusion of the Mexican-American War to protect the property and civil rights of the Spanish-American inhabitants of New Mexico, no provisions were established to enforce the provisions of the treaty. The Spanish-Americans, as a result, were treated like a conquered people. Defenseless before the dynamic legalistic, ruthless and land-hungry Anglo-American frontier culture, they were abandoned by both the American and Mexican governments . . .

Even though there were few Anglo-American residents of New Mexico before the Civil War, land loss began with their coming. Many of the first such immigrants took advantage of the unsuspicious Spanish-American residents. A Catholic Sister of Charity living in New Mexico at that time made the following observation:

In the early years of Anglo settlement in New Mexico the unsuspicious and naive Spanish Americans were victimized on every hand. When the men from the states came out west to dispossess the poor natives of their lands, they used many subterfuges. One was to offer the owner of the land a handful of silver coins for the small service of making a mark on a paper. That mark was a cross which was acceptable as a signature and by which the unsuspecting natives deeded away their lands. By this means, many a poor family was robbed of all its possessions. (*At the End of the Santa Fe Trail*, by Sister Blandina Segale.)

During the 1870's and 1880's as Anglo immigration into New Mexico accelerated, the territory gradually fell under the political and the economic control of a small group of Anglo-American lawyers, politicians, judges, public employees, merchants, ranchers and newspaper editors known as the "Santa Fe Ring." Infiltrating both political parties and highly influential in Washington, D.C., the leaders of the Ring came to control the economic and political destinies of New Mexico from the 1880's to the 1900's. With component county rings throughout New Mexico the Santa Fe Ring reaped rich benefits from the political and economic development of New Mexico.

From the Land Grant Ring grew others, as the opportunities for speculation and plunder developed. Cattle Rings, Public Land Stealing Rings, Mining Rings, Treasury Rings and Rings of almost every description grew up, till the affairs of the territory came to be run almost exclusively in the interest and for the benefit of combinations organized and headed by a few longheaded, ambitious and unscrupulous Americans. (*The Far Southwest*, by Howard R. Lamar, Yale University Press, 1966) . . .

Those who would like to understand the reasons for the existence of the Alianza Federal de Mercedes would do well to study the history of the Santa Fe Ring . . .

One source estimates that the Spanish-Americans have lost since 1854 well over 2 million acres of private lands, 1.7 million acres of communal land, 1 million acres taken by the State, and vast acres acquired by the federal government. This land loss is still continuing on a massive scale and has already been responsible for the destruction of the traditional Spanish-American rural upper and middle class groupings, has accelerated the cultural breakdown, and has caused high rates of immigration . . .

If a comprehensive dialogue can be developed between the poor Spanish-American groups on the one hand, and the State and Federal governments and Anglo leaders on the other, problems may be resolved and unrest prevented. If a successful dialogue does not develop, many Spanish-American organizations could well begin to move down the long road to civil disobedience.

MY COW, SHE WAS ALMOST ARRESTED

by Tobias Leyba

Of the 1,715 land grants made by the Spanish and Mexican governments before the conquest of the Southwest by the United States, "over 80 per cent were lost to their owners" in New Mexico alone (*The Public Domain in New Mexico* by Victor Westphall, Albuquerque, N. Mex., University of New Mexico Press, 1966). The villagers, who did not understand the English language and laws which "clearly violated the spirit of the Treaty of Guadalupe Hidalgo" (*California Almanac*), soon were almost landless. In recent years the Federal government has further diminished this land base by the establishment of national forests and parks. Tobias Leyba, a village farmer and land-grant heir, writes with poignant humor and bitter anger of his beleaguered land. ("My Cow, She Was Almost Arrested," by Tobias Leyba, *El Grito del Norte*, Vol. 3, No. 5, April 29, 1970.)

My cow she was almost arrested last week. The Forest Service was going to arrest her because she walked over the line and ate some grass. She got a little better head, my cow, than the forest ranger, but still she can't read the signs and she doesn't see the lines too pretty good.

I keep my cows on private land near the Echo Amphitheatre. This land is private where my cows are and it is across the road from where the Forest Service has its park for the tourists. The State Highway Department has land along both sides of the road and there is a little bit of forest land that goes across the road. Next to where my cows are, there is land that the University of New Mexico says it owns. All this once belonged to the people.

Now, mira my cow is eating the grass and it looks the same, and the land looks the same, so I guess she thinks it is still the same—the land still belongs to all of the people. But this ranger, a gauvacho who doesn't know much about the land—or the people—he's watching my cow. And when she steps over the line, he sends me a letter saying he's going to arrest my cow, he's going to "impound" her.

This ranger says my cow has walked over onto the University of New Mexico land and over another line of the forest and he is going to arrest her. This land the University of New Mexico has, it is just sitting there, but the university, it doesn't let the people use it. How many taxes does the university pay for that land? I tell you: Nada. But they keep it, and the rangers, they keep the people off of it. Like police.

It is the same with the Highway Department land. What is it used for—nada. How many taxes are paid—nada. But the rangers keep the people off.

My cow, she doesn't understand such things and she can't read the signs. But the ranger says he saw her cross the lines and I get a letter saying she's going to be arrested in two weeks, she and six other cows I have there. I don't know if they were eating the grass too, because the ranger says he saw only this one walk from the university to the forest and back. But he says he's going to arrest them all.

Why do they do this? Why does the University of New Mexico do this? Why can't the people use these lands of the university, which are doing nothing now? Why can't the poor people use the Highway Department land for their cows, when it is just sitting there? Porque? Why does the forest and the university and the highway all work together to hurt our people and keep us off the land?

I would laugh at him, but when they do this, they hurt our people. They have the land, and our people have become poor. When they arrest the people's cows, people have to get them back by paying. To get your cow back, it costs $20. Mira, here in the North, that's a lot of money. This ranger, he says he's going to arrest seven of my cows. That would cost $140 to get them back. Hijo, where am I supposed to get that much money? Where would any of the poor people get that much money to pay the rangers?

It is like the Presbyterian Ghost Ranch. Why can't the people use the water that's over there a little north of Ghost Ranch? It is because all that water, the Forest Service, they give it to the Ghost Ranch for nothing. Only they can use it. The people, they tell the people they can go to hell.

The university is doing the same thing. This ranger, he was called by *El Grito* and he told the paper this: "It was the university land that caused this letter (the letter that said they were going to arrest my cows). They were on the forest when we saw them, but they were walking back and forth."

How come this ranger is working as a police for the university? Why can't the people use the university's land? Last week I hear about what they're having called EARTH DAY and at the University of New Mexico they're talking about how much they love the land. They have a big demonstration at the university about loving the earth and the people. At the same time, they're arresting my cow. I don't hear about any demonstrations about my cow being almost arrested.

Tobias Leyba and his cattle have lived in Canjilon a long time, all of his life. And this ranger, he is a stranger. What does this ranger know about the land and the people? The way it is, Tobias Leyba and the ranger, they can't never have between each other any real trust. Because Tobias Leyba doesn't have any use for the ranger. The ranger is like he is a policeman for the forest, the university, the highway, the state, the U.S. Government in Washington. The ranger, he is just a police to keep the people off of the land.

For my little bit of land, I have to pay taxes. What does the university pay in taxes for our children in the schools in the North—nada. What does the highway pay—nada. What does the forest pay—nada. But they have the land, and these rangers, they are their police. The poor people pay their taxes, and this money is used to keep us poor.

I remember once I saw this ranger and another one, two of them, driving one cow. It cost the people more than $20 to get that cow back. They were poor people. They paid because they needed that cow and because they were afraid of the rangers. I don't think the rangers have a right to do this to our people. Now they send me this letter. It seems like they want Tobias Leyba to eat some mierda.

And they have put notices in the paper saying they are going to arrest the people's cattle if they cross the lines. It seems like they are saying to our Spanish people—"You just go on and just get out, get out of this land."

No, no, no, no, no—not me, not Tobias Leyba, not my people. This land is ours, and we will be here when these rangers, they are all gone.

[Tobias Leyba, the father of sixteen children, has lived all of his life in Canjilon. He is one of the eight men of the North who face charges from the so-called courthouse raid of 1967.—eds.]

THE ALIANZA: A HOPE AND A DREAM
by Father Robert G. Garcia

In seeking the legal return of the lost land grants the Alianza of Reies Tijerina was joined by thousands, among them the wife of the governor of New Mexico. Then came the apocalypse. On a summer day in June, 1967, a handful of armed farmers raided the courthouse of Tierra Amarilla. They sought to make a citizen's arrest of the district attorney and to free Alianza members who had been arrested at one of their meetings. The raid electrified the Chicano communities as nothing had since the Huelga of Cesar Chavez. A few weeks before these same men, in that same courthouse, had voted to re-establish their ancient land-grant government and had elected their own local officials. That event, in turn, had electrified the authorities and led to the arrests and subsequent raid. Father Robert G. Garcia, then State Director of the New Mexico OEO, gives the background of the Alianza and the raid. (*Statement to the Subcommittee on Rural Development*, U.S. Congress, House, June 12, 1967.)

On Monday afternoon, June 5, 1967, a group of men attacked the county courthouse in the small mountain town of Tierra Amarilla in New Mexico. There was much shooting and some destruction of property. Twenty hostages were held for about one and a half hours, then released. Two State police officers were seriously wounded, and two other men were allegedly taken away as hostages, one escaping and the other released shortly afterwards. Two police cars were ruined, according to one witness, mainly by one man using a machine gun. About one and a half hours or so after the shooting started the group fled towards the mountains.

State police were summoned and the National Guard was mobilized.

Using troopers and tanks, the guardsmen surrounded the village of Canjilon, apprehended about 50 people believed to have been involved and held them in the town of Canjilon.

Other arrests followed, and then Governor David Cargo ordered the removal of National Guard troops and two tanks in the area. The leader of the disbanded Alianza, Reies Tijerina, was taken into custody Saturday, June 10, and at the present time only a few purported members of the attacking groups remain at large.

I would like to outline the basic reasons for the recent violence and the danger of a recurrence that even now exists, as well as describing the efforts being made to solve the problems. Although the current crisis has been pinpointed to northern areas of the state, I am certain that underlying factors have caused similar responses and reactions in most rural areas of New Mexico. Because of this, I feel that these observations will serve for the entire state. It should be stressed that the attack on the Tierra Amarilla courthouse was essentially an explosion of a smouldering economic and social problem that has existed for decades in the rural areas of the state.

The current scope of the rural problems of New Mexico certainly transcends the present position of the leader of the Alianza who headed the Alianza from the beginning.

Tijerina formed his Alianza through claims of ancient Spanish Land Grants that would give back to the people vast areas of New Mexico, Texas, and Arizona.

He gained his membership and following through offering the hope of returning land that had been taken away from the Spanish people years ago. His following in large measure includes the poorest of the poor.

This statement is not to debate the issue of the land grants. Nor is it to comment on the movement led by Reies Tijerina.

This statement does not stress that the Alianza's promise of remuneration for lost land represented ideas that had never been injected into many of the rural poverty areas. It represents a hope and a dream for something better.

People in the extreme rural poverty areas are not aware of the democratic process and are definitely suspicious of state and Federal courts.

They feel economically depressed and defeated. They do have a deep sense of justice, but have never been given the opportunity to learn the full intricate workings of modern law as we know it. The recent outburst at Tierra Amarilla was a result of deeply rooted resentments along with a sense of hopelessness as to present conditions.

Following the incident of violence, many gross violations of civil rights were reported. About 50 people, old men, women, some with infants and children, were enclosed in a sheep pen for 30 hours. They were given C-rations to eat by

the National Guard, were not allowed to leave for the rest-
room at night, they had to sleep on the ground and they had
to drink water from a small reservoir used for the sheep.
Many houses were broken into without warrants. Cars were
stopped and searched without warrants. Seven defendants
apparently were kept in jail for 50 hours before a lawyer
was allowed to see them. These violations, alleged, of civil
rights were in the wake of mass arrests at small villages adja-
cent to the aforementioned town, and angered the people.
Among those apprehended there existed a pathetic lack of
understanding of the circumstances and certainly a lack of
resources to retain adequate legal protection.

The surge of people in poverty to join the Alianza stems
from an innate desire to attain first class citizenship. If they
have not been treated as full citizens thus far by the U.S.
community, symbolically they are seeking to attain it by creating their own community with its own government.

We are not dealing with educated Spanish-speaking people, nor are we dealing with people who understand the
complexities of our government and our society. But we are
dealing with people living in an abject economic state. Your
Appalachia has nothing on New Mexico's rural communities. To step into many of these communities is to step back
one or two hundred years. However, we are dealing with
people who have experienced hope for the first time in their
lives and who will be extremely reluctant to relinquish this
hope.

I appeal to the state and Federal governments to help
these people following upon their symbolic attempt to help
themselves. This is explicitly why programs must be pursued
which should be tailored to their needs expressed by themselves, basic as they are.

They were told after the Economic Opportunity Act that
help would be forthcoming provided they organized, voiced

their needs and submitted proposals. They organized and submitted many proposals, most of them excellent and which struck at the core of their poverty. Then they were told that there were no funds. Could it be that OEO has in a sense contributed to their frustration? Few as their OEO programs may be, they have a certain amount of hope for them. In some rural areas, CAA's are the only functioning organization.

Jobs, job training, social services and the basic knowledge necessary for a person to be self-sustaining and productive are still the hopes in many of these communities.

I will state that the OEO programs in rural areas have attained only a limited success. Relatively speaking, however, many of these programs are good, even excellent. These programs have touched on many of the existing problems, but have not solidly reached the real roots of their problems. OEO programs have made a good beginning, but they have barely scratched the surface. In rural New Mexico there has existed for 100 years a discrimination by neglect on the part of Federal and state governments. These people have been virtually ignored.

The resentment that has led to the recent conflict with law enforcement officers is a resentment that can be eliminated only by providing adequate and realistic services and an economic base which they have heretofore been deprived of.

There are many aggravating factors stemming from the inflexible regulations and policies of Federal and state agencies. Range management practices in national forests have caused a reduction in the number of grazing permits. The poor, uneducated owner of a small herd upon which he partly depends as a supplement for a bare subsistence does not understand this. Range management may be necessary but there appears to be a lack of sufficient consideration given to the fact that these grazing permits represent financial income and food for people in extreme poverty conditions. The existence presently of a huge gap between the Forest Service and these people is appalling.

Another point is that there exists a great difficulty in proving land ownership through lack of legal abstracts. This prevents any solid development either on the part of the individual owner or in terms of industrial growth. These people are anxious to improve themselves and their situation. The recent incident at the Tierra Amarilla courthouse indicates the intensity of their frustration.

One thing that is not commonly understood or known is that the philosophy of Anglo-American law is very different from New Mexico's Spanish philosophy of law. Anglo-American law is legalistic, highly technical, aggressive. The law that they were used to was humanistic, and based on tradition, de facto ownership and a consideration for the right of every individual to own property and to earn a living. Much consideration was given to the good of the family, inheritance, and the good of the community. The failure of these people to understand a new system of laws imposed upon them by the Anglo-American has caused a collapse of their rural economy. We are witnessing the great hardships they are experiencing in adjusting to the modern world. When these people do leave and try to live in the outside world, they very often cannot survive. They suffer great problems in the areas of juvenile delinquency, a breakdown of the family structure, and most often they return to their original community. From then on they are convinced that society is not ready to accept them or help them. Very often they tend to withdraw from society, and at this point they are lashing back at the society that has treated them with apathy and even hostility.

Any new programing to assist these people, then, must be

begun by these people themselves. They must be included in the planning and the decision-making. This, of course, has not been done. Community action is their first experience in this field. In spite of the lack of funds, they have still organized and are prepared to forge ahead. However, programs for the future must be concerned with functional factors. Their culture and their history and background must be of paramount concern. Their language also must be utilized and respected. In the present school system an attempt is made to treat them and to lead them to middle-class Anglo-American standards. Children are forbidden to speak Spanish in school, and the results are tragic when one considers that Spanish is spoken at home. Education, therefore, seems to be defeating its own purpose by causing unnecessary and damaging tension.

In their economic development their culture must likewise be considered. Tourism and recreational projects which would take water away from the small farmer and land from the small rancher would do more harm than good. Roads in the forests which practically lead nowhere, while failure to improve roads to schools does nothing for the improvement of their lives. A welfare system which prevents job seeking and stifles their iniative to add income to their families likewise does them no good. It is the people and the villages themselves who must gain the experience of planning for their own needs. . . .

OUR TIME HAS COME

> If the Huelga gave Raza a sense of pride, then the Alianza gave it a sense of power. Since then the Chicano movement has moved increasingly from protests to the building of cooperatives, credit unions and independ-

ent school boards and political parties, and the creation of barrio institutions. One such is the farm cooperative La Cooperativa Agricola del Pueblo de Tierra
Amarilla, which together with a health clinic, La Clinica del Pueblo, has been established in the village
where the raid on the courthouse took place. ("La
Cooperativa," by Valentina Valdez Tijerina, *Motive*,
Vol. XXXI, No. 5, March, 1971.)

La Cooperativa

by Valentina Valdez Tijerina

People talk about how it used to be *mas antes* in Tierra
Amarilla. They talk about how people used to work together—how they used to respect each other. It was true
brotherhood then. I suppose it was the same in the other
land grants, too.

In those times, the people used to get together and farm.
Nine or ten families would get together with their teams of
horses and plant acres and acres of land. And after it had
grown and needed weeding, they would get together to
weed and cultivate it. When it was time to harvest, they
would do that together and all share the food. Their crops
were good and didn't betray them. They stored enough food
until the next harvest, and sometimes even stored enough
for two years in case of famine.

If a family needed a house or barn, everyone would help
to build it. Everything was done communally—even the
making of blankets and mattresses, and drying and canning
food.

In the winter, there were chores to do such as milking the
cows, feeding the animals, and chopping wood. When these
were done, there was time to visit with each other. They

would sit around the stoves or fireplaces toasting and eating pinon nuts, telling *chistes* (jokes) or *cuentos* (stories) to the children, or talking about witches and hidden treasures.

But even though they had happy times, there was also time for respect. When someone said he would do something for someone, he didn't have to write it down. That was his word; he would rather die than break his promise.

The Land was also held communally in the land grants. This type of land grant is called *ejido*. There were no fences on this communal land. People would graze as many sheep and cows as they needed on this communal land, without anybody saying anything. And even though there were a lot of animals grazing on the sierra, the grass was high, as high as a horse's back, the people say. I've heard them say that the grass was so high that you couldn't even see the animals unless you were on horseback.

The people say that it used to rain and snow a lot more than now. The reason, they say, is that there were a lot more animals then than now. They say that animals have a lot of electricity on their fur, and that the electricity attracts humidity from the atmosphere, making it rain or snow.

There were a lot of animals then. None of the land was going to waste. Now the mountains and hills are bare. There are hardly any animals on them. The grass isn't as high as it used to be, and it doesn't rain or snow as much as it used to.

Then, the people used to go to the sierra to get wood for building or for fuel, but they only took as much as they needed. They weren't like the lumber companies that strip and bulldoze all the trees from the mountains, leaving them ugly and bare. The lumber companies care little that they are destroying the water reserve because of their greediness.

Our ancestors combined cultures and learned much from the Indian. The Indian taught us how to plant by the moon.

The Indian also taught us how to preserve the land. (The White man is still trying to teach us how to preserve the land. But he has not set a very good example.)

The people *mas antes* had everything they needed. They had their own houses. They had enough meat and food. And most important they had their land. Now the people don't have anything because their land was stolen from them.

In 1832, more than 580,000 acres of land belonged to the heirs of the Tierra Amarilla land grant. By 1969, the people only had 10,000 acres left. In the San Joaquin Land Grant, the heirs owned 500,000 acres in 1806. Today they have only 1,411. People ask, "But how could the land be stolen?" It was stolen in various ways.

In California, the land was grabbed up by gold-hungry diggers. In Texas, people were evicted or murdered to release the land. In New Mexico, the process was somewhat slower. Professor Clark Knowlton and Dr. Frances Swadish have written about this process in various research papers. The following is taken from their research as reprinted in *El Grito del Norte* Vol. 1, No. 4, a movement newspaper printed in northern New Mexico.

A Catholic sister of charity wrote, "In the years of Anglo settlement in New Mexico, the unsuspicious native Spanish Americans were victimized on every hand. When the men from the states came out west to dispossess the poor natives of their lands they used many subterfuges. One was to offer the owner of the land a handful of silver for the small service of making a mark on a paper. The mark was a cross which was accepted as a signature and by which the unsuspecting natives deeded away their lands. By this means, many a family was robbed of all its possessions."

According to these sources, merchants allowed the people unlimited credit from the store. When they couldn't pay, they would collect the land. Texans who came to New Mexico in the 1880's were perhaps the worst of all. They brought with them violence against the Indo-Hispanians with their traditions of peaceful community life. They treated the people as if they had no rights that needed to be respected. They drove off the people's cattle and scattered their sheep. Often they just took land with their six-shooters, killing people who resisted.

Through the years the people were cheated out of the land and its abundance in various ways. There was a case in Texas where a gringo hired a family to farm for him with the agreement that the family would get half the profit from the harvest. The poor family worked all summer planting, weeding and irrigating. When everything was harvested, the Texan took out his rifle and chased the poor family out. The family went to the sheriff, but all he said was that they were lucky to be alive. The poor family didn't have a place to go. They had to leave their animals behind, carrying with them only a few of their belongings.

A lot of Indo-Hispanos didn't take this robbery sitting down. Some of the people in the villages started fighting. A group called *La Mano Negra* (the Black Hand) was started in Rio Arriba Country. In Mora and San Miguel Counties the *Gorras Blancas* (White Caps) were started. These groups fought for their rights of honor, respect, land, and to hold onto their culture and language. They cut fences, burned haystacks, killed animals of the invaders, and sometimes hanged the men who were oppressing the people.

According to Professor Knowlton and Dr. Swadish, "The railroads opened the west more and more. By the 1880's New Mexico was full of ranchers and lawyers known to the Spanish Americans as 'black vultures,' for they cheated and fooled the people into giving up their lands.

"Some of the people started taking their demands to the courts. The Anglo solution to this threat was simple: hundreds of documents which might prove people's claims were burned up in mysterious fires, accidentally thrown out in trash and so forth!"

This ring of lawyers introduced the well-known idea of an economic system based on competition and "free enterprise." This idea has destroyed the old village values of co-operation, unity, respect, and honor.

Some of the land which the lawyers and landgrabbers stole was subsequently bought up by the federal government. Now the people have to pay for permission from the forest service to graze their animals. They can seldom afford to graze more than nine or ten cows on forest service lands. At the same time, the rich Texan has maybe 300 heads of cattle grazing in the National Forest. The lumber companies get rich on the lumber they take from the National Forest, while the people are lucky enough to get a few sticks for firewood.

The people don't earn enough to buy meat at the store. Yet if they are caught hunting deer for food for their families, they face a sentence of a five-year imprisonment. They have often watched the Texan who takes his deer-head for a trophy and leaves the meat to rot.

The people have little choice. If you own land, even if it's just five acres, you can't get welfare. If you have a small piece of land for grazing your animals, you don't have enough to farm. If you have enough to farm, you don't have enough to graze your animals. The people have been squeezed onto small plots of land which is all they own.

An economic, social, and educational survey by John Berma and Davie Williams published in *El Grito del Norte* Vol. 1, No. 2, reports about the quantity of land owned by the federal government. "Rio Arriba and Taos Counties together contain some 8,111 square miles which is federally owned. This is 69.1 percent of their total area." This survey also reports about the poverty of the people in the rural areas. "In 1959, almost half of the people (43 percent) in both counties received less than $1,000 income a year!"

People who live under these conditions suffer from everything. Their health is bad because their nutrition is bad. They can't afford to go to the regular doctors and clinics. Because the children are undernourished, they can't learn as quickly.

This isn't the only reason that their educational level is lower. Since the land was taken over, the educational system itself has been bad for the children. Our children are taught in school that the white man was the only civilized human being that came to America, and that the people he found here were lazy, ignorant savages. We are taught in school only about Davy Crockett, Kit Carson, and a blonde-haired Sally, Dick, and Jane. We are told constantly not to speak our own language. The educational system teaches us to grow up ashamed of ourselves, of the color of our skin, of our parents, and our whole way of life.

The report by Berma and Williams also states that life in these counties wasn't always as bad as it is today. There were huge quantities of corn and wheat once grown on these lands. There were huge herds of cattle. As the report states, "At one time there were flocks under single ownership (by members of the communal land grant) which were as large as the present lamb crop of the entire county."

The thing that I want to point out is that by losing the land, we also lost our culture and language. This is one reason why so many of our people are juvenile delinquents, dope addicts, and alcoholics. These are the most sensitive of people who have felt the racism in school, in jobs, and in the movies, and have been made to feel ashamed of themselves. The government continues to do investigations, spending money to try and figure out why there is so much juvenile delinquency, and so many riots, failing to recognize that they are also responsible.

These are some of the reasons the *Cooperativa Agricola del Pueblo de Tierra Amarilla* got started. The people wanted to hold on to what little culture and language they had left. There aren't too many places in the United States where people speak Spanish from birth.

One of the biggest problems is that our youth must leave the area and go to the city to find work. In fact, our people for years have been working for others—for other ranchers and other farmers. They've gone to work in the rich Anglo-owned potato fields in Colorado, and the Anglo has done what he wants with our people. He has given them poor living conditions and poor wages. When they come back, they've already spent their money just paying the rent and buying food where they've worked. The Agriculture Cooperative in Tierra Amarilla, a community owned and operated project, is one attempt to reverse these conditions.

During the first year of La Cooperativa, which was begun in 1969, we planted potatoes, wheat, corn, onions, peas, and other vegetables. Some of the land had been used for grazing land and hadn't been planted in thirty-five years. The ground was so hard that the tractor would almost stand on end when we tried to plow it. Some of the land had never been worked and a lot of *chamiso* (sagebrush) and trees had to be cleared. People from the community donated their little plots of land that were scattered all over. Some were as far as ten miles away.

Young volunteers came to help from Denver, San Francisco, and Espanola (New Mexico), and we had visitors from all over the world. All summer long we lived in tents, camping in the mountains and cooking in the open air. We really enjoyed it except when it rained. After dinner we would chat together around the fire. Sometimes we would listen to guitar and sing.

One of the biggest jobs was weeding the potatoes which were about a mile from the camp. We would walk over there, stopping to admire the view on the way. Then we would cross the river, sometimes getting our feet wet, and begin hoeing.

In the middle of that summer we heard that the doctor in Tierra Amarilla was putting his clinic up for sale. Dr. Dabbs had just returned from Vietnam where he had served with the Air National Guard, and had decided to sell his clinic.

For three years the people of this area, a distance of 90 miles from Durango, Colorado, to Espanola, New Mexico, had been without a regular doctor. There was a baby clinic open one day a week, but it only treated babies, except in an emergency.

When accidents happened, people sometimes died on the two-hour drive to the Espanola Hospital. And the ambulance often takes an hour to get to the scene of the accident. People in this area are not in the habit of going to the doctor for any little reason. This is not just because of the distance. Once they get there, they are charged more than they can afford. For example, if a pregnant woman goes to the clinic or a doctor, she is charged $5 for a visit, $12 for a blood test, $12 for a urine test, and an additional charge for medication. The delivery costs $300. At this rate the people are in debt for the rest of their lives. And worrying about their debts causes high blood pressure and ulcers.

The people of the cooperative decided that a doctor was

badly needed in the area. They decided to buy the clinic and run it as a community owned and operated clinic.

La Clinica del Pueblo de Rio Arriba was set up to offer the people better and cheaper services. For example, if a family can't afford to pay, they can pay La Cooperativa with stock or produce, or do volunteer work at the clinic. But some people don't like to see the poor start something of their own.

On the night of September 3, 1969, the clinic was burned down by arsonists. The people in the community were at the same time sad and furious. A few days before, a doctor from San Francisco had come to visit and had given first-aid classes to all the members. Two doctors practicing at a public health clinic at the Apache reservation in Dulce, New Mexico, about 30 miles from Tierra Amarilla, had promised to work in the Clinica two days a week. People in the community were getting excited over the prospect of having a doctor again. But then the fire set us back at least six months.

Maybe the arsonists thought the people were too poor to rebuild the clinic. Maybe they thought the people would get discouraged and not go on with the clinic. But to the contrary, the fire only united the people more. Right after the fire a 24-hour guard was set up, and the clinic has been guarded ever since.

Because of the fire company and friends who helped put out the fire, the clinic wasn't completely destroyed. Several attempts were made after the fire to finish it off, but because of the guards nothing happened. When people would come to see the clinic, they would say, "Who could have done such a thing? Who would want to burn the only clinic in this whole area?" One of the guards said that a woman came who didn't say anything. When she saw the ruins, she started crying.

After the fire, we planned to rebuild the clinic right away, but unfortunately we ran into problems. The Chama National Bank, located about fifteen miles from Tierra Amarilla, held the mortgage to the clinic and tried to foreclose. We were not delinquent on our payments: we had paid three months in advance, but the bank just didn't want the community-owned clinic around. Luckily, a few friends who support the clinic loaned us money to pay off the Chama Bank and changed the mortgage to another bank. This delayed us several months, but finally we started rebuilding the clinic, with the insurance money.

But this didn't stop the powerful Anglos in Chama. When they couldn't take the clinic away from the community, they decided to open another clinic in Chama. This clinic is run by people who make no attempt to reach out to the poor community.

La Clinica has finally been rebuilt, and has a full-time dentist working through VISTA. He was prevented from working for several months while the New Mexico Board of Health was deciding whether to give him a license. So now the dental program is working at full speed. People from all over the county come here to get their teeth fixed. People pay according to their ability to pay. If a family is large and has a low income, the family is given a discount.

But we need a license to get medicaid and medicare. La Clinica would like to have a free program but since it has to become self-sufficient, and has lots of expenses and plans for new things, like mobile units, etc., we have to charge people. People are really amazed by the low fees the Clinica charges. Getting a doctor has been more of a problem . . . The doctors who had promised to come from Dulce before La Clinica was burned and donate several nights a week were prevented from so doing by their commanding officer. Finally a doctor arrived in December and the Clinica began full-time operations in early January.

In addition to rebuilding La Clinica, work has continued with La Cooperativa. The first year's harvest was very good. We planted 60 100 lb. sacks of potatoes and harvested 300 100 lb. sacks of potatoes. This year's harvest was also good and we harvested a good amount of wheat, potatoes, turnips, lettuce, and beets. La Cooperativa is also building housing for volunteer workers and has started a hog farm which now has forty-six hogs of assorted sizes. We will butcher the hogs for lard, ham, bacon and sausage. We are also trying to raise some for the market. We are also trying to open a cooperative store. We have many other plans, one of which is a machine shop.

We have suffered by having our land stolen and our culture raped and our language destroyed. But through La Clinica and La Cooperativa we will go on struggling. Viva La Causa! Todo Poder A La Gente!

OUR ALLEGIANCE IS TO THE LAND

by Alex Mercure

The century-old struggle from the land has culminated in a new village- and barrio-based cooperative movement. It has taken many forms. One of its pioneers is Alex Mercure, the former director of HELP (Home Education Livelihood Program of New Mexico), who helped establish over seventy marketing, farming, and educational cooperatives in the villages of the state. Mercure himself has returned to the mountain village of El Rito, where he directs a vocational school. (From an interview in *La Raza: The Mexican Americans*, by Stan Steiner.)

Villages are not dead. Some of the experts believe that rural life is no longer functional. That rural life has collapsed beyond any possibility of rebuilding. It is not so!

Our villages have many human resources. People! Communal life still exists in the villages. It is not entirely the shadow that the experts see from the outside. It is a reality. And that communal life may be our greatest strength. These are the seeds of the revival of village life. Can these seeds be regenerated? I think so.

Gandhi in India advocated a cottage industry. That may have been all right for India. But not here. What is cottage industry in an industrial country such as this, but handicrafts and art crafts. It won't help a whole village. That benefits just one man. And a Giftie Shoppe. It is archaic. It won't help a whole village. Look what the government's Indian Arts and Crafts program has done to stop poverty on the reservations. Not much.

We need village industry. Small village industry that can revive the village. A village does not need a large plant, or a huge investment. That would only destroy the village completely. No, we need native industry that would employ maybe ten, or twenty, people. Because ten jobs would feed one hundred people. That will mean jobs in the grocery store, the post office, the gas station, the tavern. That's all a village needs to survive . . .

Too many decisions are forced [on the poor], and consequently are resented rather than responsibly met. If you want to help people let them tell you what they need. Let them decide. Never impose your needs on them. You are only fooling yourself that you are helping them. You aren't fooling them.

All this middle class nonsense of trying to teach people to be middle class on $1,500 a year. What good does it do?

Rural people don't need [it]. Learning to push an elevator button! Now what good does that do a farmer?

We want to do something *for* you, they say. They can't do anything *for* us. They don't understand that.

Our allegiance is to the land. The villager couldn't care less about the politics in the United States, or even Mexico. He cares about his land. Sometimes people will ask me why the villager doesn't move. There is nothing in the village, they say. There are no jobs. That may be so. But it is our homeland. It is the land we were born on, and where we have lived for hundreds of years . . .

Life in the villages may be a resource for the entire country. Cybernetics and the computer revolution may soon mean that most workers won't have anything to do. Then we will be in a real crisis. We may be in it already. We, in the villages, may then have to teach the country how to live in leisure. Riots in the cities may be a symptom of this age of cybernetics. The ghetto people who have "nothing" to do, who have no jobs, are taught to feel ashamed, useless, to feel guilty. So they try to assert their manhood, to do something, anything. They riot. It's this neurotic idea city people have that "doing nothing" is somehow a crime.

In the villages we know how to "do nothing". To live at a leisurely pace. To enjoy life. No one has to teach the villager how to live in the age of cybernetics. He is ready, willing and able. He is not neurotic about "doing nothing." That's one of the strengths of the village, and one of the reasons the village has endured. So, if the villages disappear our nation may lose its most precious resource—the solution to its urban problems.

The villages had better be rebuilt. Where else can urban man go to find peace of mind?

IX. LA CAUSA: LA MUJER (THE WOMAN)

THE ACT OF LOVE

from the Aztec Codices

"Our mother was the Indian; our father was the Spaniard," says Reies Tijerina. "Through this marriage we were born." It was the Mexican Indian woman, Malinche, who was lover and guide of the Conquistador Hernando Cortez. She was the mother of the mestizo, the modern Mexican—Indian in "blood and soul," Spanish in "language and civilization," as the philosopher Jose Vasconcelos has written of the origin of La Raza Cosmica. And yet this homage to the Indian mother was mocked by the social and sexual codes the Aztecs forced upon women. These codes were a duality for men, at once ascetic and lustful ("Do Not Throw Yourself upon Women," *Aztec Thought and Culture*, Leon-Portilla, from *Codice Florentino*, book VI). For women they decreed "grievous happiness": "On earth there is no happiness, no pleasure"; the "act of love" merely "sweetens life so that we are not always weeping" ("Must We Live Weeping?," *Pre-Columbian Literatures of Mexico;* Leon-Portilla; from *Codice Florentino*, book VI).

Do Not Throw Yourself upon Women

Do not throw yourself upon women
like the dog which throws itself upon food.
Be not like the dog
when he is given food or drink,
giving yourself up to women before the time comes.
Even though you may long for women,
hold back, hold back with your heart
until you are a grown man, strong and robust.
Look at the maguey plant.
If it is opened before it has grown
and its liquid is taken out,
it has no substance.
It does not produce liquid; it is useless.
Before it is opened
to withdraw its water,
it should be allowed to grow and attain full size.
Then its sweet water is removed
all in good time.
This is how you must act:
before you know woman
you must grow and be a complete man.
And then you will be ready for marriage;
you will beget children of good stature,
healthy, agile, and comely.

Must We Live Weeping?:
A Father's Advice to His Daughter

Here you are, my little girl, my necklace of precious stones, my plumage, my human creation, born of me. You are my blood, my color, my image.

Now listen, understand. You are alive, you have been born; Our Lord, the Master of the Close and the Near, the maker of people, the inventor of men, has sent you to earth.

Now that you begin to look around you, be aware. Here it is like this: there is no happiness, no pleasure. There is heartache, worry, fatigue. Here spring up and grow suffering and distress.

Here on earth is the place of much wailing, the place where our strength is worn out, where we are well acquainted with bitterness and discouragement. A wind blows, sharp as obsidian it slides over us.

They say truly that we are burned by the force of the sun and the wind. This is the place where one almost perishes of thirst and hunger. This is the way it is here on earth.

Listen well, my child, my little girl. There is no place of well-being on the earth, there is no happiness, no pleasure. They say that the earth is the place of painful pleasure, of grievous happiness.

The elders have always said: "So that we should not go round always moaning, that we should not be filled with sadness, the Lord has given us laughter, sleep, food, our strength and fortitude, and finally the act of love."

All this sweetens life on earth so that we are not always moaning. But even though it be true that there is only suffering and this is the way things are on earth, even so, should we always be afraid? Should we always be fearful? Must we live weeping?

But wee, there is life on the earth, there are the lords; there is authority, there is nobility, there are eagles and tigers (knights). And who is always saying that so it is on earth? Who goes about trying to put an end to his life? There is ambition, there is struggle, work. . . .

THE PIONEER WOMEN

by Fabiola Cabeza de Baca

In the deserts of Arizona during the expedition of Don Juan Bautiste de Anza in the year 1775, an infant was born to a woman who died in childbirth. Her son was perhaps the first Chicano born on the road to California. The earliest pioneer women of the West were these women of La Raza who began coming across the Jornada del Muerto with Onate in 1598. In the frontier villages the women were not only the wives and mothers, but the doctors (*curanderas* or medicine women), teachers, tailors, and psychologists of La Raza as well, as is recalled in the memoirs of Fabiola Cabeza de Baca, who describes these women in her memoirs of pioneer life in New Mexico (*We Fed Them Cactus*, by Cabeza de Baca).

The women on the *Llano* and *Ceja* played a great part in the history of the land. It was a difficult life for a woman, but she had made her choice when in the marriage ceremony she had promised to obey and follow her husband. It may not have been her choice, since parents may have decided for her. It was the Spanish custom to make matches for the children. Whether through choice or tradition, the women had to be a hardy lot in order to survive the long trips by wagon or carriage and the separation from their

families, if their families were not among those who were
settling on the Llano.

The women had to be versed in the curative powers of
plants and in midwifery, for there were no doctors for two
hundred miles or more.

The knowledge of plant medicine is an inheritance from
the Moors and brought to New Mexico by the first Spanish
colonizers. From childhood, we are taught the names of
herbs, weeds and plants that have curative potency; even
today when we have doctors at immediate call, we still have
great faith in plant medicine. Certainly this knowledge of
home remedies was a source of comfort to the women who
went out to the *Llano,* yet their faith in God helped more
than anything in the survival.

Every village had its *curandera* or *medica* and the ranchers rode many miles to bring the medicine woman or midwife from a distant village or neighboring ranch.

Quite often, the wife of the *patron* was well versed in
plant medicine. I know that my grandmother, Dona Este-
fana Delgado de Baca, although not given the name of *medica,* because it was not considered proper in her social class,
was called every day by some family in the village, or by
their *empleados* (servants, or *hacienda* workers), to treat a
child or some other person in the family. In the fall of the
year, she went out to the hills and valleys to gather her supply of healing herbs. When she went to live in La Liendre,
there were terrible outbreaks of smallpox, and she had
difficulty convincing the villagers that vaccination was the
solution. Not until she had a godchild in every family was
she able to control the dreaded disease. In Spanish tradition,
a godmother takes the responsibility of a real mother, and in
that way grandmother conquered many superstitions which
the people had. At least she had the power to decide what
should be done for her godchildren.

From El Paso, Texas, she secured vaccines from her cousin, Doctor Samaniego. She vaccinated her children, grandchildren and godchildren against the disease. She vaccinated me when I was three years old and the vaccination has passed any doctor's inspections.

As did my grandmother, so all the wives of the *patrones* held a very important place in the villages and ranches on the *Llano*. The *patron* ruled the *rancho,* but his wife looked after the spiritual and physical welfare of the *empleados* and their families. She was the first one called when there was death, illness, misfortune or good tidings in a family. She was a great social force in the community—more so than her husband. She held the purse strings, and thus she was able to do as she pleased in her charitable enterprises and help those who might seek her assistance. . . .

The women in these isolated areas had to be resourceful in every way. They were their own doctors, dressmakers, tailors and advisers.

The settlements were far apart and New Mexico was a poor territory trying to adapt itself to a new rule. The *Llano* people had no opportunity for public schools, before statehood, but there were men and women who held classes for the children of the *patrones* in private homes. They taught reading in Spanish and sometimes in English. Those who had means sent their children to school in Las Vegas, Santa Fe, or Eastern states. If no teachers were available, the mothers taught their own children to read and many of the wealthy ranchers had private teachers for their children until they were old enough to go away to boarding schools. . . .

Without the guidance and comfort of the wives and mothers, life on the *Llano* would have been unbearable, and a great debt is owed to the brave, pioneer women who ventured into the cruel life of the plains, far from contact with the outside world. Most of them have gone to their eternal rest, and God must have saved a very special place for them to recompense them for their contribution to colonization and religion in an almost savage country.

SONGS OF SORROWS

Love was a "grievous happiness" in the poverty of the barrios of the Southwest, where the weeping of women became a myth. She was *la Llorona* who haunts the nights of love. In the melancholy *corrido* of the *Tejas vaquero*, love was a "vice" of the poor ("El Abandonado"), while the women prayed in "La Firolera" that their husbands soon be dead, and in hell "for the kicks he gave me everyday." And yet, love, in the freer spirit of the frontier, where women had greater independence and freedom, was likened to a hat, in "El Sombrero Ancho." These songs are translated by Stan Steiner.

El Abandonado

Ay, you abandon me, woman,
For I am very poor
This is my disgrace
For I am a man of passion.

Well, what am I to do
If I am the abandoned one?
Well, whatever I do
Is for the love of God.

There are three vices
There are three sins

That I have enjoyed:
Drinking, gambling and loving.

Well, what am I to do
If I am the abandoned one?
Well, whatever I do
Is for the love of God.

But, I become desolate
If my love denies me,
If some other man is
Playing with my love.

Well, what am I to do
If I am the abandoned one?
Well, whatever I do
Is for the love of God.

La Firolera

My man is lying in bed
And I am by his bedside
With my rosary in my hand
Praying to God he will
   die . . .

Firoliroli, firoliroli, firoliroli,
Firoliroli, firoliroli, firoliroli,
Ven aca, firoliroli!
Ven aca, firoliroli!
Tu marido esperandote 'sta!

CHORUS

My man has now died.
The devil has taken him.

Surely, he is paying
For the kicks he gave me
    every day . . .

El Sombrero Ancho

Pepita no longer will sew
Neither will she crochet—
She longs for the gringo way,
With a man in a cowboy hat.

I have an embroidered hat
Richer than Don Pancho's—
My beloved embroidered it,
She loves my old sombrero.

MADRE

On the hill where Juan Diego, the humble *indio,* saw
his vision of La Virgen de Guadalupe, there had been
a temple to Tonantzin, the goddess of fertility. The *indios* of Mexico often still call their patron saint Guad-
alupana-Tonantzin. And La Virgen is sometimes depicted as stepping on a snake, as the Earth Goddess
did in the temple pictographs. Mexican scholar and
philologist Dr. Domingo Martinez Paredes has said the
name Guadalupe derives from *Coatl* (*culebra,* or
snake) and *U Pechack ma* (*pisado,* or stepped on)—
Coatl U Pechack ma (She Who Stepped on the Snake).
In this way the two ancient, supremely Mexican symbols are wedded—El Aguila y La Serpiente (The Eagle
and the Serpent) and La Virgen de Guadalupe—to
symbolize the fecundity of man and earth. And La Vir-

gen is depicted not as immaculate and white, but warm and brown; not merely the Mother of Christ, but *Nos Madre*—the Mother of Us All. In his poem *"La Jefita"* (The Little Mother), Jose Montoya recalls his mother as a symbol of life-giving sacrifice (*El Espejo–The Mirror: Selected Mexican-American Literature,* Quinto Sol Publications, 1969). The farm worker-poet Augustin Lira, in his poem "Cruz," creates an image of holiness and earthiness in the figure of his mother, the weeping woman (previously unpublished).

La Jefita

by Jose Montoya

When I remember the campos
   Y las noches and the sounds
Of those nights en carpas o
Bagones I remember my jefita's
   Palote
   Clik-clok; clik-clak-clok
   Y su tocesita.

(I swear, she never slept!)

Reluctant awakenings a la media
Noche y la luz prendida,

   PRRRRRRINNNNGGGGGGG!

A noisy chorro missing the
   Basin.

Que horas son, ama?
Es tarde mi hijito. Cover up

Your little brothers.
Y yo con pena but too sleepy,

    Go to bed little mother!

A maternal reply mingled with
The hissing of the hot planchas
Y los frijoles de la hoya
Boiling musically dando segunda
A los ruidos nocturnos and
The snores of the old man

    Lulling sounds y los perros

Ladrando—then the familiar
Hallucinations just before sleep.

    And my jefita was no more.

But by then it was time to get Up!

My old man had a chiflidito
That irritated the world to
Wakefulness.

    Wheeeeeeeeeet! Wheeeeeeet!

Arriba, cabrones chavalos,
Huevones!

    Y todavia la pinche
    Noche oscura

Y la jefita slapping tortillas.

    Prieta! Help with the lonches!
    Calientale agua a tu 'apa!

(Me la rayo ese! My jefita never slept!)

Y en el fil, pulling her cien
Libras de algoda se conreis
Mi jefe y decia,

That woman—she only complains
in her sleep.

Cruz

by Augustin Lira

ave maria madre de dios
ruega por nosotros los pecadores
ahora y en la hora de nuestra muerte amen.
     black shawled women in encantation
     flat monotone sounds speaking in prayer
     for cadaver dead.
candles adorn the walls giving off a mellow cool,
                            cold light.

touching rays caress the cracked walls,
they slide and slither
almost lovingly
against the box—a coffin.
the prayers continue and trail on
"padre nuestro que estas en los cielos
santificado sea tu nombre
venganos . . .
          venganos
y bendito es el nombre de tu vientre jesus.
cry women
men be strong
let not a tear come screaming out of your red eye
after all . . . are you not a man?
          amen
          amen
          amen.

silently the wind blows on the adobe wall
a rat scampers quickly

stopping only to shoot a look,
nervously jolting his head
this way towards the rosary house,
home of the dead . . .

                silence
                darkness blessed-cold darkness
                            hides it
                a rat
                flickering damp light escapes the
                            adobe house
                home of the dead.

into the night goes cruz
rosary dangling in her hands
her black shawl kissed by the wind,
sweet wind.
        the rat looks at the dark form
        it crouches and only its eyes move,
        voices adorn the night . . .
        "buenas noches cruz"
        the paid mourner mutters through wet eyes
        "de nada"
        cruz responds and walks on . . .
        the hum of voices in unison continue
        as if a drone of bees were speaking,
        the dark prayers crawl upon the earth
        "y bendito es
                el nombre
                      de tu
                            vientre jesus."

the rat slides away into an arroyo
food . . .
it eats forcing the decayed pile of shit into his stomach,

its eyes gleam and it is full,
the moon sees the rat,
it does not laugh,
it smiles proudly
                    silence.

she will always be remembered that way
"ey cruz, fijese nomas que se murio el senor jose"
(can you imagine, senor jose died.)
"jose? no me diga?"
"no, si."
black shawled woman spreading truth,
another night of prayers
cadaver dead,
            et nominae
                        et patrie
                                et filio sanctu
                                        amen.
she will always be remembered that way
someone died?
get the rosary
the bible and the black shawl,
she never got paid for her prayers
she was not a professional mourner
but she was there . . . praying,
she will always be remembered that way.

one day the sun was hot
melting spirits away
but for cruz it was night, always night, endless night.
            the flies buzzed around her body
            they licked her pouring sweat
            they droned around her bed,
            smoke from the religious candle tickled the brown
                                    adobe wall,

　　　　　　　　　　the smoke listened to the
　　　　　　　　　　sounds of the day.
but for cruz it was night
away they took her into the hot hills
　　"campo-santo" croaked a professional mourner.
　　"campo-santo" the birds seemed to chirp.
　　"to the burial place" said an old man.
　　"Sacred camp" smiled the earth and opened its mouth
　　to greet her.

the rat comes slowly into the sacred camp, its whiskers
　　　　　　　　　　　　　　　　　　　　　　stand
briskly outward,
it goes to the freshly dug grave,
it digs soundlessly into the moist earth,
in the far distance can be heard still the prayers for cadaver
　　　　　　　　　　　　　　　　　　　　　　dead,
the wind touches the evening
and turns it into night
it whispers with cool breaths
　　　　　　　　　　amen
　　　　　　　　　　　　amen
　　　　　　　　　　　　　　amen.

THE NEW CHICANA

In the "Raza Renaissance," there are few "leading men" who do not have a woman devotedly and actively by their side. But, as a leader of the Chicano movement has explained, "Our women are equal with the men. If they stay one step back." The new Chicanas in the universities and barrios no longer accept this separate, but unequal, heritage of the Aztec and the Spaniard; nor do they express the "silent strength" of the pioneer women of La Raza; nor do they acquiesce to the "goddess/mistress" imagery of the male ego— his *machismo*. In a village in the mountains of New Mexico, Enriqueta Longauez y Vasquez, a writer and activist, seeks to wed the ancient cultural strengths to the modern "liberation" of the new Chicana ("The Women of La Raza," *El Grito del Norte*, Vol. 2, No. 9, July 6, 1969). And Mary Lou Espinosa, in her hard-lined poem, evokes the elemental "life from within" that women bear to strengthen their status in contemporary life ("La Madre de Aztlan," *El Grito del Norte*, Vol. 2, No. 17, Dec. 24, 1969).

The Woman of La Raza

by Enriqueta Longauez y Vasquez

While attending a Raza conference in Colorado this year, I went to one of the workshops that were held to discuss the role of the Chicana woman. When the time came for the women to make the presentation to the full conference, the only thing that the workshop representative said was this: "It was the consensus of the group that the Chicana woman does not want to be liberated."

As a woman who has been faced with having to live as a member of the "Mexican-American" minority as a breadwinner and a mother raising children, living in housing projects and having much concern for other humans leading to much community involvement, this was quite a blow. I could have cried. Surely we could have at least come up with something to add to that statement. I sat back and thought, why? Why? I understood why the statement had been made and I realized that going along with the feelings of the men at the convention was perhaps the best thing to do at the time.

Looking at our history, I can see why this would be true. The role of the Chicana woman has been a very strong one, although a silent one. When the woman has seen the suffering of her peoples she has always responded bravely and as a totally committed and equal human. My mother told me of how, during the time of Pancho Villa and the revolution in Mexico, she saw the men march through the village continually for three days and then she saw the battalion of women marching for a whole day. The women carried food and supplies; also, they were fully armed and wearing loaded "carrilleras." In battle they fought alongside the men. Out of the Mexican revolution came the revolutionary personage "Adelita," who wore her rebozo crossed at the bosom as a symbol of a revolutionary woman in Mexico.

Then we have our heroine Juana Gallo, a brave woman who led her men to battle against the government after having seen her father and other villagers hung for defending the land of the people. She and many more women fought bravely with their people. And if called upon again, they would be there alongside the men to fight to the bitter end.

And now, today, as we hear the call of the Raza and as the dormant, "docile" Mexican-American comes to life, we see the stirring of the people. With that call, the Chicana woman also stirs and I am sure that she will leave her mark upon the Mexican-American movement in the Southwest.

How the Chicana woman reacts depends totally on how the "Macho" Chicano is treated when he goes out into the so-called "Mainstream of Society." If the husband is so-called successful, the woman seems to become very domineering and demands more and more in material goods. I ask myself at times, "Why are the women so demanding?" But then I realize: this is the price of owning a slave.

A woman who has no way of expressing herself and realizing herself as a full human has nothing else to turn to but the owning of material things. She builds her entire life around these and finds security in this way. All she has to live for is her house and family and she becomes very possessive of both. This makes her a totally dependent human. Dependent on her husband and family. Most of the Chicana women in this comfortable situation are not particularly involved in the movement. Many times it is because of the fear of censorship in general. Censorship from the husband, the family, friends and society in general. For these reasons she is completely inactive.

Then you will find the Chicana with a husband who was not able to fare so very well in the "Society" and perhaps has had to face defeat. She is the woman that really suffers. Quite often the man will not fight the real source of his problems, be it discrimination or whatever, but will instead come home and take it out on his family. As this continues, his Chicana becomes the victim of his machismo and woeful are the trials and tribulations of that household.

Much of this is seen particularly in the city. The man, being head of the household and unable to fight the system he lives in, will very likely lose face and for this reason there will often be a separation or divorce in the family. It is at this time that the Chicana faces the real test of having to confront society as one of its total victims.

There are many things she must do. She must: (1) Find a way to feed and clothe the family. (2) Find housing. (3) Find employment. (4) Provide child care. And (5) find some kind of social outlet and friendship.

(1) In order to find a way to feed and clothe her family she must find a job. Because of her suppression, she has probably not been able to develop a skill. She is probably unable to find a job that will pay her a decent wage. If she is able to find a job at all it will probably be only for survival.

Thus she can only hope to exist; she will hardly be able to live an enjoyable life.

Even if she does have a skill, she must all at once realize that she has been living in a racist society. She will have much difficulty in proving herself in any position. Her work must be three times that of the Anglo majority. Not only this, but the competitive way of the Anglo will always be there. The Anglo woman is always there with her superiority complex. The Chicana woman will be looked upon as having to prove herself even in the smallest task. She is constantly being put to the test. Not only does she suffer the oppression that the Anglo woman suffers as a woman in the market of humanity, but she must also suffer the oppression of being a minority with a different set of values. Because her existence and the livelihood of the children depend on her conforming to an Anglo society, she tries very hard to conform. Thus she may find herself even rejecting herself as a Mexican-American. Existence itself depends on this.

(2) She must find housing that she will be able to afford. She will very likely be unable to live in a decent place, it will be more the matter of finding a place that is cheap. It is likely she will have to live in a housing project. Here she will be faced with a real problem of being able to raise children in an environment that is conducive to much suffering. The decision as to where she will live is a difficult matter as she must come face to face with making decisions entirely on her own. This, plus having to live them out, is very traumatic for her.

(3) To find a job she will be faced with working very hard during the day and coming home to an empty house and again having to work at home. Cooking, washing, ironing, mending, plus spending some time with the children. Here her role changes to being both father and mother. All of this

plus being poor is very hard to bear. Then, on top of this, to have a survey worker or social worker tell you that you have to have incentive and motivation and get ahead! These are tough pressures to live under. Few men could stand up under them.

(4) Child care is one of the most difficult problems for a woman to have to face alone. Not only is she tormented with having to leave the raising of her children to someone else, but she wants the best of care for them. For the amount of money that she may be able to pay from her meager wages, it is likely that she will be lucky to find anyone at all to take care of the children. The routine of the household is not normal at all. She must start her day earlier than an average worker. She must clothe and feed the children before she takes them to be cared for in someone else's home. Then, too, she will have a very hard day at work for she is constantly worrying about the children. If there are medical problems, this will only multiply her stress during the day. Not to mention the financial pressure of medical care.

(5) With all of this, the fact still remains that she is a human and must have some kind of friendship and entertainment in life and this is perhaps one of the most difficult tasks facing the Chicana alone. She can probably enjoy very little entertainment as she can not afford a baby-sitter. This, plus she very likely does not have the clothes, transportation, etc. As she can not afford entertainment herself, she may very often fall prey to letting someone else pay for her entertainment and this may create unwanted involvement with some friend. When she begins to keep company with men, she will meet with the disapproval of her family and often be looked upon as having loose moral values. As quite often she is not free to remarry in the eyes of the Church, she will find more and more conflict and disapproval and she continues to look upon herself with guilt and censorship.

Thus she suffers much as a human. Everywhere she looks, she seems to be rejected.

This woman has much to offer the movement of the Mexican-American. She has had to live all of the roles of her Raza. She has had to suffer the torments of her people in that she has had to go out into a racist society and be a provider as well as a mother. She has been doubly oppressed and is trying very hard to find a place. Because of these facts she is a very, very strong individual. She has had to become strong in order to exist against these odds.

And what usually happens to this woman when she tries to become active in the "Causa"? One would think that the movement would provide a place for her, one would think that the organizations would welcome her with open arms and try to encourage her to speak up for her Raza. One would think that because of her knowledge and situation the groups would think of liberation schools with child care for the victims of broken homes, in order to teach them culture and history so that they may find self-identity. But, NO. Instead one finds that this woman is shunned again by her own Raza. When she tries to speak of Machismo, she is immediately put down and told "We know all about it, there are many many books written on the subject." She receives nothing but censorship again. She tries so hard to say, "yes, there is much on Machismo, but can't you Machos look at the women and children who are the VICTIMS of your Machismo?" She tries so much to speak up and instead finds herself speaking to deaf ears and a completely closed mind.

Then she tries other ways, perhaps to offer her skills and knowledge in some way. This too is difficult. If she does a good job, she will have to walk lightly around the men for she may find herself accused of being "Agringada" or "Agabachada" (Anglocized). To top this off, quite often the men will accept or allow an Anglo female to go in and tell them how to run things. The Anglo will perhaps be accepted and be allowed more freedom than the Raza woman. Through all of this one sees a discouraged Chicana woman. One that hungers and bleeds to help her people and is turned away and discouraged. What is to become of her? Will she be forced into being a skeleton in the closet that one does not want to see?

The Mexican-American movement is not that of just adults fighting the social system, but it is a total commitment of a family unit living what it believes to be a better way of life in demanding social change for the benefit of mankind. When a family is involved in a human rights movement, as is the Mexican-American, there should not have to be a woman's liberation movement within it. There should not have to be a definition of a woman's role. We should get down to the business at hand. Do we want a liberation for the Raza? Is this supposed to be a total liberation?

The woman must help liberate the man and the man must look upon this liberation with the woman at his side, not behind him, following, but alongside of him leading. The family must come up together. The Raza movement is based on Brotherhood. Que no? We must look at each other as one large family. We must look at all of the children as belonging to all of us. We must strive for the fulfillment of all as equals with the full capability and right to develop as humans. When the man can look upon "his" woman as HUMAN and with the love of BROTHERHOOD and EQUALITY, then and only then, can he feel the true meaning of liberation and equality himself. When we talk of equality in the Mexican-American movement we better be talking about TOTAL equality, beginning right where it all starts, AT HOME. . . .

La Madre de Aztlan

by Mary Lou Espinosa

Equality respects the function of
man as father
woman as mother
and both as an independent
human capable of change.

A Chicana woman springs out of her
Indian and Spanish cultural and
historical heritage.
From Indian comes strong mother figure
From Spanish comes dominant father figure.

True woman's liberation must happen first
in the mind of the woman.
No woman can expect nor demand
to be thoroughly accepted as equal
in a man's eyes, nor be given equal recognition,
if she first does not believe that
her potential and the man's potential
are equally realizable given the
opportunity.

Man cannot change his attitude
toward woman until the woman
perceives her deep psychological
self as independent and asserted
from man.

Socio-economic and political
conditions can help
the process of woman's full
assertion in the movement and

in society, but the woman has first
to want to make herself free.

Woman's contribution is essential.
A woman, a mother, knows life
from within because of her function.
Our society is sadly masculine oriented;
it does not know life from within
because men alone make it.

Creative solution to social change
comes with people who have
creative life within themselves,
a free woman can creatively
contribute with radical solutions
because she knows life from within.

X. LA CAUSA: THE CHICANOS

THE EMERGENCE OF THE NEW CHICANO

by Guillermo Fuenfrios

Chicano is a new word, not yet in the dictionary. Who is he? How many are there? The U.S. Census (1970) has estimated there are five and a half million, while a former director of the President's White House Committee on Mexican American Affairs has estimated eight to twelve million. The Chicano is born of contrary forces in our history; he is conqueror and conquered, *gachupin* and *indigena, patron* and *peon,* "Aztec Prince and Christian Christ." He has internalized all of them. "In our hearts Cortez still tortures Cuauhtemoc," says a Chicano writer; and Rodolfo "Corky" Gonzales, in his epic of modern Chicanismo "I Am Joaquin," says, "I ride with Revolutionists/ against myself." The word Chicano is born of these contradictions. Some of the older generation object to the term for they say it derived from *chicaneria* (chicanery). Some say it referred to the lowest of the low, the street people of the burro alleys and goat hills. Some say it originated in barrio slang for a *mexicano* from Chihuahua—thus, a Chi-cano. Some have dignified it with ancient origins, saying it comes from the Nahuatl word *Mexicanoob,* referring to the god Quetzalcoatl, in which the *x* was pronounced *sh,* and mispronounced by the Spaniard: *Meshicano* became *Mex-*

icano, and finally *shicano* became *chicano.* The young Chicano Guillermo Fuenfrios eschews the semantic game and says simply that he is a "pluralistic man" who stands on "the bridge of history" and who defines himself by what he has become and is becoming. (*The Emergence of the New Chicano,* by Guillermo Fuenfrios.)

Octavio Romano has pointed out in his remarkable essay on the historical and intellectual presence of the Mexican-American, the emergence of a new kind of Chicano. The young bilingual college student who, through reading of Latin American authors, has discovered the full range of the meaning of biculturalism. This new Chicano is able to enter into a full and comprehensive understanding of both of the dominant cultures of the American continent, and yet by his link to his origins is in contact with the full social range from the fields to the ivory tower. He is an amalgam of indigenous America: "razgos indigenos, the scars of history on my face and the veins of my body . . . (Alurista)" of Europe and Africa through his Spanish heritage and by education. Anglo-America.

He is by nature a pluralistic man, a universal man, combining the racial strains and cultures of the entire world in his own person. Jose Vasconcelos coined the term "La Raza Cosmica" to describe him. The term is apt. With the possible exception of the Hawaiian, there are no people on earth with a more legitimate claim to universality. It is no wonder that he has successfully resisted the best efforts of the North American crucible to melt him down into a mere American.

All this universality, however, has had its price in pain, suffering and isolation. He has paid with his toil in the fields and sweat shops, his tears of rage and humiliation, and his blood at the hands of lynch mobs and on the battlefields of World War II, Korea and Vietnam. The memory of peonage in Mexico and the agony of the Mexican revolution are still fresh in his mind. He lives as an exile in a land that belonged to his fathers. Despised equally by Mexican (see Paz—*The Labyrinth of Solitude*) and American, is it any wonder that in his search for identity he has rejected both labels and picked up the term Chicano from the dust of opprobrium where it had languished for years? Formerly denoting derision of the indigenous origins of the Mexican peon, it is now the proud symbol of militancy and newfound pride of origin for students and activists throughout the Southwest. In conjunction with indigenous roots is the resurrection of the ancient Aztec myth of Aztlan, the ancient northern homeland of the Nahuatl-speaking peoples. The intellectual and spiritual direction of the Chicano movement appears to be toward revindication of the American past after four hundred years of its debasement of European ethnocentric racism. As a result, the Chicano is becoming consciously tricultural.

The question which confronts us now is: What are the implications of this phenomenon for the Chicano, the Mexican and the European descendants in the New World?

It is significant that this emergence from the subconscious into the conscious of the non-European element of "la Raza Cosmica" should come about at a moment of crisis in Western Civilization unparalleled in human history. Cortazar, Fuentes, Paz, Borges, Marcuse, Norman O. Brown, McLuhan, William Burroughs, Leslie Fiedler, as well as many other writers, painters, musicians and scientists from all over the world, have pointed out the apocalyptic nature of the times in which we live. The somewhat unreal threat of the atomic is now being overshadowed by more inevitable threats such as population explosion and ecology disaster. All of these mind-boggling horrors can be traced directly to the success of modern technological society, of which the United States is the most spectacular example. We have seen in our time the total impotence of Western-Christian-Marxist-Humanism to curb the disastrous long-range effects of technological development. The emergence of the Humanists from the Ivory Towers and Churches into the streets of Selma, Washington and Chicago has only hastened their demise by making them more easily eliminated. The spread of the Capitalist-Marxist technological materialist society can be denoted in every urban center in the world.

Norman O. Brown refers to this process as the victory of linear rational thought, or Protestant literalism, over symbolic and poetic thought. Marcuse calls it the success of the performance principle. In Freudian terms it is the victory of the Ego over the Id, the rational suppressing the non-rational. The process began in eighteenth-century France, and men of prophetic vision have pointed to its dangers since the first: Rousseau, Jefferson, Blake, Schopenhauer, Baudelaire, Nietzsche, Jose Enrique Rodo, and more recently, those mentioned beforehand. Western society, while tolerating these Isaiahs at best, and persecuting them at worst, has generally accused them of being enemies of progress and has paid them little heed. The magic of technology is more theatrically effective than that of the poets.

But now, the non-rational element in man, having been banished from his consciousness, threatens to completely dominate his actions. A glance at the morning paper is all the proof we need. Zodiac Killer, Vietnam, professional football, the freeway crunch, ad infinitem. Twenty-four hours in Los Angeles is sufficient to bring to the surface the forgotten words of the Biblical prophet speaking of the Apocalypse: "The sun shall be turned into darkness and the moon into blood." Echoes of Nazism are heard in the words of our freely-elected dignitaries. Spiro Agnew, Julius Hoffman, Judge Chargin, of San Jose. Dressed in the cloak of sweet reason and law and order, the Beast of Revolutions seems to stalk our land.

Where, where, one asks one's self, can one look for hope? Casting about in the darkness, I am reminded of the words of St. John of the Cross: "Admirable cosa es que, siendo tenebrosa, alumbrase la noche." The darkness of night, by blinding our most rational sense, illuminates our most rational sense, illuminates our spirit. Brown, in *Love's Body*, points to the need for a change of consciousness from linear literalism to poetic symbolism, "to rise from history to mystery."

Marcuse, in *Eros and Civilization*, calls for the resurrection of the spirit of Orpheus and Narcissus. Octavio Paz, in *Corriente Alterna*, says: "La actitud occidental es enfermiza. Es moral. Gran aisladora, gran separadora, la moral parte en dos a hombre. Volver a la unidad de la vision en reconciliar cuerpo, alma y mundo." And thus we see all about us efforts to escape from the tyranny of reason and return to mystical and symbolic forms of thought. The phenomenon of drugs is no coincidence: it is a direct response to the psychic oppression of our culture. It is only part of a great spiritual reawakening which has led our most prophetic thinkers to the study of both Eastern and Western mysticism. Bab Ras Dam, formerly Richard Alpert relates a remark made to him by a Tibetan holy man: "God came to America in the form of LSD." Certainly the simultaneous discovery of the Sacred Mushrooms of Mexico and the invention of LSD in a Swiss laboratory point to a similarity with other outcroppings of the Zeitgeist such as the multiple simultaneous inventions of the automobile, the airplane, etc.

By this time the reader must be asking himself, OK, OK, but what does all this have to do with the Chicano? Very well, the Chicano stands squarely at the point where both East and West meet. He has access to the occidental modes of rational thought, he is heir to the lyrical and poetic tradition of the Mediterranean, and he has recently discovered the dignity and wonder of the non-rational indigeneous mind.

For the Chicano, Indian forms and symbols are no affectation. They are in his blood, his religion and his culture. Who but the Chicano is better suited to bridge the gap between Western rationalism and non-Western symbolism? To translate technology into poetry? Is he not in the position to remember the body, the spirit and the world, put asunder by a technological imperialism?

Oh, Chicano: you are here at the crisis of man's existence on the earth, the legitimate heir to the culture of the entire community of man. Wandering Jew, exiled Arab, dispossessed Indian, Spanish bastard and American orphan, you have in your language all the cultures of Europe; in your blood the mystery and wisdom of Native America and the Orient and Africa—the "Cosmic Race." Find your voice and sing and you will save the world.

EL GRITO

by Guadalupe de Saavedra

Reies Tijerina has defined the Chicanos as a "New Breed"—like "the Hebrews in Egypt," he has said. The rites of passage from the hyphenated man, the "passive" Mexican-American "who drank the blood of Christ," to the Chicano, who "will not crawl" and who desires "to be a man," have historically been the path of the youth. And so the journey begins in the schools. In his "grito," the young barrio poet Guadalupe de Saavedra voices the student's restlessness, anger, frus-

tration, and pain as he moves from personal rebellion
to the ideology of Chicanismo. ("El grito," *La Raza
Yearbook*, Sept., 1968.)

>   to worms and the educator raised
>   in boyle heights who hides behind
>   the thin veil of anonymity

until yesterday you called me a good chicano. . . . .

i was meek, humble, god-damned ignorant.
i was young, passive,
          another pawn in a game you play.
i bent my knee, smiled, echoed,
          "my country . . . right or wrong."
i squatted, listened, as a bastard beagle preached,
          "come now, let us reason together."
i drank the blood of christ,
          yet vendidos bled me dry.
i was a good american,
          i licked the hand that fed me crumbs.

until yesterday you called me a good chicano. . . . .

now the years have fled, i'm back,
          you crawl——behind a skirt.
i spit my greetings upon you,
          denier worm seek a coward's grave.
i stand before you——humbly,
          i am Saavedra: a writer, a poet

a man re-born a man,
          has learned to stand up, bear the
          burden of his people on his back.
i——no longer dead, i——alive.

      my heart cries to my people:
numberous,
united we shall be but one voice.
for our great grito. . . .
      ADELANTE MIS TIGERES ANGELINOS!
      ARRIBA MI RAZA DE BRONZE . . .
                              QUERIDA!
      QUE VIVA MI RAZA. . . . . . . !
                  MI RAZA QUERIDA!

see my people rising,
      my peasant blood sings with pride.
see my people refuse to bend,
      prostitutes for an anglo dog.
see a multitude of clenched fists,
      casting off shackles of death.
see brothers joined hand in hand,
      muscular and strong, march before the sun.
tender the flame of justice,
      forge the swords of tomorrow.
see, feel silver raindrops,
      run down my cheeks of brown.

until yesterday you called me a good chicano. . . . .
today you refer to ours as a bad chicano. . . . .
you label me a disgrace,
            because i dare to speak of truth,
            because i dare not be silent,
            because i dare destroy the image
                you have built of me,
            because i choose not to live
                or end my life in an eternal siesta.

you point at me as militant,

because i will not crawl,
because i have learned to walk,
because i seek to uproot the hell
   of being the system's dog,
patten on the head . . . "NICE BOY,
                     PANCHO,"
   while a finger is jammed right up my ass,
because i desire to be a man.

listen. . . . . . . listen. . . . . . .

   there is a message in the wind,
   as a people cry against the rains of injustice
each day new voices join
             in a united front,
to take the lead in a common cause.
         ADELANTE TIGERES ANGELINOS

EDUCATION AND DE-EDUCATION

In the schools the young Chicanos have engaged in a "struggle for their souls." The anguish of high drop-out rates, "illiteracy in two languages," and drug addiction is reflected in the rueful irony of "The Writing on the Blackboard" by teenage students in Los Angeles (*Con Safos*, Fall, 1968). Education is de-education to the Chicano child, for he has been taught to forget his language and his culture, writes Professor Sabine R. Ulibarri in "The Word Was Made Flesh" (*Cultural Heritage of the Southwest*, Cabinet Committee Hearings on Mexican-American Affairs, El Paso, Oct., 1967). To some educators the "learning problems of most Mexican-American children generally arise from the home situation" (*Education of the Mexican-American*, Rueben E. Aguirre), but the U.S. Office of Education's National Advisory Committee on Mexican American Ed-

ucation has indicted the educational system in general
("The Mexican American Child: How Have We failed
Him?" *Quest for Equality*, U.S. Office of Education,
National Advisory Committee on Mexican American
Education, Dr. Amando Rodriguez, director, 1968).
And the Chicano students have voiced their own opin-
ion of the schools in a barrio-wide strike of the Los An-
geles high schools under the slogan "Education, Not
Eradication" ("The Blow Outs!," *Chicano Student
News*, March 15, 1968).

The Writing on the Blackboard

Students of Los Angeles

i am
a chicano
one of that lovely race
a race bred on love but fed hate
i am

Michael Sanchez, age 15

The only thing you have to do is die
Baby, don't let them tell you anything else;
You don't have to lower your hems.
You don't have to pay your taxes.
They may boot you and send you to jail,
But you don't have to let them,
You can run, defend yourself, or end it all
in this wicked world. . .

Olga Ceballos, age 15

CHINO

I knew some guy named Chino. He was real nice. He was a
Cholo. He was from Clover. He used to always get loaded,
loaded on anything. He didn't really care about anything.
He would always get torcide in and out. I remember one
time me and him and my cousin Dimples went to a party.
There was a gang fight. He beat up some guy. He was real
nice. He was going to get married with my cousin Dimples.
He loved her a lot. He loved her so much he put a tatoo on
her. It said CHINO just like that. The last time I saw him was
at his funeral. He was 19 years old before he died. My
cousin had broke up with him. He told me that he was still
looking for her. He was never going to give her up because
he loved her alot, and his kid, his daughter. It was chicken
the way he died. The guys from 3rd killed him with guys,
knifes, chains. He was real nice. He could have been my
cousin in law.

Hilda Leal, age 13

I love a hamster because we had these
hamsters and they died. I hate my
school because there are bad people
over there. The End.

Genevieve Diaz

THE GIRL THAT EARN MONEY

Once upon a time there live an old lady that had one child. Her child's name was Betty and was 10 year old. They were pour and needed some food so Betty went to get a job. She earn $5.00 a week. They save $2.00 and spend $3.00. When Betty was 14 year old she had save $85.00 and they were not pour anymore and they live happily ever after.

Renee Jaun

WE HAD A DISCUSSION . . .

Our discussion was about children of Germany. They were of Therisienstadt Consertration Camp. They were captured by the bad Germans. They were taking into rooms of gas and smoke. Their parents were taking from them and their uncles and aunts. They were all killed in the gas. The children were about 6 years old to 16 years old. They were killed too.

They said they'll never see their homes again. But they just prayed and prayed until at last they were sent into the gas. Before they were sent in the gas, they drew a picture of their homes. And when the men went there in the tents they found the children's bodys. I thought that was sad. I hope that will not happen to us.

Marta Enriquez

The Word Was Made Flesh:
Spanish in the Classroom

by Sabine R. Ulibarri

In the beginning was the Word. And the Word was made flesh. It was so in the beginning, and it is so today. The language, the Word, carries within it the history, the culture, the traditions, the very life of a people, the flesh. Language is people. We cannot even conceive of a people without a language, or a language without a people. The two are one and the same. To know one is to know the other. . . .

It is all a matter of language. It is a matter of economics. It is a matter of rural versus urban societies. Hispano children speak Spanish. Most of them are poor. Many of them live in the country. Many have recently moved to the city. Consequently, they are predestined to failure, frustration and academic fatigue in our national public schools.

The Hispano child begins with a handicap the very first day he shows up in the first grade. English is the language of the classroom. He speaks no English, or he speaks inadequate English. The whole program is designed to make him an Anglo. He doesn't want to become an Anglo, or he doesn't know how. He comes from a father-dominated home and finds himself in a female-dominated classroom. The Anglo concepts and values that govern and prevail are unintelligible to him. In all likelihood he comes from a low social and economic class, and there he is in an Anglo middle class environment. Much too frequently he is fresh out of the country, and the city in general, and the school in particular, might just as well be in another planet. He probably feels very uncomfortable in the unfamiliar clothes he's wearing. He looks about him. The teacher, far from representing a mother image, must seem to him a remote and

awe-inspiring creature. The children around him so friendly
with one another and so much at ease, look at him with suspicion. There is nothing in the atmosphere from which he
can draw any comfort. Everything he sees is foreign. The
climate of sound is confusing, and frightening. The Hispano
kid, Jose Perez, finds himself in a hostile environment indeed. He will never, ever, forget this day, and this day will
influence everything he does from then on. So the very first
day in school, before he comes up to bat, he has two strikes
against him. Before the coin is tossed, he has a penalty of a
hundred yards against him. He has to be something very
special, a star, a hero, in order to win.

Amazingly enough, he does much better in the primary
grades than one would expect. It is later when he gets into
deep trouble. In the primary grades the language of the
classroom is primarily what the linguists call "sign language," that is, the kind of language a dog would understand: "stand up," "sit down," "go to the blackboard,"
"open your books," "let's sing." The Hispano kid falls behind in the first grade, but not too much; his intuition and
native intelligence keep him afloat.

Each successive year he falls farther behind, and as time
goes on, as the language becomes more abstract and more
transparent, the gap of deficiency becomes wider and
wider—until he becomes a drop-out. We hear a great deal
about the high school drop-out. We are going to hear more
and more about the university drop-out. Imagine if you will
the young Hispano with his high school diploma in his hot
little hand who appears at the university. He's highly motivated, eager and full of illusions. He has been more successful than most. His family is very proud of him. He is going to
be a somebody. Then comes the shock. He finds out. He
doesn't know how to read! His teachers never taught him
how to read. How could they? They didn't know Spanish.

They didn't understand his culture. No teacher can teach a second language effectively without knowing the native language of her students and understanding their culture. So the kid is suspended. No one can blame him if he feels cheated, betrayed and frustrated. He earned that high school diploma in good faith, and he put in more than the normal effort to earn it. And a valuable asset to our society is lost in anger and despair. . . .

Above all the Hispano should be educated in his own culture, his own history, his own contribution to the life-stream of his country. An American citizen of Jewish extraction, who is proud of being a Jew, is worth more to himself, to his people and to the United States than one who is not. An Hispano who doesn't speak Spanish must choke on his chile. . . .

The Mexican American Child: How Have We Failed Him?

from a Report of the U.S. Office of Education

There are more than five million Mexican Americans in the United States, 80 per cent of whom live in California and Texas. Most of the others are found in Arizona, Colorado, New Mexico, Illinois, and Ohio. In excess of four million of these people live in urban areas.

The Mexican American is the second largest minority group in the United States and by far the largest group of Spanish-speaking Americans. The fact that most of them have learned Spanish as their first language and that millions are not fluent in English makes them no less Americans. Their interests, attitudes, and aspirations differ little from those of other Americans.

Yet they have been denied the opportunities that most

other Americans take for granted. Suffering the same problems of poverty and discrimination of other minority groups, the Mexican American is additionally handicapped by the language barrier. The typical Mexican American child is born of parents who speak little or no English, and thus Spanish becomes his only language. When he reaches school age, he is enrolled in a public school where only English is accepted. Bewildered and ashamed of his "backwardness," the Mexican American child is quickly discouraged and drops out within a few years, enlarging the ranks of the uneducated, unskilled, and unwanted.

Let's look at some shocking statistics.

The average Mexican American child in the Southwest drops out of school by the seventh year. In Texas, 89 per cent of the children with Spanish surnames drop out before completing high school!

Along the Texas-Mexico border, four out of five Mexican American children fall two grades behind their Anglo classmates by the time they reach the fifth grade.

A recent study in California showed that in some schools more than 50 per cent of Mexican American high school students drop out between grades 10 and 11; one Texas school reported a 40 per cent dropout rate for the same grades.

Mexican Americans account for more than 40 per cent of the so-called "mentally handicapped" in California.

Although Spanish surnamed students make up more than 14 per cent of the public school population of California, less than ½ of one per cent of the college students enrolled in the seven campuses of the University of California are of this group.

These facts give tragic evidence of our failure to provide genuine educational opportunity to Mexican American youth; and today there are nearly two million of these children between the ages of 3 and 18.

It can't be said that nothing has been done for these youngsters. The Federal Government, through the Elementary and Secondary Education Act (ESEA), has given a good deal of financial aid to schools for the purpose of improving the education of Mexican Americans. Although a few million of dollars have been spent, hundreds of millions still need to be spent—and for hundreds of thousands of Americans it is even now too late. State and local agencies have spent respectable sums of money—and even more energy— in behalf of the Mexican American but none has given the problem the really massive thrust it deserves.

Money is only one problem. Perhaps an even more serious one is the problem of involuntary discrimination—that is, our insistence on fitting the Mexican American student into the monolingual, monocultural mold of the Anglo American. This discrimination, plus the grim fact that millions of Mexican Americans suffer from poverty, cultural isolation, and language rejection, has virtually destroyed them as contributing members of society.

Another problem is that we have not developed suitable instruments for accurately measuring the intelligence and learning potential of the Mexican American child. Because there is little communication between educators and these non-English speaking youngsters, the pupils are likely to be dismissed as "mentally retarded." Common sense tells us that this is simply not so. The chasm that exists between the teacher and the student in the classroom is even wider between the school and the home, where there is virtually no communication. Such lack of understanding soon destroys any educational aspiration the pupil might have or that his parents might have for him.

Blueprint for Action

Once we have faced up to the critical issues and recognized the imperatives, the Committee recommends specific action on several fronts.

1. We must immediately begin to train at least 100,000 bilingual-bicultural teachers and educational administrators.

2. We must make use of current knowledge and encourage further research to assist in creating educational programs that promise learning success for the Mexican American.

3. We must agitate for priority funding by the U.S. Office of Education to develop educational programs immediately.

4. We must see that testing instruments are developed that will accurately measure the intelligence and achievement potential of the Mexican American child.

5. We must promote programs to assist state legislatures in taking the necessary action to permit instruction in languages other than English.

6. We must help the various states to recognize the need for statewide programs in bilingual education.

7. We must provide assistance, through Federal funds, to Mexican American students in pursuit of a college education.

8. With the leadership of the Federal Government, we must increase the adult basic education and vocational programs to equip the Mexican American adult with skills and knowledge necessary to become a partner in our economic society.

9. We must encourage parental involvement at the state and local levels.

10. We must encourage state and local education agencies to use more effectively the Mexican American personnel on their staffs.

11. We must foster a joint effort of the Federal Govern-

ment and private enterprise to produce instructional materials that are designed expressly for Mexican American students.

The Blow Outs!

from the Chicano Student News

BLOW OUTS were staged by us, Chicano students, in the East Los Angeles High Schools protesting the obvious lack of action on the part of the LA School Board in bringing ELA schools up to par with those in other areas of the city. We, young Chicanos, not only protested but at the same time offered proposals for much needed reforms. Just what did we propose?

To begin with, we want assurance that any student or teacher who took part in the BLOW OUTS——WILL NOT be reprimanded or suspended in any manner. You know the right to protest and demonstrate against injustice is guaranteed to all by the constitution.

We want immediate steps taken to implement bi-lingual and bi-cultural education for Chicanos. WE WANT TO BRING OUR CARNALES HOME. Teachers, administrators, and staff should be educated; they should know our language (Spanish), and understand the history, traditions and contributions of Mexican culture. HOW CAN THEY EXPECT TO TEACH IF THEY DO NOT KNOW US? We also want the school books revised to reflect the contributions of Mexicans and Mexican-Americans to the U.S. society, and to make us aware of the injustices that we, Chicanos, as a people have suffered in a "gabacho" dominated society. Furthermore, we want any member of the school system who displays prejudice or fails to recognize, understand, and appreciate us, our culture, or our heritage removed from ELA schools.

Classes should be smaller in size, say about 20 students to 1 teacher, to insure more effectiveness. We want new teachers and administrators to live in the community their first year and that parents from the community be trained as teacher's aides. We want assurances, that a teacher who may disagree politically or philosophically with administrators will not be dismissed or transferred because of it. The school belongs to the community and as such should be made available for community activities under supervision of Parents' Councils.

There should be a manager in charge of janitorial work and maintenance details and the performance of such duties should be restricted to employees hired for that purpose. IN OTHER WORDS NO MORE STUDENTS DOING JANITORIAL WORK.

And more than this, we want RIGHTS—RIGHTS—STUDENT RIGHTS—OUR RIGHTS. We want a free speech area plus the right to have speakers of our own choice at our club meetings. Being civic minded citizens we want to know what the happenings are in our community so we demand the right to have access to all types of literature and to be able to bring it on campus.

The type of dress that we wear should not be dictated to us by "gabachos," but it should be a group of Chicano parents and students who establish dress and grooming standards for Chicano students in Chicano schools.

Getting down to facilities. WE WANT THE BUILDINGS OPEN TO STUDENTS AT ALL TIMES, especially the HEADS. Yeah, we want access to the Heads at all times. . . . When you get right down to it, WE ONLY DEMAND WHAT OTHERS HAVE. Things like lighting at all ELA football fields, swimming pools. Sports events are an important part of school activity and we want FREE ADMISSION for all students. We, CHICANO STUDENTS, BLEW OUT in protest. Our proposals have been made. The big question is will the School Board take positive action. If so, WHEN?

IF NOT————BLOW OUTS————BABY————BLOW OUTS!!

THE CHICANO MOVEMENT: A NEW BREED

In the barrios there has traditionally been a euphoria of *familia*, religious, fraternal, and social organizations. East Los Angeles alone has more than three hundred of these groups. With the rise of the Chicano movement a new type of barrio organization has arisen—often from the streets. One of these is the Brown Berets, a self-defense and service youth group founded by David Sanchez, the former chairman of the Mayor's Advisory Youth Council of Los Angeles ("The Brown Berets," *La Raza Yearbook*, Sept., 1968). In seeking a deeper cultural identification with La Raza history, a group of Brown Berets created La Junta "to promote and advance the culture and heritage of our people" ("La Junta," *La Raza Yearbook*, Sept., 1968). And in the mountain villages of New Mexico a youth group, similar in purpose, but very different in spirit, was formed by Chicanos who identified with the "renegades of the plains"—the *comancheros*—in the rugged tradition of the frontier ("Los Comancheros del Norte: For Machos Only," *La Raza Yearbook*, Sept., 1968).

The Brown Berets

Ten Point Program

1. Unity of all of our people, regardless of age, income, or political philosophy.

2. The right to bi-lingual education as guaranteed under the Treaty of Guadalupe-Hidalgo.
3. We demand a Civilian Police Review Board, made up of people who live in our community, to screen all police officers, before they are assigned to our communities.
4. We demand that the true history of the Mexican-American be taught in all schools in the five (5) Southwest States.
5. We demand that all police officers in Mexican-American communities must live in the community and speak Spanish.
6. We want an end to "Urban Renewal Programs" that replace our barrios with high rent homes for middle-class people.
7. We demand a guaranteed annual income of $8,000 for all Mexican-American families.
8. We demand that the right to vote be extended to all of our people regardless of ability to speak the English language.
9. We demand that all Mexican-Americans be tried by juries consisting of only Mexican-Americans.
10. We demand the right to keep and bear arms to defend our communities against racist police, as guaranteed under the Second Amendment of the United States Constitution.

The Brown Berets are not a gang, car club, or private social group; it is an organization of young Chicanos dedicated to serving the Mexican-American community.

The purpose of the Brown Berets is summed up in its motto:

To serve

To give vocal as well as physical support to those people and causes which will help the people of the Mexican-American communities.

To observe

To keep a watchful eye on all federal, state, city and private agencies which deal with the Mexican-American, especially the law enforcement agencies.

To protect

To protect, guarantee, and secure the rights of the Mexican-American by all means necessary. How far we must go in order to protect these rights is dependant upon those in power. If those Anglos in power are willing to do this in a peaceful and orderly process, then we will be only too happy to accept this way. Otherwise, we will be forced to other alternatives.

Why a Brown Beret?

The brown beret was chosen because it is a symbol of the love and pride we have in our race and in the color of our skin. The BROWN BERET also acts as a symbol of unity among chicanos.

La Junta

La Junta is a group of vatos from different barrios that have come together to try and bring the barrios together. Up to now no group has been able to bring us together so we have taken it upon ourselves to bring peace between the barrios. JUNTOS we will be stronger and the vatos will now be heard. It will be de aguellas cuando un chicano can go anywhere in the BARRIOS and be accepted like a CARNAL. We are all carnales and will someday work together. Why not now CARNAL!

LA JUNTA NEEDS YOU, you are the people, help us do our thing carnales.

The vatos locos and the viejas locas have long been neglected by society and as a whole Psychologists, social workers, teachers and the placa have been treating us like "pendejos" because they do not understand us. To them, we are rebels without a cause. But times are changing. Society has put down our people because we are individualists and society doesn't understand our way of thinking because we reject their false values. The vato loco has truly been at the forefront of the Chicano Revolution but without realizing it.

The vatos have been the victims of the most jacked-up schools, shitty jobs and messed-up chantes. We have had no choice in making decisions that affect our lives. The vatos are no longer going along with the program. The only way we could express our pride in LA RAZA was putting our placas on walls, buses and other places. Today the placas still go up on walls, but we are also learning other ways to show our pride in LA RAZA. The vatos locos now know who is their real enemy.

STATEMENT OF PURPOSE

It is the purpose of this organization to spread a cultural consciousness among our people which will result in a political force for the advancement and well being of La Raza. It is our belief that we, as a people, cannot contribute fully to this society or to our community without an awareness, knowledge, and pride in our racial and ethnic origin. In keeping with this organization, it is our intention to promote and advance the culture and heritage of our people.

We will promote the purposes of La Junta by following a 4 point program:

1. By setting up Chicano Libraries in the barrios which will carry books dealing with the History, Heritage and Culture of La Raza.

2. By setting up educational classes dealing with such subjects as: Culture, History, Spanish, English, Reading, Writing and Organizing.

3. By setting up programs for community involvement such as dealing with Educational Reform, Police Malpractice, Drug Addiction, the High School Drop-Out, Unemployment, etc.

4. By working in the creative arts such as the Teatro Chicano, Music Poetry, Painting and Film Exhibitions. This would be for the purpose of gaining a free and open expression of the true sentiments of La Raza in the Southwestern United States.

We will strive to preserve the Spanish Language in the Southwest; not only because it is a part of our heritage, but also because it is one of the great ties binding La Raza.

We will stress pride in our people not only by teaching and learning of our history, but also by showing the great contributions of La Raza to civilization.

In working towards our goals, we will conduct ourselves and La Junta in a free and democratic manner, in keeping with the great traditions of the Americas.

Los Comancheros del Norte: For Machos Only

Listen, man, you from Bernalillo or Chama or Taos or wherever you are. Listen, you think you're so macho because you fight with your blood brother—because you get drunk—because you treat women like things. You think you're macho, but I tell you that you're a jerk, because all those things are just what the Anglo enemy wants you to do. He wants you to fight with your own brothers so that you'll be divided and not fight against him, he wants you to get blind drunk so that you won't know what you're doing and then he can do anything he wants with you. And you think you're so macho! If you really were some kind of man, you would be fighting to pull up your people, you would be fighting for your people, you would be forming groups like the Brown Berets in Albuquerque or like the Comancheros in Rio Arriba. We don't need machos. We need guys with fresh blood and fresh ideas who can go all the way in the struggle and by any means necessary. You don't know how? That's no excuse. Here is something to show you what other guys like you are doing:

LOS COMANCHEROS
A Declaration

The purpose of Los Comancheros is:

TO SERVE: To serve the Indo-Hispano people (sometimes called Mexican-Americans or Spanish-Americans or La Raza) of New Mexico by telling them about their rights and protecting them by all means necessary.

TO OBSERVE: To keep a watchful eye on all federal, state, city and private agencies and prevent them from taking advantage of the Indo-Hispano people.

TO EDUCATE: To open the eyes of the Indo-Hispano people because they have been blinded to the truth by the

Anglo people, by the politicians, by the law enforcement agencies, and by the educational system.

TO UNITE: To unite our people regardless of age, income or political philosophy.

The meaning of the name Los Comancheros:

Los Comancheros is a youth organization which takes its name from the original Comancheros of the Southwest, who were the militant vanguard of the New Breed. The original Comancheros were of Indo-Hispanic blood, despised by both the pure Indians and the pure Spaniards. They were outcasts in the 18th and 19th centuries. Spain and later the United States (Texas Rangers) tried to wipe them out; the Comancheros retaliated. Many of them were descendants of landholders, and they fought to get back the lands taken away from them—just as the Alianza Federal de los Pueblos is today fighting to get back stolen lands. Thus the Comancheros represented a high point in the history of the New Breed—the Indo-Hispano people of the Southwest. With the same militant spirit as that of the original Comancheros, the new Comancheros will move to help people where the law fails to protect them.

The program of Los Comancheros:

1. We demand an educational system which gives our people a thorough knowledge of the Spanish language and which teaches the true history of the Indo-Hispano people.

2. We demand that all police officers in Indo-Hispano communities live in the community and speak Spanish.

3. We demand a decent standard of living for the Indo-Hispano people, and especially the return of our lands with

compensation for the loss of income during the many years when we were deprived of our lands.

4. We demand an end to the preferential hiring of out-of-town and out-of-state labor. Jobs must be given first to people in our communities, and only afterward to outsiders.

5. We demand that all Indo-Hispano people be tried by juries consisting only of Indo-Hispanos.

6. We affirm the right to keep and bear arms to defend our homes and communities against racist police, as guaranteed under the Second Amendment of the Constitution.

THE CHICANO MOVEMENT: A CONTROVERSY

"I do not ask for freedom. *I am freedom,*" writes the poet Alberto Alurista. This concept of La Raza Cosmica, in which the universality of man is inherent, differentiates the Chicano movement from minority protest movements. And this creates a "philosophy of nationalism in human form," says Rodolfo "Corky" Gonzales, leader of the Crusade for Justice in Colorado. The "tool of nationalism" has similarly been used by Jose Angel Guitierrez in building MAYO (Mexican American Youth Organization) and the La Raza Unida political party in Texas, which defeated the two major parties to win an important election in Crystal City. So angered were the traditional political leaders by the youths' rhetoric and "tool of nationalism" that Congressman Henry Gonzales (Dem., Texas) accused them of "Reverse Racism" (*Congressional Record,* April 28, 1969). In California, however, the oldest political journal of the Chicano movement defended those young people ("The Youth Will Be Heard," *Carta Editorial,* Vol. 6, No. 4, April-May, 1969).

Reverse Racism

by Congressman Henry Gonzales

It is virtually impossible for any man of reason, intelligence and sensitivity not to see every day the destructive and corrosive effects of racism. It is virtually impossible for any man who has seen and acknowledges the existence of racism and its terrible results not to fight against it.

Racism is based on feelings that are beyond my power to fathom; it is fear, hatred and prejudice combined into a poison that divides men who under their skin are identical; it causes some to believe that they are superior to others, simply because they are one thing and others are not; and racism has given us all a burden of dishonor, guilt and grief.

The passions of racial hatred have been fanned high by fanatics and demagogues long since gone, but the poisons they disseminated remain with us still. Who can forget the contorted, hateful faces of people attacking innocent children who sought nothing more than to obtain equal educational opportunity, to enter schools freely without regard to the color of their skin? And who can forget the shameful defiance of law by George Wallace's stand in the doors of a great university, or the deadly riots at the University of Mississippi? And who can forget the fire hoses of Birmingham? Who among us did not feel shame on the day of the incident at Selma bridge? The passions that fueled those incidents, and that have bombed schools and churches, and that have created night riders and slick demagogues are with us still. The fears that created Jim Crow are still around, and we are burdened yet with the disaster that frightened *Plessy vs. Ferguson;* dozens of court decisions and hundreds of judicial orders have yet to erase the stain that decision placed on our legal system.

There is in physics a series of laws having to do with motion. There is a law of inertia which states that a mass that is headed in a given direction is inclined to continue in that direction until its force is spent or some superior force deflects or overcomes it. There is another law that states that for a given force there is an equal and opposite force; for every action there is an equal and opposite reaction. In the laws of civilizations gone by we can observe these same kinds of phenomena; and injustice will continue until its force is spent or until society rectifies it; and an injustice on one side may lead to another injustice on the other. Even as the poisons of racism are with us still, though its legal foundations be destroyed and gone for all time to come, so too can racism produce an equally deadly, opposite poison that can be called reverse racism. I say it can produce that opposite effect, for the laws of politics are not so precise as the laws of physics; in social interaction there are no immutable laws. It is true that inertia exists in political and social systems, much as it does in physics, but an opposite action, a reaction, will occur only when the force of inertia is so great that only legitimate force can change it.

I believe that we are attacking the forces of hate and bigotry, and I believe that however slowly and painfully we may be doing it, our country is overcoming the forces of racism. I believe that the impetus of racism is spent, or very nearly so, and that it is possible that justice in this land can be achieved within legitimate means.

I do not believe that violence is necessary to obtain justice, and I do not believe that hatred is necessary either; I do not believe that there is any reason why despair should be so great that reverse racism can be justified. Yet reverse racism, and reverse racists exist and their voices are loud, if largely unheard.

No man ought to either practice or condone racism; every man ought to condemn it. Neither should any man practice or condone reverse racism.

Those who would divide our country along racial lines because they are fearful and filled with hatred are wrong, but those who would divide the races out of desire for revenge, or out of some hidden fear, are equally wrong. Any man, regardless of his ambitions, regardless of his aims, is committing an error and a crime against humanity if he resorts to the tactics of racism. If Bilbo's racism was wrong—and I believe that it was—then so are the brown Bilbos of today.

Fifteen years ago as a member of the City Council of the city of San Antonio, Texas, I asked my fellow Council members to strike down ordinances and regulations that segregated the public facilities of the city, so as to end an evil that ought never to have existed to begin with. That Council complied, because it agreed with me that it was time for reason to at long last have its day. Eleven years ago I stood almost alone in the Senate of the State of Texas to ask my colleagues to vote against a series of bills that were designed to perpetuate segregation, contrary to the law of the land. I saw the beginnings then of a powerful reaction to racist politics, and I begged my colleagues to remember: "If we fear long enough, we hate. And if we hate long enough, we fight." I still believe this to be true. Since then there has been vast progress in Texas. I did not know how to describe to you the oppression that I felt then; but I can tell you that the atmosphere today is like a different world. Injustices we still have aplenty, but no longer is there a spirit of blatant resistance to just redress of just grievance. Yet despite this change in the general atmosphere, despite the far healthier tenor of public debate and public action today, I felt compelled almost exactly a year ago to address the United States House of Representatives on the continuing and alarming practice of race politics, and what I chose to call the politics of desperation.

There are those in Texas today—and I suppose elsewhere as well—who believe that the only way that the problems of the poor, and the problems of ethnic minorities, will be solved, is by forcing some kind of confrontation. This confrontation can be economic, or it can be direct and personal, but whatever form it may take, the object is to state in the most forceful possible terms what is wrong, and to demand immediate and complete corrective action. This tactic leaves no room for debate and often no room for negotiation, however reasonable that might be. It is the tactic of drawing a line and saying that it is the point where one system ends and another begins. This may not sound unreasonable in itself, and in fact the tactics of confrontation may have a place in political life. But the problem is that this deliberate and very often sudden confrontation might or might not be reasonable, and the demands presented might or might not be legitimate. The fact is that the tactic deliberately attempts to eliminate alternatives to violence, and it is therefore risky at best and at worst it can lead to disaster. This sort of politics is only one step removed from rebellion.

When the politics of race are added to the politics of confrontation, the makings of tragedy are abundantly clear. Race politics is itself highly unstable, and the same is true of the politics of confrontation. When the potent mixtures of long held passions are met on a hard line, but with justice obscured or perhaps lost in the midst of empty slogans, then great and perhaps irreparable damage can result.

There are those in Texas who believe that reverse racism can be mixed with the politics of confrontation, and that the result will be justice—or if not justice at least revenge. One cannot be certain whether the new racists want justice or revenge; only one thing is certain and that is that you cannot have both.

Probably the leading exponent of the new racism in Texas is the current president of the Mexican-American Youth Organization. This young man is filled with passions that may be obscure even to himself; he is ready to accuse anyone who does not help him of being a "turncoat" and anyone who opposes him of having "gringo tendencies" and concludes that most of the citizens of Texas are racists. Indeed, if he is opposed, he says, ". . . within a few years I will no longer try to work with anybody." He is not certain of what he wants, except that he does not want to "assimilate into this gringo society in Texas." He wants to be "Mexicano" but not "Mexican." He wants to expose and eliminate "gringos," and by that he means killing if "it doesn't work." Of course, I am told that this young man never meant to make such threats, though he clearly uttered them. But those who utter threats and who clearly mean them, must be prepared to be challenged. And I do not believe that anyone who claims any position of responsibility, or anyone who pretends to leadership can make threats of killing and still be expected to be called responsible.

This young man and his followers have attempted to find settings in Texas to practice their militance, and in particular to test out their theory of confrontation.

They distribute literature that is replete with hatred, and which builds on the supposed romance of revolution; too often one finds a photo of Juarez running alongside a photo of Che Guevara in MAYO literature. It would be hard to find a broader appeal than that to build a myth based on Guevara. They print such patent nonsense as "there is no bad luck, just bad gringos." They like to label enemies: "If you label yourself a gringo then you're one of the enemy." They give the overall impression that anyone the MAYO leadership disapproves of is either a gringo or has "gringo tendencies" or is a "turncoat." Only one thing counts to them: loyalty to *la raza* above all else, and MAYO next. Of course they reserve the right to judge who is loyal and who is not.

Filling people with the bright phrases of revolution and the ugly phrases of race hate, MAYO seeks to find a confrontation. They sought it at Del Rio, Texas on Palm Sunday, but did not find it. Some of them sought it at Denver that same weekend, but did not find it. When they do, they have every likelihood of doing great harm to themselves and the cause they supposedly are trying to advance. The fuel of tension and the flame of passion make a dangerous mix.

I do not favor repression, because I do not believe that order is something that can be forced, at least not in an open and free society. I believe that there is enough good will and enough determination in this country that justice will prevail, and without resort to violence on one side or the other.

The young racists want to promote and exacerbate fears that already exist; they want to destroy what they perceive as an equilibrium, or a stalemate, that militates against their perception of justice. I do not think they will succeed. I believe that most Americans believe, as I do, and as Sandburg did, that:

> Across the bitter years and howling winters
> The deathless dream will be the strongest
> The dream of equity will win.

This is no land of cynics, and it is no land of demagogues; it is a land wherein I believe reason can prevail; if it cannot succeed here, it can succeed nowhere.

I oppose this new racism because it is wrong, and because it threatens to destroy that good will, that sense of justice that alone can bring ultimate and lasting justice for all of us. This new racism threatens divisions that cannot be soon healed, and threatens to end whatever hope there may be— and I think that hope is considerable—of peaceful progress toward one country, indivisible, with liberty and justice for all.

I do not want to see Texas riots and burned buildings; and I do not want to see men beaten, men killed, and fear rampant. I have seen it happen in other cities; I have seen fear and hate and violence destroy that essential impetus toward full justice. I have seen the ugliness of division and violence. I do not want to see it again, and I do not want again to have to fight against blind unreasoning intolerance. It is not necessary and it is not inevitable.

But the fruit of racism is not prejudice, fear and distrust. There can be no benefit from it, no matter how you color it with romance, or the new techniques of confrontation. There can only be tragedy from it. If MAYO gets its confrontation, it will not "crush any gringo who gets in (the) way" —"squashing him like a beetle"—and it will not "kick the door down." It will only find itself beaten in the end, and with it, the hopes of many innocent people who follow their false banner.

The new racists, if they succeed in their divisive efforts, will in the end only unloose destructive forces that may take generations to control, for those who plumb the well-springs of hate and break the dams of passion always learn too late that passions and hatreds are far easier to open than they are to close. It is not possible to pursue a just cause with unjust tactics, and it is not possible to justify cruel and deceitful actions by the end hoped for. It is not possible to expect sympathy or justice from those whom you threaten with hatred and destruction and it is self-deluding to think that there is no alternative to inviting violence.

I stand for justice, and I stand for classless, raceless politics. I stand for action, and I stand for freedom. I stand against violence, racism, and anyone or anything that threatens our ability in this land to govern ourselves as a free people.

The Youth Will Be Heard

from Carta Editorial

Two curious and possibly interrelated reactions regarding minority youth have been aired in the last month or two from within the minority community itself. In Texas, Congressman Gonzalez is leading a charge against what he calls "reverse racism." His main target is MAYO, a Mexican American Youth Organization which has chapters in Texas and which is very outspoken regarding the poverty and the discrimination against the Mexican people. This attack by Gonzalez bounces off to strike at others especially the newly created voice which is now being heard from one end of the country to the other . . . the "Chicano" press. The people who produce these periodicals and newspapers work hard utilizing their resources to inform the people what is going on in the Mexican communities across the country, and in this manner overcoming the censorship which has prevented one community from knowing what the others are doing.

With respect to the press . . . it is interesting to note that the Negro "traditional leaders" are also alarmed over the growth of community press in their areas. According to the National Hotline (Los Angeles Sentinel) "Black publishers around the country are expected to start asking questions about the presence of community-grass-root-newspapers springing up around the country and being financed by government money through poverty programs. Federal law forbids financing any type of media. Look for fireworks on this score."

Congressman Gonzalez, in addition to attacking MAYO, has lent himself for an attack on the community press and has raised the question of inspection of tax free foundations in relation to funds provided for community action programs.

First a look at the charges of Gonzalez is making and then a brief look at MAYO and what is happening in Texas.

"Issue of hate" . . . in the April 18 newsletter, Congressman Gonzalez stated: "For some time now I have been concerned about the Ford Foundation's funding of certain militant types among my ethnic group in San Antonio—namely, Americans of Spanish surname and of Mexican descent, and during this week have brought this situation to the attention of Congress through speeches in the *Congressional Record*.

"As most of you receiving this newsletter realize, there are all over the Southwest new organizations springing up: some promote pride in heritage, which is good, but others promote chauvinism, which is not; some promote community relations and organization, which is good, but some promote race tension and hatred, which is not good; some seek redress for just grievances, which is good, but others seek only opportunities for self-aggrandizement, which is not good.

"About three years ago, the Ford Foundation, by far the greatest of all foundations devoted to the development of humanity, took an interest in the Mexican-American minority group. What the Foundation saw was an opportunity to help. That opportunity, coupled with the best of intentions, has produced what I could classify only as a very grave problem in the district I am privileged to represent.

"As deeply as I must respect the intentions of the Foundation, I must at the same time say that where it aimed to produce unity it has so far created disunity and where it aimed to coordinate it has only further unloosened the conflicting aims and desires of various groups and individuals. (Since my first public statements regarding this matter week before last, people from all over the Southwest have added to my samples of 'Hate Gringo' literature, and the founder of a youth organization has gone so far as to say in a televised press conference that it might be necessary to 'kill some gringos' in order to bring about their objectives.)

"If you would be interested in the full texts of my speeches on this cause for concern which have appeared in the *Record* this week, please write to me at 116 Cannon House Office Building, Washington.

"I also contacted Congressman Wilbur Mills, Chairman of the House Ways and Means Committee, this week in respect to the Ford Foundation's role. The Chairman of the Committee on which I serve (Congressman Wright Patman, House Banking and Currency) has for several weeks been investigating tax exempt foundations."

A series of speeches . . . In the first of the series Congressman Gonzalez denounced "race Hate," inferiority, second class citizenship because of race or color. He reiterated his long standing position against discrimination and the attacks he has received from the right, from the conservatives for the position he has always taken. It does not matter, he says, "what I am, or what I am called, as long as I make an honest effort to be an honest representative." However, he points out, "ironically, I now find myself assaulted from the left as well as from the right. Evil is evil . . . (and) it is just as wrong for a member of an ethnic minority to succumb to hate and fear as it is for anyone else to do so."

Attack on MAYO . . . "I cannot stand silently by if an organization like the Mexican American Youth Organization publishes hate sheets containing statements like 'the gringo took your grandfather's land, he took your father's job and now he is sucking out your soul. There is no such thing as mala suerte (bad luck); there is only malos gringos (bad gringos).' "

Congressman Gonzalez says, "I cannot accept the argument that this is an evil country or that our system does not work, or that it is foolish to expect redress of a just grievance." At the end of his remarks he inserted a newspaper story (not identified) attacking all CPA papers from Texas to California and as far away as Chicago and Wisconsin. The writer of the article (also not identified) charges that the newspapers are "cheaply printed, crudely illustrated but (that) they pack a wallop." The writer quotes Gonzalez calling these papers "hate sheets." Among those named, El Deguello, Hoy, La Revolucion . . . all MAYO publications. Other Texas papers named La Justicia Mayorista, El Malcriado (McAllen), El Yaqui and El Compass. Outside of Texas, Las Raza, Inside Eastside, Carta Editorial and Bronze from California, El Gallo from Colorado, El Papel from New Mexico, El Paisano from Arizona, LADO from Chicago and La Voz Mexicana from Wisconsin. The writer of the article admits that while the "objective is unity for Mexican Americans to gain economic, education and fair treatment goals, the language of the papers is bellicose."

Loss of perspective . . . The overall reaction to Congressman Gonzalez's behavior is mixed. The over-riding feeling, however, is that of sorrow to witness his public exhibition of insecurity and lack of understanding of his own people and his role in relation to them. The youth are angry—that is for sure. They are not only angry at the "gringo" they are also angry at their parents, at Congressman Gonzalez's generation, who they feel let them down. In this respect they are not totally justified but Congressman Gonzalez should understand the reason, the cause of their frustration. In the 24 years since WWII ended and years of relatively high degree of prosperity . . . things have not changed too much for the Mexican or for the poor. Yet the poor and the Mexican have paid with their lives (at a higher ratio) so that this country could remain free to prosper and so that a great majority might enjoy relative security and affluence.

The Mexican youth are no longer willing to sit quietly while a decent living for their family, for their children passes them by. This is the point which appears to have been lost on Congressman Gonzalez. His rejection of "unjust tactics" which he says will not produce justice should not blind him. He should be able to rise above the loud talk, the verbage and "vilification" of the majority society. After all, the society which they are attacking has used "unjust tactics" toward them in all aspects of life, from a higher percentage sent to Vietnam to no education, and only menial labor and no resource to change the situation. And all of the speeches Gonzalez makes to Congress will not change the situation nor will there be justice just because Gonzalez proclaims it.

No need to be defensive . . . either. Congressman Gonzalez does not need to feel defensive about his role in civil rights . . . his record speaks for itself. However, he has to admit that there is plenty of room for criticism. Yet he is out of tune with the movement today. He should analyze where we got lost or sidetracked.

In some of the areas we fell off the train on the question of representation . . . becoming part of the establishment as a means to bring about change. The main change which has occurred, however, was in the men elected to office. They became so busy belonging to the national government leadership that the day to day struggle for existence by the people back home became secondary in terms of priority. They became participants in the general life stream of national concerns at the expense of the problems back home.

The children in the high schools are right when they say it took them to shake up the whole question of education and they have not yet begun to fight for a decent education. Where were Gonzalez and other national and local representatives on issues such as these. Where are they on the question of the farm workers, the poor, etc. It is not enough for them to endorse a struggle, they must become part of it. By staying out Gonzalez is denying the people he represents his leadership at a time when they need it the most.

The youth are moving and insertions into the *Congressional Record* will not stop them . . . they will be heard . . . even if their language sounds uncouth to our ears, their demands for a better life are not unjustified.

VOICES OF THE CHICANOS

A folksong is a communal poem. So too is the *corrido*. The young poets of Chicanismo often continue the traditions of the *corrido* singer, going from barrio to barrio, like troubadours of old, reciting their poems. In a sense, the old *corridos* and modern poems are mother and child, in form and in theme and in mood. Omar Salinas, a *campesino* poet, embodies this tradition in his "Aztec Angel" (*Crazy Gypsy: Poems by Luis Omar Salinas*, La Raza Studies, Fresno State College, 1970). The rhythms of Benjamin Luna's "Musica de Machete" (*La Raza*, Los Angeles, Vol. 1, No. 9, Feb.,

1968) are more formal, but no less musical; while Jose
Angel Guitierrez's "22 Miles" (*El Grito*, Spring, 1968)
is a rhapsodic tour de force reminiscent of the ironic
vacilada songs. In "Jail Flashes" and "Segundo
Canto," by Roberto Vargas (*El Pocho Che*, Vol. 1, No.
1, July, 1969) the language of the urban barrios—not
Spanish, not English, but Chicanismo—begins to
emerge. In his "Poem in Lieu of Preface," Alberto
Alurista evokes an older Nahuatl form (*Aztlan, Chicano Journal of the Social Science and the Arts*, Mexican American Cultural Center, University of California at Los Angeles, Vol. 1, No. 1, Spring, 1970). Jose
Montoya's "El Louie" and J. L. Navarro's "To A Dead
Lowrider" (*Con Safos*) return to the Chicanismo of the
barrios, the pathos of the *vato* and the *pachuco*, but it
is Raul Salinas, poet and inmate of Leavenworth Peni-
tentiary, where he edits the prison newspaper, *Aztlan*,
who evokes the whole cosmos of the barrio youth
through the "art form of our slums" in his remarkable
"Trip Through The Mind Jail" (*Aztlan*, Leavenworth,
Kansas, 1970).

Aztec Angel

by Luis Omar Salinas

I
I am an Aztec angel
        criminal
            of a scholarly
                society
    I do favors
        for whimsical
                magicians
    where I pawn

my heart
for truth
and find
my way
through obscure
streets
of soft spoken
hara-kiris

II

I am an Aztec angel
forlorn passenger
on a train
of chicken farmers
and happy children

III

I am the Aztec angel
fraternal partner
of an orthodox
society
where pachuco children
hurl stones
through poetry rooms
and end up in a cop car
their bones itching
and their hearts
busted from malnutrition

IV

I am the Aztec angel
who frequents bars
spends evenings

with literary circles
and socializes
with spiks
niggers and wops
and collapses on his way
to funerals

V

Drunk
lonely
bespectacled
the sky
opens my veins
like rain
clouds go berserk
around me
my Mexican ancestors
chew my fingernails
I am an Aztec angel
offspring
of a woman
who was beautiful

Musica de Machete

by Benjamin Luna

The wild mountains of Mexico
are wild in me.
Musica de machete
toca tu son de acero.
Lover of the wild mountains
women
life

                    music
                    wild
am i.
AAAY!   AAAY!   AAAY!
Musica de machete
            toca tu son de acero.
Voices filled with sex and secret dangers
            ring throughout the wild mountains
of my Mexican soul.
Musica de machete
            toca tu son de acero.
A man like raging rivers
            toca tu son de acero.
A man like raging rivers
            a woman like mountain streams
of the huayacan tree which grow in the ravines
            sired me with their passion.
Musica de machete
            toca tu son de acero.
By ancient and despised gods of my fathers
      blessed (cursed) with love for death and poetry.
Musica de machete
            toca tu son de acero.
Savage poets of the mountains sing to me
            songs like stabs of steel.
Poems of spring and bullets
            run through my veins.

Musica de machete
            toca tu son de acero.
when i rage
      i rage unbounding.
when i love
      i love uncaring

When i sing
     i sing for sadness.
When i die
     i'll die for love
Musica de machete
       toca tu son de acero.

22 Miles

by Jose Angel Guitierrez

From 22 I see my first 8 weren't.
  Around the 9th, I was called "meskin."
    By the 10th, I knew and believed I was.
      I found out what it meant to know, to believe . . .
                    before my 13th.

Through brown eyes, seeing only brown colors and feeling
only brown feelings . . . I saw . . . I felt . . . I hated
. . . I cried . . . I tried . . . I didn't understand during
                        these 4.
      I rested by just giving up.

While, on the side . . . I realized I BELIEVED in
  white as pretty,
    my being governor,
      blond blue eyed baby Jesus,
        cokes and hamburgers,
          equality for all regardless of race, creed, or color,
        Mr. Williams, our banker.
      I had to!
    That was all I had.
Beans and Communism were bad.
         Past the weeds, atop the hill, I looked back.

Pretty people, combed and squeaky clean, on
                                                arrowlike roads.
Pregnant girls, ragged brats, swarthy machos, rosary beads,
and friends waddle clumsily over and across hills,
                                                each other,
mud, cold, and woods on caliche ruts.
At the 19th mile, I fought blindly at everything and
                                                anything.
    Not knowing, Not caring about WHY, WHEN, or
                                    FOR WHAT.
        I fought. And fought.
        By the 21st, I was tired and tried.

                        But now. . . .
I've been told that I am dangerous.
That is because I am good at not being a Mexican.
That is because I know now that I have been cheated.
That is because I hate circumstances and love choices.

    You know . . . chorizo tacos y tortillas ARE good,
                                    even at school.
    Speaking Spanish is a talent.
Being Mexican IS as good as Rainbo bread.
And without looking back, I know that there are still
                                too many . . .
    brown babies,
        pregnant girls,
            old 25 year-old women,
                drunks,
                who should have lived but didn't,
                on those caliche ruts.

        It is tragic that my problems during these past
                                        21 miles
            were/are/might be . . .

> looking into blue eyes,
> wanting to touch a gringita,
> ashamed of being Mexican,
> believing I could not make it at college,
> pretending that I liked my side of town,

> remembering the Alamo,
> speaking Spanish in school bathrooms only,
> and knowing that Mexico's prostitutes like Americans
> > better.

At 22, my problems are still the same but now I know I am
> your problem.
That farm boys, Mexicans and Negro boys are in Vietnam is
> but one thing I think about:
> Crystal City, Texas 78839
> The migrant worker;
> The good gringo:

Staying Mexican enough;
Helping;
Looking at the world from the back of a truck.
The stoop labor with high school rings on their fingers;
The Anglo cemetery,
Joe the different Mexican,
> Damn.
> Damn.
> Damn.

Jail Flashes

by Roberto Vargas

Rayos De luz
Rayos De Pena y alegria
El Dulce/Amargo beso

De la noche. . . . Y Tu
Naked lady of My Sorrows
     Elusive lady of Nirvahna/

O'wring . . . wring your hands
Shed The crystal of our mourning
for Tomorrow may be Never
yet Tomorrow may be forever/

Dance   Dance   Dance
O'Vida loca Que me acompana
Que ya El Mudo grita "las doce"
Y otra Manana abra los ojos/

O'cinnamon Maiden of Nepenthe
(Marijuana be thy Name)
Lighten My Jailhouse hours
Que ya no soy
La Torre Que Era
Am Not Now
The Tower
I Am!

Segundo Canto

by Roberto Vargas

Ay Raza Vieja
Raza nueva y orgullosa
Sun bronzed and arrogant
Con el Espiritu de Che y Sandino
Con el ardor de Malcolm X y Zapata
Now Marching Against Exploitation
Now Marching Against Shit and Frustration
Now Marching Against the Bastard Grape
Grapes of wrath/Grapes of Paradox

and bittersweet madness . . . grapes of big white houses
Grapes that mold or destroy the innocent lives of our
  children
Children that starve while Pigs feed off their backs
children of brown eyes in Delano
Delano the epitome of America/Delano of cesar el santo
  who fasts
in their consciences/Delano of the 10 o'clock Mexican
  Curfew
Delano the mississippi of California
Delano of the 3 thousand year Huelga/Huelga that Rings in
Hungers own belly/Huelga Que Inspira Revolucion y
  descubre
el vendido

Hoy Si mis hermanos

This is the year of the last stolen banana
And the Rape of Coffee Beans must cease/This is the
  year of
the bullet and frenzied Pig that Runs with Grape Stuffed
mouths/And they know Shit, yes *they* know

EN ESTE DIA DOMINGO
Y EN TODOS LOS SOLES
QUE SIGUEN————.

Poem in Lieu of Preface

by Alberto Alurista

                    it is said
            that MOTECUHZOMA ILHUICAMINA
SENT
                    AN expedition
            looking for the NortherN

                    mYthical land
            wherefrom the AZTECS CAME
                    la TIERRA
                         dE
                            AztlaN
                    mYthical land for those
                    who dream of roses and
    swallow thorns
                            or for those who swallow
                                                    thorns
        in powdered milk
    feeling guilty about smelling flowers
                        about looking for AztlaN

El Louie

by Jose Montoya

Hoy enterraron al Louie.

And San Pedro o sanpinche
are in for it. And those
times of the forties
and the early fifties
lost un vato de atolle.

Kind of slim and drawn,
there toward the end,
aging fast from too much
booze y la vida dura. But
class to the end.

En Sanjo you'd see him
sporting a dark topcoat
playing in his fantasy
the role of Bogard, Cagney
or Raft.

Era de Fowler el vato,
carnal del Candi y el
Ponchi—Los Rodriguez—
The Westside knew 'em,
and Selma, even Gilroy.
48 Fleetline, two-tone—
buenas garras and always
rucas—como la Mary y
la Helen . . . siempre con
liras bien afinadas
cantando La Palma, la
que andaba en el florero.

Louie hit on the idea in
those days for tailor-made
drapes, unique idea—porque
Fowler no era nada como
Los, 'ol E.P.T. Fresno's
Westside was as close as
we ever got to the big time.

But we had Louie, and the
Palomar, el boogie, los
mambos y cuatro suspiros
del' alma—y nunca faltaba
that familiar, gut-shrinking,
love-splitting, ass hole-up-
tight, bad news . . .

Trucha, esos! Va 'ver
pedo!
Abusau, ese!
Get Louie!

No llores, Carmen, we can
handle 'em.

Ese, 'on tal Jimmy?
Horale, Louie!
Where's Primo?
Va 'ver vatos!
En el parking lot away from
the jura.

Horale!
Trais filero?
Simon!
Nel!
Chale, ese!
Oooooh, este vato!

An Louie would come through—
melodramatic music, like in the
mono—tan tan taran!—Cruz
Diablo, El Charro Negro! Bogard
smile (his smile as deadly as
his vaisas!) He dug roles, man,
and names—like "Blackie," "Little
Louie . . ."

Ese, Louie . . .
Chale, man, call me "Diamonds!"

Y en Korea fue soldado de
levita con huevos and all the
paradoxes del soldado razo—
heroism and the stockade!

And on leave, jump boots
shainadas and ribbons, cocky
from the war, strutting to
early mass on Sunday morning.

Wow, is that 'ol Louie?

Mire, comadre, ahi va el hijo
de Lola!

Afterward he and fat Richard
would hock their Bronze Stars
for pisto en el Jardin Canales
y en El Trocadero.

At barber college he came
out with honors. Despues
empenaba su velardo de la
peluca pa' jugar pocar serrada
and lo ball en Sanjo y Alvizo.

And "Legs Louie Diamond" hit
on some lean times . . .

Hoy enterraron al Louie.

Y en Fowler at Nesei's
pool parlor los baby chukes
se acuerdan de Louie, el carnal
del Candi y el Ponchi—la vez
que lo fileriaron en el Casa
Dome y cuando se catio con
La Chiva.

Hoy enterraron al Louie.

His death was an insult
porque no murio en accion—
no lo mataron los vatos,
ni los gooks en Korea.
He died alone in a rented
room—perhaps like in a
Bogard movie.

The end was a cruel hoax.
But his life had been
remarkable!

Vato de atolle, el Louie Rodriguez.

To a Dead Lowrider

by J. L. Navarro

It seems a tragedy that he
Died the way he did.
The Pachuco, I mean.
You must have known him.
He use to come around a lot.
His name was Tito—that's all.
Just Tito. Big, brawny, and
Always raising hell.
                    Remember?
He had a way of walking, too:
Swaggering down the block like
A strident bull. Everyone moved
For Tito.
Never much cared for anything, that
Dude. He knew he lived for something,
But he never knew what for. He only
Reasoned to a limit. He didn't care
For more.
He had it good, that guy. T-bird wine
and H, and all that kind of thing.
There was always a broad standing by.
A Chola ready to let him in.
Talking his tongue to others, not
Knowing his way of life, was like
Listening to another language: "Orale,

Ese, no se aguite. Te wacho tonight
When the rucas come down with their
Chi chis hanging down to here." And
Then he'd grab his balls
                    Remember?
Good old Tito.
He use to say to us, in speaking of
His escapades: "Last night I geezed
A good one, ese. And the coloradas
Were all right. I dug the bennies, too,
Carnal. Everything was up tight."
He was a vet from long ago: Khaki pants
And Sir Guy shirts.
                    Remember?
  It's a shame the way he died.
He never had a care, that guy.
Balling and cruising and making love.
That was the trip with Tito.
On the corner he'd come around and
Say to us, "Me gusta la mota cuando
Traigo una burnena ruca."   Or: "La Valley
y la Clover are getting along."
And things like: "I kicked that
Motherfucker's ass at Bertha's
Gig the other night."
His eyes were hard and cool
With lashes long and curling;
And for a crown he had rich
Black hair that shimmered with
Three Roses. His appearance said
Chicano all the way, and if you
Didn't like it he'd bound to
Say, "Up yours, puto, do something
About it."

It's a shame the way he died.
But while he lived he stood tall
And proud, bowed his head to no man
At all.
He'd cruise and caravan the streets
With the other dudes from the Neighborhood.
He'd drive around in his lowriding short,
Digging the sounds and downing Ripple.
       And then one night the Man flashed his
lights; and there they stood in the early
Morning, staring at each other with
Vindictive looks.
              At last the cop said,
"What are you doing out so late
At night, punk?"
Tito stared back with an abject
Hate and said, "Fuck you, sissy!"
And then they fought, and in a
Flash the .38 was out, cocked
And ready . . .
              I say, carnal, it's a shame
The way he died.

A Trip Through the Mind Jail

For Eldridge
by Raul Salinas

LA LOMA
Neighborhood of my youth
   demolished, erased forever from
   the universe.
You live on, captive, in the lonely
   cellblocks of my mind.

Neighborhood of endless hills
    muddied streets—all chuckhole lined—
    that never drank of asphalt.
    Kids barefoot/snotty-nosed
    playing marbles/munching on bean tacos
    (the kind you'll never find in a cafe)
    2 peaceful generations removed from
    their *abuelos'* revolution.

Neighborhood of dilapidated community hall
    ——*Salón Cinco de Mayo*——
    yearly (May 5/Sept. 16) gathering
    of the *familias*. Re-asserting pride
    on those two significant days.
    Speeches by the elders,
    patriarchs with evidence of oppression
    distinctly etched upon *mestizo* faces.
    "Sons of Independence!"
    Emphasis on allegiance to the *tri-color*
    obscure names: JUAREZ & HIDALGO
    their heroic deeds. Nostalgic tales of war
    years under VILLA'S command. No one listened,
    no one seemed to really care.
    Afterwards, the dance. Modest Mexican
    maidens dancing polkas together
    across splintered wooden floor.
    They never deigned to dance with boys!
    The careful scrutiny by curbstone sex-perts
    8 & 9 years old. "Minga's bow-legged,
    so we know she's done it, huh?"

Neighborhood of Sunday night *jamaicas*
    at Guadalupe Church.
    Fiestas for any occasion
    holidays holy days happy days

'round and 'round the promenade
eating snowcones—*raspas*—& tamales
the games—bingo cake walk spin the wheel
making eyes at girls from cleaner neighborhoods
the unobtainables
who responded all giggles and excitement.

Neighborhood of forays down to *Buena Vista*—
Santa Rita Courts—*los* projects—friendly neighborhood
cops n' robbers on the rooftops, sneaking peeks
in people's private night-time bedrooms
bearing gifts of Juicy Fruit gum for
the projects girls/chasing them in adolescent heat
causing skinned knees & being run off for the night
disenchanted walking home affections spurned
stopping stay-out-late chicks in search of
Modern Romance lovers, who always stood them up
unable to leave their world in the magazine's pages.
Angry fingers grabbing, squeezing, feeling,
french kisses imposed; close bodily contact, thigh &
belly rubbings under shadows of Cristo Rey Church.

Neighborhood that never saw a school-bus
the cross-town walks were much more fun
embarrassed when acquaintances or friends or relatives
were sent home excused from class
for having cooties in their hair!
Did only Mexicans have cooties in their hair?
        Qué Gacho!

Neighborhood of Zaragoza Park
where scary stories interspersed with
inherited superstitions were exchanged
waiting for midnight and the haunting
lament of *La Llorona*—the weeping lady

of our myths & folklore—who wept nightly,
along the banks of Boggy Creek,
for the children she'd lost or drowned
in some river (depending on the version).
i think i heard her once
and cried
out of sadness and fear
running all the way home nape hairs at attention
swallow a pinch of table salt and
make the sign of the cross
sure cure for frightened Mexican boys.

Neighborhood of Spanish Town Cafe
first grown-up (13) hangout
Andres,
tolerant manager, proprietor, cook
victim of bungling baby burglars
your loss: Fritos n' Pepsi Colas—was our gain
you put up with us and still survived!
You too, are granted immortality.

Neighborhood of groups and clusters
sniffing gas, drinking muscatel
solidarity cement hardening
the clan the family the neighborhood the gang
NOMAS!
Restless innocents tatto'd crosses on their hands
"just doing things different"
"From now on, all troublemaking mex kids will
be sent to Gatesville for 9 months."
Henry home from *La Corre*
khakis worn too low—below the waist
the stomps, the *grena* with duck-tail
—*Pachuco Yo*—

Neighborhood of could-be artists
   who plied their talents on the pool's
   bath-house walls/intricately adorned
   with esoteric symbols of their cult,
   the art form of our slums
   more meaningful & significant
   than Egypt's finest hieroglyphics.

Neighborhood where purple clouds of *Yesca*
   smoke one day descended & embraced us all.
   Skulls uncapped—Rhythm n' Blues
               Chalie's 7th St. Club
   loud negro music-wine spodee-odees/barbecue/grass
   our very own connection man: big black Johnny
      B_____.

Neighborhood of *Reyes'* Bar
   where Lalo shotgunned
   Pete Evans to death because of
   an unintentional stare
   and because he was *escuadra,*
   only to end his life neatly sliced
   by prison barber's razor.
   Duran's grocery & gas station
   Guero drunkenly stabbed *Julio*
   arguing over who'd drive home
   and got 55 years for his crime.
   Raton: 20 years for a matchbox of weed. Is that cold?
   No lawyer no jury no trial i'm guilty.
               Aren't we all guilty?
   Indian mothers, too, so unaware
   of courtroom tragi-comedies
   folded arms across their bosoms
   saying, *"Sea por Dios."*

Neighborhood of my childhood
  neighborhood that no longer exists
  some died young—fortunate—some rot in prisons
  the rest drifted away to be conjured up
  in minds of others like them.
  For me: only the NOW of THIS journey is REAL!

Neighborhood of my adolescence
  neighborhood that is no more
  YOU ARE TORN PIECES OF MY FLESH!!!
  Therefore, you ARE.
LA LOMA—AUSTIN—MI BARRIO—
                    i bear you no grudge
i needed you then . . . identity . . . a sense of belonging.
  i need you now.
  So essential to adult days of imprisonment.
  you keep me away from INSANITY'S hungry jaws;
                    Smiling/Laughing/Crying.

i respect your having been:
  my *Loma* of Austin
  my Rose Hill of Los Angeles
  my Westside of *San Anto*
  my *Quinto* of Houston
  my Jackson of *San Jo*
  my *Segundo* of El Paso
  my Westside of Denver

Flats, *Los Marcos, Maravilla, Calle Guadalupe,*
Magnolia, Buena Vista, Mateo, La Seis, Chiquis,
El Sur, and all Chicano neighborhoods that
    now exist and once existed;
        somewhere . . . someone remembers . . .

XI. LA CAUSA: THE ARTIST

THE TOLTEC (THE ARTIST):
HE MAKES THINGS LIVE

from the Aztec Codices

One of the ancient chronicles of the Aztecs tells of a woman who embroidered the symbol of the "Seven Flowers" so badly "that she deserved to become a woman of the streets." Her crime was that she was a "bad artist," and her punishment was "to work as a prostitute," for the Aztecs demanded that the artist have "God in his heart"; he "puts divinity into things" ("The Good Painter"). The artist, be he merely a potter, does not imitate life; he creates life. "He teaches the clay to lie" and "he makes things live" ("He Who Gives Life to Clay"). In doing this he "humanize[s] the desires of people" ("He Is Whole"). In the Society of *Icniuhyotl* (friendship) the Aztec artist was both a "jester-prophet and a prime minister" to the King. (*Aztec Thought and Culture,* by Leon-Portilla.)

The Good Painter

The good painter is a Toltec, an artist;
he creates with red and black ink,
with black water . . .

The good painter is wise,

God is in his heart.
He puts divinity into things;
he converses with his own heart.

He knows the colors, he applies them and shades them;
he draws feet and faces,
he puts in the shadows,
he achieves perfection.
He paints the colors of all the flowers,
as if he were a Toltec.

He Who Gives Life to Clay

He who gives life to clay;
his eye is keen, he molds
and kneads the clay.

The good potter;
he takes great pains in his work;
he teaches the clay to lie;
he converses with his heart;
he makes things live, he creates them;
he knows all, as if he were a Toltec;
he trains his hands to be skillful.

The bad potter;
careless and weak,
crippled in his art.

He Is Whole

Amantecatl: the feather artist
He is whole; he has a face and a heart.

The good feather artist is skillful,
is master of himself;
it is his duty
to humanize the desires of the people.
He works with feathers,
chooses them and arranges them,
paints them with different colors,
joins them together.

The bad feather artist is careless;
he ignores the look of things,
he is greedy, he scorns other people.
He is like a turkey with a shrouded heart,
sluggish, coarse, weak.
The things that he makes are not good.
He ruins everything he touches.

THE ART OF THE CHICANO MOVEMENT, AND THE MOVEMENT OF CHICANO ART

by Manuel J. Martinez

God in his heart—*Dios en su corazon!*—within this sacred concept the Chicano artist has created a unique communal art. In the Spanish colonial days the art of La Raza was pervasively religious. Nowadays it tends toward "secular religiosity." "Like the modern art of Mexico, the new Chicano art is essentially an art of social protest," writes Manuel Martinez, a muralist and easel painter who has created a pulpit for Cesar Chavez's farm workers' union and covered entire houses with his murals. Little known outside the barrios of the Southwest, the work of artists such as Manuel Martinez is indigenously communal. "The painter gives life to the barrio wall," wrote a Chicano critic; "*Chilam Balam* prophesied it centuries ago. Now the time has come when the very walls, *las paredes*, will speak." ("The Art of the Chicano Movement, and the Movement of Chicano Art," unpublished paper.)

To understand the present cultural values of our people, it is necessary to understand the history of Mexico, to which we are still closely related. Mexican history and artistic expressions that bring life and cultural nationalism within emotional grasp.

Unlike many of the styles of contemporary art, many concepts and forms of Chicano art come from its own traditions. This is not to say that Chicano art is an imitation of Indian, Spanish, or Modern Mexican art, in technique or otherwise. The most *ancient* art of our history is purely Indian and is still considered the natural and most vital source of inspiration. Then following the conquest of Mexico came Colonial art which is based fundamentally on Spanish-European principles of the sixteenth and seventeenth centuries. And then came the Modern Mexican art movement dominated by artists who were Mestizo (the offspring of Indian and Spanish blood) and whose work has both Indian and European influences.

Chicano art is a newborn baby with Ancient Indian art as a mother, Spanish Colonial art as a father and Modern Mexican art as a midwife. Or we can see it as a branch extending out into the southwest United States from the great Bronze Tree of Mexican art. Taking the roots of that tree for granted as being Indian and Spanish, we can move up to the trunk of the tree which is known as Modern Mexican art.

It would be wrong if we first looked up definitions of art in textbooks and then used them to determine the past principles from the modern artistic movement of Mexico. We

should start from historical facts, not from abstract definitions.

What are some of the historical and artistic facts of the
modern art movement in Mexico? Or, from the Mexican
point of view what are some of the significant features in the
development of this movement? Despite all the conflict,
confusion, and bloodshed of the Mexican Revolution, it
created a new spirit. A revolutionary spirit that inspired
new leadership and began to be felt and expressed by the
writers, the musicians, the poets and the painters. Each felt
that it was his duty and privilege to share his talents in the
social cause of bringing about a new Mexico. Art for art's
sake began to die. The new art would no longer serve as a
privilege of the rich or a mere decoration. Since Mexico was
largely illiterate, painting had to become the medium of vis-
ual education, monumental in size, and become public
property.

Some of the more advanced artists and pioneers of this
new aesthetic concept formed a group in 1922 known as the
"Syndicate of painters, sculptors, and intellectual workers."
Among those who allied themselves into this group and who
brought forth the first original expression of Modern art on
this continent were: Ramon Alva de la Canal, Jean Charlot,
Fernando Leal, Xavier Guerrero, Carlos Medina, Roberto
Montenegro, Jose Clemente Orozco, Fermin Revueltas,
Diego Rivera, David Alfaro Sigueiros, and Maximo Pacheco.

The open-mindedness and foresight of Jose Vasconcelos,
minister of education, must be given credit for opening the
doors to the usefulness of monumental painting on the walls
of public buildings. Under his program, Vasconcelos patron-
ized the artists and they were given but one instruction: to
paint Mexican subjects. It was the first collective attempt at
mural painting in Modern art.

Then followed the fruits of the "Mexican Renaissance": the rebirth of creative enthusiasm and a time for the people to again recognize human values and their expressions in a creative form.

The Mexican painters have shown in their work the long and exciting history of the Mexican people. Great murals were done by men who sought truth and justice for their people and all of humanity. Mexican Modern art was essentially an art of the Revolution. No where else in the world can the people of a country see so much of their own story told pictorially on the big walls of their public buildings.

Like the modern art of Mexico, the new Chicano art is essentially an art of social protest. Generally speaking, however, there are two types of Chicano art. The first is an art that makes up the cultural front of the Chicano movement that is sweeping the Southwest, an art that reflects the greatness and sacrifices of our past, an art that clarifies and intensifies the present desires of a people who will no longer be taken for granted as second class citizens and whose time has come to stand up and fight for what is rightfully theirs as human beings.

The art of the Chicano movement serves as a shield to preserve and protect our cultural values from the mechanical shark of this society, that has been chewing and spitting out our beautiful language, music, literature, and art for over a hundred years. The artists use their own media in their own way to strengthen the unity of our people and they help to educate us about ourselves since the educational system has failed to do so.

The other type of Chicano art is created by artists who find it difficult to allow themselves to be used by any cause, by any institution, or by any government. They realize that the artist has spent centuries to free himself from the domination of a social hierarchy, the church, or government control. They love the past but refuse to be trapped by it. Their primary interest is to convey a point of view or an idea, whereas the Chicano artist of the movement generally uses any method to achieve his goal.

The Chicano artist who refuses to plunge into the movement, yet wishes to deal with social concerns in this society, cannot escape the realities in his life, in the lives of people around him, and in the times in which he lives. These things will inevitably begin to show in his work. Art works that are characterized as works of social protest are really just the product of the artist having to deal with the realities he sees. How does he respond to these realities? He writes a poem, a play, a song; he paints a picture, a mural; or models clay or wax.

The Chicano artist will work with his own "raw materials" of his social concerns in his own way. Most importantly, the artist is devoted to his art, and he loves color, form, composition, structure, and rhythm.

There are times when the Chicano artist, like other people, attempts to escape his humanness but cannot. His commitment is to himself and to humanity. He loves art and he loves his people. It is this love for humanity that he can reveal to others and in doing so help fulfill their humanness. This does not mean that he is not going to reveal the countless evils of our life but rather to show you that we must get back our humanness if we are to live in this world peacefully.

CHICANO THEATER

In the year of 1598 the first drama of La Raza was performed on our shores. On Ascension Day the settlers, led by Don Juan de Onate, paused on the banks of the Rio Grande and enacted a symbolic play to bless their journey. It was written for the occasion by the captain of the cavalry, Don Marcos Farfan de los Godos, and it was a "living theater" whose audience was its actors, the *espanoles mexicanos* farmers and Mexican *indios* who made up the Onate pilgrimage. In the tradition of the religious *autos* that the Catholic Church staged in Mexico in the 1500's, and in the tradition of the dance/dramas of Indian rituals, the "Chicano theater is religion," explains Luis Valdez, founder of El Teatro Campesino de Aztlan, in his "Notes on Chicano Theater" (*El Teatro*, Summer, 1970). In all its elements—its combining of song, dance, and mime, its *campesino* actors, its message of the morality play, its use of masks, its bilingual performances, its open-air stages—the farm workers' theater of Luis Valdez is a direct descendant of the religious theater of the Indians, and the "sacred comedies" of the Church ("El Teatro Campesino," *La Raza Yearbook*, Sept., 1968).

Notes on Chicano Theater

by Luis Valdez

What is Chicano theater? It is theater as beautiful, rasquachi, human, cosmic, broad, deep, tragic, comic, as the life of La Raza itself. At its high point Chicano theater is religion —the huelgistas de Delano praying at the shrine of the Virgen de Guadalupe, located in the rear of an old station wagon parked across the road from DiGiorgios' camp #4; at its low point, it is a cuento or a chiste told somewhere in the recesses of the barrio, puro pedo.

Chicano theater, then is first a reaffirmation of LIFE. That is what all theater is supposed to do, of course, but the limp, superficial, gringo seco productions in the "professional" American theater (and the college and university drama departments that serve it) are so antiseptic, they are antibiotic (anti-life). The characters and life situations emerging from our little teatros are too real, too full of sudor, sangre, and body smells to be boxed in. Audience participation is no cute production trick with us; it is a pre-established, pre-assumed privilege. "Que le suenen la campanita!"

Defining Chicano theater is a little like defining a Chicano car. We can start with a low-rider's cool Merc or a campesino's banged-up Chevi, and describe the various paint jobs, hub caps, dents, taped windows, Virgin on the dashboard, etc. that define the car as particularly Raza. Underneath all the trimmings, however, is an unmistakable production of Detroit, an extension of General Motors. Consider now a theater that uses the basic form, the vehicle, created by Broadway or Hollywood: that is, the "realistic" play. Actually, this type of play was created in Europe, but where French, German, and Scandinavian playwrights went beyond realism and naturalism long ago, commercial gabacho theater refuses to let go.

It reflects a characteristic "American" hang-up on the material aspect of human existence. European theater, by contrast, has been influenced since around 1900 by the unrealistic, formal rituals of Oriental theater.

What do Oriental and European theater have to do with teatros Chicanos. Nothing, except that we are talking about a theater that is particularly our own, not another imitation of the gabacho. If we consider our origins, say the theater of the Mayans or the Aztecs, we are talking about something totally unlike the realistic play and more Chinese or Japanese in spirit. Kabuki, as a matter of fact, started long ago as something like our actos and evolved over two centuries into the highly exacting art form it is today; but it still contains pleberias. It evolved from and still belongs to el pueblo japones.

In Mexico, before the coming of the white man, the greatest examples of total theater were, of course, the human sacrifices. *El Rabinal Achi*, one of the few surviving pieces of indigenous theater, describes the sacrifice of a courageous guerrillero, who, rather than dying passively on the block, is granted the opportunity to fight until he is killed. It is a tragedy naturally, but it is all the more transcendant because of the guerrillero's identification, through sacrifice, with God. The only "set" such a drama-ritual needed was a stone block; nature took care of the rest.

But since the Conquest, Mexico's theater, like its society, has had to imitate Europe and, in recent times, the United States. In this same vein, Chicanos in Spanish classes are frequently involved in productions of plays by Lope de Vega, Calderon de la Barca, Tirso de Molina, and other classic playwrights. Nothing is wrong with this, but it does obscure the indio fountains of Chicano culture. Is Chicano theater, in turn, to be nothing but an imitation of gabacho playwrights, with barrio productions of racist works by Eugene O'Neill and Tennessee Williams? Will Broadway produce a Chicano version of "Hello, Dolly" now that it has produced a Black one?

The nature of Chicanismo calls for a revolutionary turn in the arts as well as in society. Chicano theater must be revolutionary in technique as well as content. It must be popular, subject to no other critics except the pueblo itself, but it must also educate the pueblo toward an appreciation of *social change*, on and off the stage.

It is particularly important for teatro Chicano to draw a distinction between what is theater and what is reality. A demonstration with a thousand Chicanos, all carrying flags and picket signs, shouting CHICANO POWER! is not the revolution. It is theater about the revolution. The people must act in *reality* not on stage (which could be anywhere, even a sidewalk) in order to achieve real change. The Raza gets excited, simon, but unless the demonstration evolves into a street battle (which has not yet happened but is possible) it is basically a lot of emotion with very little political power, as Chicanos have discovered by demonstrating, picketing, and shouting before school boards, police departments, and stores to no avail.

Such guerrilla theater passing as a demonstration has its uses, of course. It is agit-prop theater, as the gabachos used to call it in the 1930's: agitation and propaganda. It helps to stimulate and sustain the mass strength of a crowd. Hitler was very effective with this kind of theater, from the swastika (卐) to the Wagneresque stadium at Nuremberg. On the other end of the political spectrum, the Huelga march to Sacramento in 1966 was pure guerrilla theater. The red and black thunderbird flags of the UFWOC (then NFWA) and the standard of the Virgen de Guadalupe challenged the bleak sterility of Highway 99. Its emotional impact was irrefutable. Its actual political power was somewhat less.

But beyond the mass struggle of La Raza in the fields and barrios of America, there is an internal struggle in the very corazon of our people. That struggle, too, calls for revolutionary change. Our belief in God, the church, the social role of women—these must be subject to examination and redefining in some kind of public forum. And that again means teatro. Not a teatro composed of actos or agit-prop but a teatro of ritual, of music, of beauty and spiritual sensitivity. A teatro of legends and myths. A teatro of religious strength. This type of theater will require real dedication; it may, indeed, require a couple of generations of Chicanos devoted to the use of the theater as an instrument in the evolution of our people.

The teatros in existence today reflect the most intimate understanding of everyday events in the barrios from which they have emerged. But, if Aztlan is to become reality, then we as Chicanos must not be reluctant to act nationally—to think in national terms, politically, economically, and spiritually. We must destroy the deadly regionalism that keeps us apart. The concept of a national theater for La Raza is intimately related to our evolving nationalism in Aztlan.

Consider a Teatro Nacional de Aztlan that performs with the same skill and prestige as the Ballet Folklorico de Mexico (not for gabachos, however, but for the Raza). Such a teatro could carry the message of La Raza into Latin America, Europe, Japan, Africa—in short all over the world. It would draw its strength from all the small teatros in the barrios, in terms of people and their plays, songs, designs; and it would give back funds, training, and augmented strength of national unity. One season the teatro members would be on tour with the Teatro Nacional; the next season they would be back in the barrio sharing their skills and experience. It would accomodate about 150 people altogether, with twenty to twenty-five in the Nacional and the rest spread out in various parts of Aztlan, working with the campesino, the urbano, the mestizo, the piojo, etc.

Above all, the national organization of teatros Chicanos would be self-supporting and independent, meaning no government grants. The corazon de La Raza cannot be revolutionalized on a grant from Uncle Sam. Though many of the teatros, including El Campesino, have been born out of pre-established political groups—thus making them harbingers of that particular group's viewpoint, news, and political prejudices—there is yet a need for independence for the following reasons: objectivity, artistic competence, survival. El Teatro Campesino was born in the Huelga, but the very Huelga would have killed it, if we had not moved 60 miles to the north of Delano. A struggle like the Huelga needs every person it can get to serve its immediate goals in order to survive; the Teatro, as well as the clinic, service center, and newspaper, being less important at the moment of need than the survival of the Union, were always losing people to the grape boycott. When it became clear to us that the UFWOC would succeed and continue to grow, we felt it was time for us to move and to begin speaking about things beyond the Huelga: Vietnam, the barrio, racial discrimination, etc.

The teatros must never get away from La Raza. Without the palomia sitting there, laughing, crying, and sharing whatever is on stage, the teatros will dry up and die. If the Raza will not come to theater, then the theater must go to the Raza. This, in the long run, will determine the shape, style, content, spirit, and form of el teatro Chicano.

Pachucos, campesinos, low-riders, pintos, chavalonas, familias, cunados, tios, primos, Mexican-Americans, all the human essence of the barrio is starting to appear in the mirror of our theater. With them come the joys, sufferings, disappointments, and aspirations of our gente. We challenge Chicanos to become involved in the art, the life style, the political and religious act of doing theater.

El Teatro Campesino

by Luis Valdez

El Teatro Campesino is a bilingual theater company created in 1965 to teach and organize Chicano farm workers. (Chicanos are Mexicans in the U.S. born on either side of the border.)

We started in a broken-down shack in Delano, California, which was the strike office for Cesar Chavez' farm workers' union. At a meeting there one night Luis Valdez, who became our director, was trying to explain theater to a group of farm workers, most of whom had never seen a play. He hung signs around people's necks, with the names of familiar character types: scab, striker, boss, etc. They started to act out everyday scenes on the picket line. These impr visations quickly became satirical. More people gathered around and started to laugh, to cheer the heroes and boo the villains; and we had our first show.

It's simple: if you want unbourgeois theater, get unbourgeois people to do it. Theater does not live in props and scenery—it reveals itself in the excitement and the laughter of the audience.

We developed what we call "actos": one-acts or skits, though skit is too light a word, dealing with the strike, the union, and the problems of the farm worker. Humor is our major asset and our best weapon: not only satire, but comedy, which is a much healthier child of the theater than tragedy or realism. Our use of comedy originally stemmed from necessity—the necessity of lifting the strikers' morale. We found we could make social points not in spite of the comedy, but through it. Slapstick can bring us very close to the underlying tragedy—the fact that human beings have been wasted for generations.

We worked with the union for two years, performing all over the West and Southwest, in fields, in labor camps, at union meetings, and at strike benefits in the cities. In 1967 we toured across country to publicize the strike, performing at universities, in union halls and civic auditoriums, at New York's Village Theater, at the Newport Folk Festival, and in the courtyard of the U.S. Senate Building in Washington, D.C. We received a 1968 Obie award, "For creating a workers' theater to demonstrate the politics of survival."

In September, 1967, we left Delano and the union to establish a farm workers' cultural center—El Centro Cultural —in Del Rey, a rural California town of 1,000 people (2,000 in the harvest season), mainly Chicanos. We wanted to concern ourselves with the cultural as well as the economic oppression of our people, whose consciousness as well as their land had been invaded by the Anglo. In Del Rey we give "History Happenings": successive chapters of Mexican and American history in actos and puppet shows, with music, free to the community; also music lessons and art classes. We take our shows to other small towns up and down the San Joaquin Valley of California. We still work with the union in its organizing efforts, but we are now independent and self-supporting (no foundation grants).

We will consider our job done when every one of our people has regained his sense of personal dignity and pride in his history, his culture, and his race.

BERNABE

A play by Luis Valdez

Of the rituals of the Aztecs none was more sacred, and dramatic, than the offering of a gift of a human heart to Huitzilopochtli, the Sun God. The sun was fed by human life, as the sun fed human life: so the poets wrote. In the life of the *campesinos* of the Southwest, toiling in the fields of the deserts, the sun retains that power of life and death, wonder and terror. *Bernabe: A Drama of Modern Chicano Mythology* depicts barrio life in a farm town in the San Joaquin Valley, in California, where the Aztec Sun God reappears "in a golden feathered headdress" as El Sol. The hero, Bernabe, a poor *campesino* and "village idiot" possessed of the "divinity of madness" asks El Sol for the body of La Tierra (The Earth). He is taunted, then tempted, by La Luna (The Moon), who appears as a *pachuco* to protect his sister, La Tierra. When the Moon asks the Sun to give the Earth to Bernabe, the Sun makes the Earth "virgin again" for the poor *campesino*. (*Bernabe*, by Luis Valdez, unpublished.)

NOTES OF THE PLAYWRIGHT

The play takes place in a small town in the San Joaquin Valley in California.

It is about the life and death of Bernabe, a village idiot, un loquito del pueblo. He appears in scene one, going to the store with his aged mother, Dona Chala. On their way they pass the local cantina, Torres' Place. Bernabe sees Consuelo, the town prostitute, coming out of the bar with a man. He gets excited at the sight of Consuelo, but his mother immediately scolds him like a child. After Consuelo and the man exit, the mother decides to send Bernabe on to the store, "la tienda del chino," without her. The sun is too hot, she says. On his way to the store, Bernabe meets his cousin Eduardo, who is talking to Torres (owner of the cantina) about his recent trip to Tijuana. Eduardo "el primo" and Torres decide to have a little fun with Bernabe by asking him about his girl friends. Bernabe responds like a true loco, and tells them he has seven and that he is going to get married "manana." After Bernabe leaves, Eduardo and Torres make a bet that the primo cannot get the loco to sleep with Consuelo.

Scene two: Later that same day, the madre is out looking

for Bernabe, who has not returned from the store. She meets Eduardo on the street, who is coming to look for Bernabe himself. She tells him how tight her financial situation is; since Bernabe had his accident (an epileptic attack in the fields), he has been unable to find work. Eduardo loans her ten dollars, and she goes on looking for her son. El Tio, Teodoro, now enters, and he too asks Eduardo for a small loan. The primo asks him about Bernabe, and Teodoro tells him that he is probably visiting with the neighbor, the "viejita gringa" who lives next door and who occasionally makes a cake or cookies and invites Bernabe to "come out of there." His mother finally finds him in the neighbor's house. Bernabe comes out, protesting his innocence, but the madre accuses him of having sexual relations with the old woman. She threatens him that "one day the luna is going to come down and eat you alive!" He runs into his house, crying like a child. The primo suggests that he and the tio should do Bernabe a favor by taking him to see Consuelo. Bernabe is thirty-one years old and has never had a woman, urges the cousin. After considering the matter, the tio agrees to help Eduardo. The primo goes to convince Dona Chala to let him take Bernabe to go see a "contratista" about work. Teodoro goes on to Torres' place to make sure Consuelo will be there.

After considerable coaxing, Bernabe finally goes in to see Consuelo. El primo and el tio go have a few beers in the cantina, and return an hour later. Consuelo is furious. Bernabe does not want to get out of her room. Eduardo finally has to go in and drag him out. During the ensuing fight, Bernabe hits the primo over the head with a chair and knocks him down. Bernabe runs out of the room, screaming he has killed the primo, out of the hotel, and down the street, without finding out that Eduardo is hurt and bleeding but not dead.

Bernabe keeps running until he finds himself in a field outside of the small town. There is a full moon.

There is a central duality in the life and character of Bernabe: there is divinity in madness.

Bernabe: A Drama of Modern Chicano Mythology

SCENE 3

An open field. Night.

BERNABE: (*Crying to himself*) Primo! Hijo 'e su tisnada madre, lo mate! I kill' the primooo! (*Pauses. Listens for sounds*) I better hide . . . 'scondeme! . . . Cabron desgraciado, I told him . . . Le dije! (*Stops, fearful. Looks at sky, sees moon*) La Luna! Me va tragar la Luna! Ahi viene, ayyy! Yo no hisce nada! 'Ama, la lunaaaaa!

BERNABE *sobs like a terrified child. Moonlight gathers into a spot focused on him. Music.* LUNA *enters, dressed like a pachuco, 1945 style: zoot suit, drapes, hat with feather, multi-soled shoes* (*calcos*), *small chain, etc.*

LUNA: Orale pues esa vato. No te escames. (BERNABE *looks up too scared to say anything*) It's me, La Luna.

BERNABE: No, chale!

LUNA: Orale pues, you can't be scared of me. You're a vato loco.

BERNABE: (*Looks up*) Yo no soy loco!

LUNA: O, simon! I din't mean it like that, carnal. I meant you're a Chicano, you know? If people don't like the way you are, tengan pa' que se mantengan! Consafos, putos. Inside you're cool, man. You're making it, sabes?

BERNABE: Simon.

LUNA: A toda madre! (*Pauses. Reaches in his pocket*) Oye, no le haces a la grifa? Here, lighten up. Have a tocazo. (*He gives* BERNABE *a joint*) No traes trolas? (*Looks for matches*) Orate, here. (*Lights the joint for* BERNABE) Alivian el esqueleto, carnal. Me and you are going to get real locos tonight. (BERNABE *gives him the joint*) Hayte llevo. (LUNA *smokes. Gives it back to* BERNABE) Here, no le aflojes. (BERNABE *takes it again*) Heh, man, you see them stars up there? Some of them got some real fine asses. (*He cracks up, laughing*) I saw you over at Torres' Place tonight, vato. How was it, perty good?

BERNABE: (*Nods*) Perty good. (*Laughs. Gives him back the joint*)

LUNA: Yeh, that Connie's a real mamasota. But tell me, ese a la bravota—was she your first piece? Chale! Don't tell me. That's none of my business, man. Here, forget I ask you nothing. (*Passes joint back*) Oye, Bernabe, sabes que? You want me to fix you up a date with my carnala? She's fine, ese. And you know what? She wants to meet you. Me la rayo. She ask me to come down a periquiar contigo.

BERNABE: Conmigo?

LUNA: She knows all about you, loco. Que tal? Wanna meet her?

BERNABE: Tu sister?

LUNA: She digs Chicano. (BERNABE *laughs*)

BERNABE: Yo soy uno.

LUNA: Orale, let me call her. (*Calls out*) Oye, sister,
            vente! There's a Chicano here who wants to
            meet you.

Music accompanies the entrance of TIERRA, *who appears as
a beautiful soldadera with cartridge belts.* BERNABE *is spell-
bound the moment he sees her.*

TIERRA: (*Staring at* BERNABE) Quien es?
LUNA: Pos who? The vato loco himself! Bernabe, this is
            my sister, La Tierra.
TIERRA: Quiboho pues, Bernabe. (BERNABE *makes a
            slight grunt, smiling idiotically*) Bueno, que no
            me vas a decir jalo si quiera?

Pause. BERNABE *is speechless, embarrassed.* LUNA *intercedes
for him.*

LUNA: Give him time, he'll do it. He just a little shy,
            que no, ese?

BERNABE *struggles to say something. His mind tries to form
words. He ends up starting to laugh moronically, from help-
lessness.* TIERRA *cuts him off.*

TIERRA: No, hombre, don't laugh. Not like that. Talk se-
            rious . . . Soy La Tierra.

BERNABE *stares at her. A sudden realization strikes him: he
is talking to the moon and the earth. Fear overwhelms him,
and he screams. He runs.*

LUNA: Epale, where you going? (*He stops* BERNABE
            with a wave of his arm) Calmala, you don't have
            to be scared. (*Pulls him toward* TIERRA) Look at
            my carnala, ese. Mira que a toda madre se wat-
            cha en la moonlight. She digs you, man. Verdad
            sister?

TIERRA: Si es macho.

BERNABE *is caught in a strange spell. He and* TIERRA *look at each other for a long moment.* LUNA *gets restless.*

LUNA: Bueno, le dijo la mula al freno. Saben que? I think I'll go for a little walk. A ver lo que 'stan chismiando las estrellas. Oye, Bernabe, I'm going to trust you with my sister, eh? Lleve sela, suave.

TIERRA *toys with* BERNABE's *hair, deliberately establishing a romantic, coquettish mood.*

TIERRA: (*Softly*) De que piensas, Bernabe? (*No answer*) What you thinking?
BERNABE: (*Struggles to say it*) I kill my primo.

TIERRA *now reacts to* BERNABE's *answer with a more characteristic earthiness.*

TIERRA: H'm, que pelado este! I thought you were thinking about me. Your cousin's alive, hombre. Todavia 'sta vivo.
BERNABE: El primo 'sta vivo?
TIERRA: Pos luego, you think that little chair was going to kill him? He's over at your house right now, looking for you.
BERNABE: For me?
TIERRA: He's not going to hurt you. The senso is even worried about you.
BERNABE: Mi 'ama, he's going to tell her! Me tengo que ir! (*Starts to go*)
TIERRA: Tu mama? Como que tu mama! Aren't you a man?
BERNABE: (*Stops*) Simon.

TIERRA: Entonces. Where you going, running like a mocoso?

BERNABE: (*Searches for answer*) El trabajo . . . I got to work tomorrow.

TIERRA: Pa' que, hombre? All you ever do is work. Mira, come here. Sit down with me. Andale, hombre, just for a little while. (BERNABE *does not move*) Don't you like me? (BERNABE *nods*) Then sit here. (BERNABE *sits*) Aver, dime . . . tell me about your work.

BERNABE: (*Shrugs*) I'm a swamper.

TIERRA: Swamper?

BERNABE: En la papa.

TIERRA: O si, you load the potato trucks.

BERNABE: Two hundred pounds! (*Proud*) Mira. (*He makes a muscle*)

TIERRA: (*Pretends*) Ay, Chihuahua, que fuerte! (BERNABE *laughs, embarrassed*) Eres muy macho, Bernabe. Muy hombre! Que no? Menso!

BERNABE: (*Taken aback*) Uh?

TIERRA: Well, what makes you so macho? The smell of your sweat? The work you do for the patron? I thought you were a Chicano!

BERNABE: Si soy!

TIERRA: How? All your life you work for nothing, como un perro, para que? The patron at least has me, Bernabe—what do you have? I bet you don't even have a girlfriend, verdad? (*Pause.* BERNABE's *head is down*) Mirame, hombre— look at me. I'm La Tierra. Do you want me? Because if you do, I'll be your mujer. (BERNABE *reaches out to embrace her*) Not so fast, pelado! I'm not Consuelo, you know. You'll have to fight to get me. Que no sabes nada? Men have killed each other fighting over me. Are you Chicano enough to kill, Bernabe?

BERNABE: Kill?

TIERRA: For me. Then I'll be tuya, and you'll protect me. Treat me like a woman . . . make love to me.

BERNABE *goes to her. He takes her in his arms and starts to lie down on the ground with her.*
LUNA *re-enters.*

LUNA: Orale, hold it there!

TIERRA: (*Peeved*) Godblessit, Luna! You're supposed to help me.

LUNA: Pos what do you think I'm doing?

BERNABE: (*A new seriousness in his voice*) Go away Luna.

LUNA: Oye, you sound different, carnal. What did my sister do to you?

BERNABE: Go away!

LUNA: Heh, man, no te caldees. I'm your friend, re-member? I brought you two together.

TIERRA: Fine, now leave us alone.

LUNA: Simon, as soon as I find out what's on his mind. Well, vato? What about my carnal, you love her?

TIERRA: (*Pause*) Of course, he does. What man doesn't?

LUNA: What man hasn't?

TIERRA: Go to hell.

BERNABE: Let her alone, Luna!

LUNA: Aw come on, ese! What you gooing to do, marry her? (*Aware of what he has just said*) Oh-oh. En la madre, la regue! (*He backs off*)

TIERRA: (*Approaches* BERNABE *who says nothing*) Well, Bernabe? Te casas conmigo?

BERNABE: (*Strangely sure of himself*) Simon.

LUNA:	Pendejo.
TIERRA:	Satisfied?
LUNA:	Chale. You can't get married without his permission.
TIERRA:	He'll give it.
LUNA:	Maybe, but Bernabe's got to ask him first.
BERNABE:	(*Pause*) Who?
LUNA:	Her father, loco, my jefito. El Sol.
BERNABE:	Sol!
LUNA:	He'll be here in a couple of minutes. It's almost morning. Watcha. There's some light by the mountains already. Sabes que, vato, just to prove I'm your friend, let me do the talking first, eh? To smooth things out. I'll tell him what a good Chicano you are.
TIERRA:	Stop treating him like that, Luna!
LUNA:	Like what?
TIERRA:	(*Pause*) He can talk for himself.
LUNA:	Orale, no hay pedo. But you know the jefito.
TIERRA:	You're going to have to ask for my hand, Bernabe. If you really love me, you'll show mi 'apa that you're a man.

BERNABE *tries to express something but fails to find the words. Unlike before he is calm, serene, unafraid. He nods.*

LUNA:	Alalva! Here he comes! Get down! And don't look at his face too much, ese. He'll blind you!

TIERRA *and* LUNA *kneel before the place where the* SUN *is rising. Music: majestic flutes and drums.* SOL *rises in the guise of Tonatiuh, the Aztec Sun God. A golden disk rises above the mountains; it turns to reveal a bearded face in a golden feathered headdress. The music ends just as* SOL *faces his children. There is authority in his voice.*

SOL:	Buenos dias, mis hijos!
TIERRA:	(*Head down*) Buenos dias, papa.
LUNA:	(*Head down*) Buenos dias, jefe.
SOL:	Luna! Como va mi pleito con las estrellas? Cuidaste mi cielo por toda la noche?
LUNA:	Si, jefe, todo sta bien.
SOL:	Y tu hermana? La cuidaste a ella?
LUNA:	Si, senor, como no?
SOL:	Pues como? Ya te conosco. Hasta se me hace que a veces cuando no estoy aqui, te metes alla arriba con las estrellas, no?
LUNA:	No, jefe, nunca!
SOL:	Calla pues!
TIERRA:	(*Sweetly*) Papasito?
SOL:	Si, hija, digame.
TIERRA:	There's somebody here who wants to talk with you.
SOL:	Who is it?
TIERRA:	Un hombre. (*Whispers to* BERNABE) Go on!

BERNABE *stands before the sun, somber and serious.*

BERNABE:	It's me, senor.
SOL:	Who are you?
BERNABE:	(*Facing him*) Bernabe!
SOL:	(*With godly disdain*) What do you want from El Sol, Bernabe?
BERNABE:	(*Glances at* TIERRA) I want La Tierra.
SOL:	Mija!
BERNABE:	Pos for my wife, no?
SOL:	Many years have passed Bernabe, since men had the courage to ask for the bride, como es debido. Why do you come before me now?
BERNABE:	I'm a man.
SOL:	Y que? What is that to me!

BERNABE: I love her.

SOL: (*With disgust*) Muchos hombres have loved her. Do you think you're the first? Ella es la chingada!

TIERRA: Papa!

SOL: (*With mounting anger*) No, hija, callese. Do you hear me, Bernabe? She has been married before. She has even been raped! Many times. Look at her—this is La Tierra who has been many things to all men. Madre, prostituta, mujer. Aren't you afraid?

BERNABE: (*Defiantly*) No, senor, of what?

SOL: (*Furious*) Of her padre, desgraciado, El Sol!! (*There is a tremendous flash of light and sound.* BERNABE *runs and hides*) Look at him, corriendo como un cobarde! Malora! I should kill you for what your kind has done to mija.

BERNABE: It was not me, senor.

TIERRA: Por favor, papa, es inocente!

LUNA: She's right, jefe, he's never done nothing to her. It was others.

SOL: (*Calms down*) What work do you do, Bernabe?

BERNABE: I work in the fields.

SOL: You are poor then?

BERNABE: Si, senor.

SOL: Then what do you expect to do for mija? You have no money. You have no power.

BERNABE: Senor, yo no soy nadie. I am nobody. In town people even say I am crazy. But I do know that if somebody has done wrong to La Tierra, it has not been the pobres. It has been the men with money and power.

SOL: Dices bien. (*Pause*) Once there were men like you, Bernabe—de tus mismos ojos, tu piel, tu sangre. They loved La Tierra and honored her padre above all else. These men were mis hijos. They pierced the human brain and plunged into the stars and found the hungry fire that eats of itself. They saw what only a loco can understand: that life is death, and death is life. Que la vida no vale nada porque vale todo. That you are *one* so you can be two, then four, then eight, then sixteen, and on and on until you are milliones, billones, then you look inside yourself and find nothing, so you fill up the space with *one* again. Me comprendes, Bernabe? They had the power of the Sun! (*Pause*) If you marry mija, you will have this power. And you will be my son, un hijo del Sol. (*Pause*) Tierra, do you love this man?

TIERRA: Si, papa!

SOL: Bernabe, do you love La Tierra?

BERNABE: Con todo el corazon!

SOL: Corazon? No, hijo, not with your heart. You may love her with your body, your blood, your seed, but your corazon you will give to me. Estas listo para morir?

BERNABE: (*Frightened*) Morir?

SOL: Para vivir.

BERNABE *is momentarily confused. He looks at* TIERRA *for help, then at* LUNA.

TIERRA: I can't help you, Bernabe.

LUNA: It's up to you, ese.

SOL: Hijo, I offer you the power of the Sun! You have been nothing, you will be everything. I am the beginning and the end of all things. Believe in

me, and you shall never die. Will you give me
your corazon?

BERNABE: (*Pause*) Si, senor.

SOL: Que sea asi!

Drums sound with a rapid beat. Flutes cry out. LUNA *strips*
BERNABE *of his shirt and grabs his arms from behind, bend-*
ing him backward. SOL *slashes down with his great macana,*
pointing down at BERNABE's *exposed chest. A clash of cym-*
bals. BERNABE *dies. Silence.*

SOL: (*After a pause*) Bernabe, levantate!

BERNABE *rises. His appearance has changed.* LUNA *hands*
him an Indian robe. BERNABE *is puzzled but serene. He puts*
on the robe and notices his leg is no longer crippled.

SOL: La Tierra is virgin again, Bernabe. She is yours:
take her!

TIERRA: Bernabe! (*She embraces him*)

LUNA: Ora-LEH! Congratulations, ese, you did it! A
toda madre, man! This calls for a celebration,
loco. Toma, hechate un pisto de wine. (*Pulls out
wine bottle.* BERNABE *drinks, then* LUNA)

BERNABE: Gracias!

LUNA: Anytime, cunado. Salud! (*Drinks*)

TIERRA: (*Hugging him*) Mi esposo, mi Bernabe!

LUNA: Vivan los novios! (*He lets out a grito*)

SOL: Silencio pues! (*Silence*) I am still here! Mas res-
pecto, eh Luna? Don't you see the day is dying?
The time has come for me to go. Mis hijos, I
bless your marriage. Los dejo con mi bendicion.
(*Blesses them*) Luna, take care of my sky during
the hours of darkness. Y dale luz a tu hermana,
eh?

LUNA: Si, jefe, like always.

SOL:	Bueno, me voy pues. (*He starts to sink*) Bernabe . . . Tierra, do not waste the night . . . Have hijos . . . muchos hijos.
TIERRA:	Si, papa, pase buenas noches.
LUNA:	Buenas noches, jefe!
SOL:	Buenas noches, . . . hijos.
BERNABE:	Buenas noches, senor!
SOL:	(*Sinking fast*) Buenas . . . noches . . . Bernabe! (*He is gone*)

There is silence. TIERRA *shivers, then* LUNA.

TIERRA:	It's cold! (*She goes to* BERNABE. *He puts his arm around her*)
LUNA:	Simon, it always gets chilly when the jefito leaves. How about lighting a fire and finishing the wine, eh?
TIERRA:	No!
LUNA:	Oh yeah, I forgot. This is your honeymoon, huh? Orale, what kind of light you want? Soft, low, romantic?
TIERRA:	Why don't you just go away.
LUNA:	Mirala, mirala—just because she's a virgin again.
BERNABE:	Mira, hermano, no andes con insultos. Como antes fui loco, ahora soy hombre. Y La Tierra es mi mujer.
LUNA:	Okay, 'ta bien pues! I got to work anyway. (*Looks up*) Pinches estrellas, I bet you they're just itching to move in on the jefito's territory. I better go check. Goodnight, you two, don't do nothing I wouldn't do, eh?
TIERRA:	(*Pause*) Bernabe? (*Her back to him*)
BERNABE:	Que?
TIERRA:	Will you always love me?

BERNABE: Always.

TIERRA: Hasta la muerte? (*She turns. Her face is a death mask*)

BERNABE: Hasta la muerte. (*He lies down beside her*)

(*End of scene*)

XII. LA CAUSA: GOD AND CHURCH

THE DESTRUCTION OF THE AZTEC TEMPLES: I OVERTURNED THE IDOLS

by Hernando Cortez

In Renaissance Spain the Catholic Church was "a Spanish, national Church, controlled from Madrid," Dr. Frederick B. Pike, of Notre Dame, has written; it was "an appendage of the State." So in the New World the Conquistadors established an "ecclesiastical government," recorded Icazbalceta, a historian of the origins of Mexican Catholicism; Cortez thus ordered the destruction of the Aztec temples and idols. The religion of the Indians was adapted to Catholicism, but Catholicism was also adapted to the religion of the Indians. Four hundred years later Archbishop Lucey of San Antonio was to comment ruefully on the problem of " 'Christianizing' Mexican Catholics." And a Chicano writer noted that "We took your Virgin Mary and made her our Virgin of Guadalupe. It meant more than making a white statue brown. It meant making her Mexican. And *Indio!*" ("I Overturned the Idols," *Conquest: Dispatches of Cortes from the New World,* edited by Irwin Blacker and Harry Rosen, New York, Grosset & Dunlap, 1962.)

This great city contains many mosques, or houses for idols, very beautiful edifices situated in the different precincts. The principal ones house the priests of the religious orders.

All these priests dress in black and never cut or comb their hair from the time they enter the religious order until they leave it. The sons of all the principal families are placed in these religious orders at the age of seven or eight years and remain till they are ready for marriage. This applies more frequently to the first born, who inherits the property. They have no access to women, who are not allowed to enter the religious houses; they abstain from eating certain dishes, particularly at certain times of the year.

There is one principal mosque which no human tongue can describe. It is so large that within the high wall which surrounds it a village of five hundred houses could easily be built. All around it are very handsome buildings with large rooms and galleries where the priests are lodged. There are as many as forty very high and well-built towers, the largest having fifty steps to reach the top; the principal one is higher than the tower of the chief church in Seville. I have never seen anything so well built. . . .

I overturned the idols in which these people believe the most and rolled them down the stairs. Then I had those chapels cleansed, for they were full of blood from the sacrifices; and I set up images of Our Lady and other Saints in them. This disturbed Montezuma and the natives a good deal, and they told me not to do it. They said that if it became known, the people would rise against me, as they believed that these idols gave them all their temporal goods. If the people allowed them to be ill-treated, they would be angered and give nothing, and would take away the fruits of the soil and cause the people to die of want. . . .

The figures of the idols exceed in size the body of a large man. They are made of all the seeds and vegetables which they eat, ground up and mixed with one another, and kneaded with the heart's blood of human beings. The breasts are opened while these unhappy creatures are still alive; the hearts are removed, and the blood which comes out is kneaded with the flour to make the quantity necessary for a large statue. When the statues are finished the priests offer them more hearts, which have also been sacrificed, and smear the faces with the blood. The idols are dedicated to different things. To obtain favors in war these people have one idol, for harvests another, and for everything they desire they have special idols whom they honor and serve.

GOD AND MAN

In the mountains of New Mexico the *Penitente* villagers still adhere to the teachings of the Third Order of Saint Francis. Fray Angelico Chavez, a Franciscan monk, has explained that these teachings urge simplicity and humility and brotherhood in religion, as in life; Patrocino Barela's writings show that in the mountains a man is face to face with his life, his fellows, and his God. ("Sayings," *Patrocino Barela: Taos Wood Carver*, Taos Recordings and Publications, 1962). A mountain village priest said: "Priests are men. Why do we hide our manhood behind the skirts of the Church? Here a man is a man. Look what Saint Augustine was trying to tell us: the way to God is through the flesh of man." And Fecundo Valdes, a village community organizer in the mountains: "In religion we are individualists to a degree the Anglo cannot comprehend. We do penance when we decide to. We atone for our own sins." These thoughts are expressed in the modern parable "I Believe in God. But Not in Priests" by Cleofas Vigil, an ex-*Penitente* and village farmer (*La Raza*, by Steiner).

Sayings of Patrocino Barela

NOT UNTIL HE MADE A CONFESSION

A man
always carries around
with him
The weight
of all the things
he has done wrong
all his life
Not until he makes
a confession
of these wrong things
will they change
over
Their upside down
position
And be right again

SACRED HEART

A good heart
keeps you safe
When Christ traveled
in those days
there were no rifles or pistols
to keep himself safe
Only
a good heart

MAN WHO STANDS BY HIS OWN

This man stands
on his own ground
on his own particular place
in this world
With half-closed eyes
and upraised arm
he declares this
This is what he holds
which is his
by natural right
received from above
This is his own
which is
what he stands by

HOPES AND THANKS TO GOD

Simple to pray
when you feel like it
You pray
hopes and thanks
The way you feel
Not in
the hands and arms

I Believe in God. But Not in Priests.
by Cleofas Vigil

I believe in God. But not in priests. If you go to confession
to the priest, he forgives you. But who is he to forgive you?
It is not for him to forgive, but who you have sinned against.

Maybe I do something wrong. If I steal your watch how can the priest forgive me? Was it his watch?

No, I have to confess to you. To ask forgiveness of you whom I have wronged.

And I will say, "Stan, I have stolen your watch."

And you will say, "Why did you do that, Cleofas? Why didn't you ask me for it?"

And I will say, "Well, I was ashamed."

And you will say, "But I need my watch. It cost me a lot of money. What did you do with it?"

And I will say, "I sold it."

And you will say, "That was wrong."

And I will say, "Yes, it was wrong. I know it. But I needed the money. I will pay you back when I can. Will you forgive me?"

And you will say, "Yes, Cleofas, I forgive you."

Maybe I will never pay you back. But I have confessed to you and you have forgiven me. That is being Christian. That is Christ's way. Who the hell are the priests to tell us that if we do this we will go to hell? Aren't the poor living in hell now?

GOD IS BESIDE YOU ON THE PICKETLINE

On their "Pilgrimage to Sacramento," the capital of California, the grape strikers walked behind the banner of the Virgin of Guadalupe, as had the army of Zapata. God was with them. Was there not a sign in the union hall in Delano that said: GOD IS BESIDE YOU ON THE PICKETLINE. The *campesino* has a "religion oriented culture," wrote Cesar Chavez; his protest is also a penance (*Peregrinacion, Penitencia, Revolucion* by Cesar Chavez, mimeographed, undated). In ending his twenty-five-day fast for "non-violent struggle," in which he broke bread with the late Robert Kennedy, who was soon to be assassinated, Cesar Chavez spoke of his personal credo of sacrifice (*To Be a Man Is to Suffer for Others. God Help Us to be Men!* by Cesar Chavez, mimeographed, undated).

Peregrinacion, Penitencia, Revolucion

by Cesar Chavez

In the "March from Delano to Sacramento" there is a meeting of cultures and traditions; the centuries-old religious tradition of Spanish culture conjoins with the very contemporary cultural syndrome of "demonstration" springing from the spontaneity of the poor, the downtrodden, the rejected, the discriminated against bearing visibly their need and demand for equality and freedom.

In every religion-oriented culture "the pilgrimage" has had a place: a trip made with sacrifice and hardship as an expression of penance and of commitment—and often involving a petition to the patron of the pilgrimage for some sincerely sought benefit of body or soul. Pilgrimage has not passed from Mexican culture. Daily at any of the major shrines of the country, and in particular at the Basilica of the Lady of Guadalupe, there arrive pilgrims from all points—some of whom may have long since walked out the pieces of rubber tire that once served them as soles, and many of whom will walk on their knees the last mile or so of the pilgrimage. Many of the "pilgrims" of Delano will have walked such pilgrimages themselves in their lives—perhaps as very small children even—and cling to the memory of the day-long marches, the camps at night, streams forded, hills climbed, the sacral aura of the sanctuary, and the "fiesta" that followed.

But throughout the Spanish-speaking world there is another tradition that touches the present march, that of the Lenten penitential processions, where the *penitentes* would march through the streets, often in sack cloth and ashes, some even carrying crosses, as a sign of penance for their sins, and as a plea for the mercy of God. The penitential procession is also in the blood of the Mexican-American, and the Delano march will therefore be one of penance— public penance for the sins of the strikers, their own personal sins as well as their yielding perhaps to feelings of hatred and revenge in the strike itself. They hope by the march to set themselves at peace with the Lord, so that the justice of their cause will be purified of all lesser motivation.

These two great traditions of a great people meet in the Mexican-American with the belief that Delano is his "cause," his great demand for justice, freedom, and respect from a predominantly foreign cultural community in a land where he was first. The revolutions of Mexico were primarily uprisings of the poor, fighting for bread and for dignity. The Mexican-American is also a child of the revolution.

Pilgrimage, penance, and revolution. The pilgrimage from Delano to Sacramento has strong religio-cultural overtones. But it is also the pilgrimage of a cultural minority which has suffered from a hostile environment, and a minority which means business.

To Be a Man Is to Suffer for Others: God Help Us to Be Men!

by Cesar Chavez

We are gathered here today not so much to observe the end of the Fast but because we are a family bound together in a common struggle for justice. We are a Union family celebrating our unity and the non-violent nature of our movement. Perhaps in the future we will come together at other times and places to break bread and to renew our courage and to celebrate important victories.

The Fast has had different meanings for different people. Some of you may still wonder about its meaning and importance. It was not intended as a pressure against any growers. For that reason we have suspended negotiations and arbitration proceedings and relaxed the militant picketing and boycotting of the strike during this period. I undertook this Fast because my heart was filled with grief and pain for the sufferings of farm workers. The Fast was first for me and then for all of us in this Union. It was a Fast for non-violence and a call to sacrifice.

Our struggle is not easy. Those who oppose our cause are rich and powerful and they have many allies in high places. We are poor. Our allies are few. But we have something the rich do not own. We have our own bodies and spirits and the justice of our cause as our weapons.

When we are really honest with ourselves we must admit that our lives are all that really belong to us. So, it is how we use our lives that determines what kind of men we are. It is my belief that only by giving our lives do we find life. I am convinced that the truest act of courage, the strongest act of manliness is to sacrifice ourselves for others in a totally non-violent struggle for justice.

To be a man is to suffer for others. God help us to be men!

THE CHURCH AND THE CHICANOS

"God is alive and well in the heart of the Chicano!" Luis Valdez has written. Yet the Church is troubled. "Our Church has always been two Churches," explains a barrio priest in Texas; "we have always had a conservative hierarchy, first from Spain, then from the Anglos. In the poor parishes we have had revolutionary priests." The dichotomy of the wealth of the Church and the poverty of the barrios is set forth in "The Church and La Raza" (*El Grito del Norte*, Vol. 3, No. 2, February 11, 1970). This dichotomy provoked demands of Chicano Catholics in California that title to a Church campground be given to the community ("Campo Cultural de La Raza" by Alberto Alurista). In their statement of religious principle, the Catolicos por La Raza (*La Raza*, February, 1970) appear both as supplicants and ecclesiastic militants, appealing to the Church to remember that Christ "not only washed and kissed the feet of the poor," but that He "did all in His power to feed and educate the poor." Dolores del Grito, in her "Jesus Christ as a Revolutionist" (*El Grito del Norte*, February 11, 1970), chastises those who, in Christ's words, have turned the "house of prayer" into "a den of thieves."

The Church and La Raza

It is common knowledge that the Catholic Church is a block of power in society and that the property and purchases of the Church rate second only to the government. True Christianity demands that this institutional power and wealth of the Church be brought to bear in solving the current Chicano urban and rural crisis . . . The religious dollar must be invested, without return expected, in the barrios. . . .

The Church must come to realize that her commitment to serve the poor today means the investment of land and seed money for La Raza's self-help projects such as housing development corporations, management development corporations, small business corporations, credit unions and coops, the profit from which will be used to further our own barrios. . . .

Spanish surnamed clergy and laity should determine the priorities of goals and objectives in a given barrio. Financial assistance must be provided without stringent controls and bureaucratic attachments.

Because of the incredibly high dropout rate among Mexican-American students, tutorial services, study halls, bilingual programs, programs for dropouts, etc., must be initiated and funded.

In conclusion, to build power among Mexican-Americans presents a threat to the Church; to demand reform of Anglo-controlled institutions stirs up dissension . . . However, if representatives of the Church are immobilized and compromised into silence, the Church will not only remain irrelevant to the real needs and efforts of La Raza in the barrios, but our young leaders of today will continue to scorn the Church and view it as an obstacle to their struggle for social, political and economic independence.

Campo Cultural de La Raza

by Alberto Alurista

The Mexican-American constitutes 23% of the total Catholic population in the U.S. and 67% of the Catholics in the five Southwestern states. Yet we are totally unrepresented in the official national and Diocesan appointments. To be oblivious to the needs of the poor is to be responsible for their poverty. The church must now account for its lack of responsibility to the poor people of the Barrios.

After all, what people in the United States have been historically and at the present more faithful to the Catholic faith than our peoples? The Catholic Church is the strongest and richest institution in the world. Do you really think that if the Catholic Church had all along demanded social and economic justice for our people that we would be in our present predicament? It has done the opposite because it has chosen to be silent although it knows we have been and continue to struggle for a place in the sun. Indeed, we know that the Catholic Church in Los Angeles alone has over one billion dollars in property and other assets (that's right, $1,000,000,000). And we can prove it! Compare such wealth to the plight of our people and you begin to wonder, as CPLR (Catolicos por La Raza) has wondered, just who has taken on the vow of poverty—the Chicanos or the Catholic Church. Compare such wealth further to the creator of Christianity, Jesus Christ, who was born in a manger, died for poor people, washed their feet—*in short truly loved the poor*—and you further realize that the Catholic Church is not even Christian.

The Chicano community demands the immediate transfer of the title [of the "Centro"] from the Catholic Church to the Chicano community, and that the Catholic Church fund the operation of the "Centro" with respect to upkeep and resource input.

The Chicano community hereby makes notice that the Catholic Church is not absolved of further damage, that this is only the beginning, and that scholarships, open enrollment, free textbooks, free uniforms, be provided to the Chicano, and that Self-Determination be the sole right of the Chicano.

The "Centro" will commence plans for reprinting studies of the Mexican-American in the Southwest U.S. and will cover all aspects of the Mexican-American with particular emphasis on the Chicano movement. The "Centro" will concentrate on Chicano crafts and its culture, conferences in the unification of Chicano learning, consultation services, and sensitizing sessions as it relates to "Chicanismo." The "Centro" will emphasize a recreational retreat where people can come to learn about "Chicanismo" and LA RAZA, and will serve as a research center.

Catolicos por La Raza

We wish to share with you the feelings which gave rise to Catolicos por La Raza. As Mexican-Americans and as Catholics you have a right to know.

Members of Catolicos por La Raza (CPLR) are Catholics. We have gone to Catholic schools and understand the Catholic tradition. Because of our Catholic training we know that Christ, the founder of Catholicism was a genuinely poor man. We know that he was born in a manger because His compatriots refused Him better housing. We know that He not only washed and kissed the feet of the poor (Mary Magdalen) but did all in His power to feed and educate the poor. We also know that one day He rode through Jerusalem on a jackass and was laughed at, spat upon, and ridiculed. We remember, from our Catholic education, that Christ, our hero, did not have to identify with the poor but chose to do so. We also were taught that one day Christ went to the established church, a church which identified with the rich people, with people who were never ridiculed or laughed at or spat upon, and He took a whip and used it upon the money-changers of His day who, in the name of religion, would dare to gather money from the poor. And, finally, we know, as all Christians know, His love for the poor was so great that He chose to die for poor people.

We know these things because our Catholic education has taught us that these were the things Christ did, Christ who founded the Catholic Church. And we know further that if you or I claim to be Christian we have the duty to not only love the poor but to be as Christlike as possible.

It is these feelings within us, as members of Catolicos por La Raza, which led us to look at our Catholic Church as it presently exists: a Church which, for example in Los Angeles, would dare to build a $3,500,000 church on Wilshire Boulevard when you and we know that because of our poverty our average education is 8.6 years and many, too many of our people, live in projects. How many churches, let alone million-dollar churches, did Christ build? We looked further and found that, although as a matter of faith all of us are members of the Catholic Church, nonetheless no Chicanos are able to participate in decisions within the Church, which are not of purely religious nature. Would you have voted for a million-dollar Church?

So many other considerations led to the creation of Catolicos por La Raza. We do not have the time or the money to print them all. But we do ask you to remember, as Mexican-Americans, as Catolicos, as Chicanos, that as members of the Catholic Church, it is our fault if the Catholic Church in the Southwest is no longer a Church of blood, a Church of struggle, a Church of sacrifice. It is our fault because we have not raised our voices as Catholics and as poor people for the love of Christ. We can't love our people without demanding better housing, education, health, and so many other needs we share in common.

In a word, we are demanding that the Catholic Church practice what it preaches. Remember Padre Hidalgo. And remember that the history of our people is the history of the Catholic Church in the Americas. We must return the Church to the poor. OR DID CHRIST DIE IN VAIN?

Jesus Christ as a Revolutionist

by Dolores del Grito

"And he went into the temple, and began to cast out them that sold therein, and them that bought.

"Saying unto them, it is written, my house is the house of prayer; but ye have made it a den of thieves." (Luke 19: 45–46.)

It seems that people are taking a good close look at their Church. They now question the real meaning of Christianity. Why are the Blacks DEMANDING reparation from the Church? Why have the Young Lords in Harlem taken over a church for a community center? Why did Raza in Los Angeles enter a church on Christmas Eve? Why is UMAS in Denver picketing the Church? Why are groups seen picketing various churches of our country today?

People have come to the point where they know the difference between CHURCH, CHRISTIANITY, and a real SPIRITUAL LIFE. Where a church was said to be a house of God people now realize that that house is built brick by brick on human exploitation, huge land holdings throughout the world, major stockholders in business, wars, bloodshed, political maneuvering and out and out hypocrisy. People have come to realize that one church is a CORPORATION FOR PROFIT, and one of the world's richest corporations.

So now the house of God, the rock of Peter, is a house of commerce, and people know the difference between this business and love of God. People now know the temple of God is within each and every one of us.

Christianity is being looked at in a different light. Jesus Christ is being seen as the radical he really is. He is seen as a revolutionist through the eyes of the revolutionaries, for it is from him that we draw strength. When we see the teachings of Jesus Christ we see what he fought, we see him become angry with money merchants, and again we see where after his lifetime of teaching those in power turned around and built bigger and stronger the very same type organizations he fought. The church institutions are the biggest BLAS-PHEMISTS of all.

Spiritual life is what we know we have. This is what guides us in our day to day living. The church has too often played the role of a powerful patron who is not interested in ministering to all of the needs of the people. The Church has remained uninvolved and uninterested in the social conditions of the world. It has preached with deaf ears. It seems to serve as a pacifier. It talks of a way of life completely contrary to the society we live in. Yet it does nothing about our human needs; it only rakes in the gold to add to its bricks of the impenetrable tower.

THE NEW CHRIST

Poems by Abelardo Delgado

"Pobres de Mexico, tan lejos de Dios, y tan cerca de los Estados Unidos"—President Porfirio Diaz, of Mexico. "The poor of Mexico, so far from God, and so near the United States." On the border, in El Paso, Texas, there is the Barrio of the Seven Hells. It was during Lent in 1968 that Abelardo Delgado, a barrio poet, mystic, and Chicano activist, fasted for forty days on the streets of Seven Hells. He fasted for "the children, so they do not have to grow up in tenements," for "love of neighbor," for "peace in Vietnam," and for "the Churches to get involved with us." In his poem "The Fast" he wrote:

Maybe my empty belly
Will serve as a drum
On which I can drum messages
To a distant God.

Abelardo Delgado sees the Chicano movement as a "New Church." He seeks a "New Christ" who will "humanize the desires of people," and who will bear a "New Cross"—"made of love." ("The Organizer" and "A New Cross" by Abelardo Delgado, published privately, undated.)

The Organizer

"And the flock shall be one"
The job that should be done
Was not issued by
The U.S. government
But by a gent full of light
And full of obscure ideas
A classless society idea
Is full of the same message,
One flock,
And can you imagine
Anything sillier
That buddhism crossed up
With Christianity
And catholics sharing a bed
With protestants
and agnostics
And atheists eating off
The same plate

With believers
And yes
What is even more beautiful
Is the gathering
On the same floor
Of whores and homosexuals
Sadists, nymphos, masochists,
Thieves, adulterers and murderers
With saints,
How does that strike you?
A flock———
E pluribus unum
The jig saw puzzle God
Fullfilled by us salmons upstream bound
Who having never been lost cannot be found.

A New Cross

CHRIST, your cross sure ain't impressing nobody no more
Get a new one, run, don't walk, to your nearest store.
But before let me suggest a few new models
How about one made out of three H-bombs
You sure could convey the idea of power,
Or one made out of petrified dollar bills
You always looked well in green,
Maybe one of cemented birth control pills
To signify your power over life,
Better yet one made of solid gold
That's the "in" thing with nations,
If you care to reach the masses
Your cross would have to be
N.B.C., C.B.S. and A.B.C.
You always did go for the poor

So maybe we can find
A slum shaped like a cross
To fit you on,
What about the turned-on generation
Maybe flowers could appeal,
Or a psychedelic one with neons
And sound effects
Or one with acid running through,
Man, I can't begin to exhaust
The possibilities,
But let's face it,
A wooden cross leaves us cold,
Would you believe one
With hot and cold running blood
For war makers and soldiers?
Personally, I prefer one twice as brilliant as the gun,
Made of love; if you find it, buy that one.

XIII. AZTLAN

THE CHILDREN OF THE AZTEC: THE VISION OF MOTECUHZOMA

> It is thought that the Aztecs, before they marched south to conquer people of Central Mexico, had come from the land of Aztlan. The word, in Nahuatl, may refer to "the land to the north," or "the land of the white reeds." Some believe the land of Aztlan was located in the valley of the Lower Colorado River in the present-day United States. In the vision of Emperor Motecuhzoma which is as much folklore as prophecy, the Aztec ruler forecast the day when his descendants "will rise up"—"the newly risen tribes, like trodden grass"—and there will be a "new birth." ("The Children of the Aztec," *Warriors of the Rainbow* by William Willoya and Vinson Brown, Heraldsbury, Cal., Naturegraph Books, 1952.)

To the world I have said farewell. I see its vanities go from me one by one. Last in the train and most loved, most glittering, is power—and in its hands is my heart. A shadow creeps upon me, darkening all without, but brightening all within; and in the brightness, lo, I see my People and their future!

The long, long cycles—two—four—eight—pass away, and I see the tribes newly risen, like the trodden grass, and in their midst a Priesthood and a Cross. An age of battles more, and, lo! there remains the Cross, but not the priests; in their stead is *Freedom and God.*

I know the children of the Aztec, crushed now, will live, and more—after ages of wrong suffered by them, they will rise up, and take their place—a place of splendor—amongst the deathless nations of the earth. What I was given to see was revelation. Cherish these words, O Tula; repeat them often; make them a cry of the people, a sacred tradition; let them go down with the generations, one of which will, at last, rightly understand the meaning of the words FREEDOM AND GOD, now dark to my understanding; and then, not till then, will be the new birth and new career.

EL PLAN ESPIRITUAL DE AZTLAN

Chicano Liberation Youth Conference

In the summer of 1969, three thousand young Chicanos met in the Crusade for Justice in Denver, Colorado, at the Chicano Liberation Youth Conference. They adopted a resolution proclaiming that the day of Motecuhzoma's "new birth" had come. "We are a Nation. We are a Union of free pueblos. We are Aztlan," they declared. They then went on to detail their goals —through the reborn symbol of Aztlan—for "a nation autonomously free." ("El Plan Espiritual de Aztlan," *El Grito del Norte,* Vol. 2, No. 9, July 6, 1969.)

In the spirit of a new people that is conscious not only of its proud historical heritage, but also of the brutal "Gringo" invasion of our territories: We, the Chicano inhabitants and civilizers of the northern land of Aztlan, from whence came our forefathers, reclaiming the land of their birth and consecrating the determination of our people of the sun, declare that the call of our blood is our power, our responsibility, and our inevitable destiny.

We are free and sovereign to determine those tasks which are justly called for by our house, our land, the sweat of our brows and by our hearts. Aztlan belongs to those who plant the seeds, water the fields, and gather the crops, and not to the foreign Europeans. We do not recognize capricious frontiers on the Bronze Continent.

Brotherhood unites us and love for our brothers makes us a people whose time has come and who struggle against the foreigner "Gabacho," who exploits our riches and destroys our culture. With our heart in our hands and our hands in the soil, We Declare the Independence of our Mestizo Nation. We are a Bronze People with a Bronze Culture. Before the world, before all of North America, before all our brothers in the Bronze Continent, We are a Nation, We are a Union of free pueblos, We are Aztlan.

March, 1969—Adopted at
Chicano Youth
Conference, Denver, Colorado

Aztlan, in the Nahuatl tongue of ancient Mexico, means "the lands to the north." Thus Aztlan refers to what is now known as the southwestern states of this country.

El Plan espiritual de Aztlan sets the theme that the Chicanos (La Raza de Bronze) must use their nationalism as the key or common denominator for mass mobilization and organization. Once we are committed to the idea and philosophy of El Plan de Aztlan, we can only conclude that social, economic, cultural, and political independence is the only road to total liberation from oppression, exploitation and racism. Our struggle then must be the control of our barrios, campos, pueblos, lands, our economy, our culture, and our political life. El Plan commits all levels of Chicano society— the barrio, the campo, the ranchero, the writer, the teacher, the worker, the professional—to la Causa.

I.   Punto Primero: Nationalism

Nationalism as the key to organization transcends all religious, political, class, and economic factions or boundaries. Nationalism is the common denominator that all members of La Raza can agree upon.

II.   Punto Segundo: Organization Goals

1. Unity in thought of our people concerning the barrios, the pueblo, the campo, the land, the poor, the middle class, the professional is committed to liberation of La Raza.

2. Economy: economic control of our lives and our communities can only come about by driving the exploiter out of our communities, our pueblos, and our lands and by controlling and developing our own talents, sweat, and resources. Cultural background and values which ignore materialism and embrace humanism will lend to the act of cooperative buying and distribution of resources and production to sustain an economic base for healthy growth and development. Lands rightfully ours will be fought for and defended. Land and realty ownership will be acquired by the community for the people's welfare. Economic ties of responsibility must be secured by nationalism and the Chicano defense units.

3. Education must be relevant to our people, i.e., history, culture, bilingual education, contributions. Community control of our schools, our teachers.

4. Institutions shall serve our people by providing the service necessary for a full life and their welfare on the basis of restitution, not handouts or beggar's crumbs. Restitution

for past economic slavery, political exploitation, ethnic and cultural psychological destruction, and denial of civil and human rights. Institutions in our community which do not serve the people have no place in the community. The institutions belong to the people.

5. Self-defense of the community must rely on the combined strength of the people. The front line defense will come from the barrios, the campos, the pueblos, and the ranchitos. Their involvement as protectors of their people will be given respect and dignity. They in turn offer lives for their people. Those who place themselves on the front for their people do so out of love and carnalismo. Those institutions which are fattened by our brothers to provide employment and political pork barrels for the Gringo will do so only by acts of liberation and la Causa. For the very young there will no longer be acts of juvenile delinquency, but revolutionary acts.

6. Cultural values of our people strengthen our identity and the moral backbone of the movement. Our culture unites and educates the family of La Raza towards liberation with one heart and one mind. We must insure that our writers, poets, musicians, and artists produce literature and art that is appealing to our people and relates to our revolutionary culture. Our cultural values of life, family, and home will serve as a powerful weapon to defeat the gringo dollar value system and encourage the process of love and brotherhood.

7. Political liberation can only come through an independent action on our part, since the two party system is the same animal with two heads that feeds from the same trough. Where we are a majority we will control; where we are a minority we will represent a pressure group. Nationally, we will represent one party, La Familia de La Raza.

III. Punto Tercero: Action

1. Awareness and distribution of El Plan espiritual de Aztlan. Presented at every meeting, demonstration, confrontation, courthouse, institution, administration, church, school, tree, building, car, and every place of human existence.

2. September 16th, on the birthdate of Mexican Independence, a national walkout by all Chicanos of all colleges and schools to be sustained until the complete revision of the educational system—its policy makers, its administration, its curriculum, and its personnel—to meet the needs of our community.

3. Self-defense against the occupying forces of the oppressors at every school, every available man, woman, and child.

4. Community nationalization and organization of all Chicanos re: El Plan espiritual de Aztlan.

5. Economic program to drive the exploiter out of our communities and a welding of our peoples combined resources to control their own production through cooperative effort.

6. Creation of an independent local, regional, and national political party.

Punto Cuarto: Liberation

A nation autonomously free, culturally, socially, economically, and politically will make its own decisions on the usage of our lands, the taxation of our goods, the utilization of our bodies for war, the determination of justice (reward and punishment), and the profit of our sweat.

EL PLAN DE AZTLAN IS THE PLAN OF LIBERATION!

ACKNOWLEDGMENTS

The editors gratefully acknowledge the following sources:

"The Heart of Earth," from *Popol Vuh: The Sacred Book of the Ancient Quiche Maya,* by Adrian Recinos. Copyright 1950 by the University of Oklahoma Press.

"In A Time Nobody Exactly Remembers: The Olmecs"; "Where Are the Roots of Men?"; "Must We Live Weeping?"; from *Pre-Columbian Literatures of Mexico,* by Miguel Leon-Portilla, translated from the Spanish by Grace Lobanov and the author. Copyright 1969 by the University of Oklahoma Press.

"What Greater Grandeur" and "I Overturned the Idols," reprinted from *Conquest: Dispatches of Cortez from the New World,* by Irwin R. Blacker and Harry M. Rosen. Copyright © 1962 by Irwin R. Blacker and Harry M. Rosen. Published by Grosset & Dunlap, Inc.

"Greater than Constantinople and Rome," from *The Discovery and Conquest of Mexico,* edited by Gennaro Garcia, translated by A. P. Maudsley, New York, Farrar, Straus & Cudahy, copyright © 1956. Reprinted with permission of publisher.

"Aztec Democracy: In Favor of the Common Man"; "Aztec Imperialism: Tlacaelel and Human Sacrifice"; "Does Man Possess Any Truth?"; "One Day We Must Go"; "Who Am I?"; "It Is Not Proper That This Book Be Published: A Royal Cedula of Philip II"; "Do Not Throw Yourself upon Women"; "The Toltec"; from *Aztec Thought and Culture,* by Miguel Leon-Portilla, translated by Jack Emory Davis. Copyright 1963 by the University of Oklahoma Press.

"The Blood Was Fulfilled," from *The Book of Chilam Balam of Chumayel,* by Ralph L. Roys. New edition copyright 1967 by the University of Oklahoma Press.

"Death Emerges From Life, Life Emerges From Death," from *El Popol Vuh Tiene Razon,* by Domingo Martinez Paredes, Mexico, Editorial Orion, 1968. Reprinted with permission of author.

"We Come as Friends: The Meeting of Motecuhzoma and Cortes"; "The Fall of Tenochtitlan"; "Broken Spears"; "Flowers and Songs of Sorrow"; from *The Broken Spears: The Aztec Account of the Conquest of Mexico,* edited by Miguel Leon-Portilla, copyright © 1962 by the Beacon Press; Originally published in Spanish under the title of *Vision de los Vencidos,* copyright © 1959 by Universidad Nacional Autonoma de Mexico. Reprinted by permission of Beacon Press.

"The Last Judgment" and "The King Must Pay," from *The Life and Writings of Bàrtolome de las Casas* by Henry Raup Wagner and Helen Rand Parish, copyright © 1967 University of New Mexico Press.

"The Thoughts That Clothe the Soul of a European" and "Our Countrymen, These Slave Catchers," from *Interlinear to Cabeza de Vaca,* edited by Haniel Long, copyright © 1969, Frontier Press.

"How Onate Took Possession of the Newly Discovered Land," from *A History of New Mexico* by Gaspar Perez de Villagra. Courtesy The Rio Grande Press, Inc., Reprint edition 1962.

"The Vow of Poverty," from *Relaciones* by Zarate Salmeron, translated by Alicia Ronstadt Milich. Copyright © 1966, Horn & Wallace Publishers.

"Sonora Is Our Motherland"; "The Vaquero"; "Joaquin Murrieta"; from *The Vaquero,* by Arnold Rojas, copyright © 1964. Reprinted by permission of the publisher, McNally & Loftin, Publishers, Santa Barbara.

"The Simple Pastoral Life (Texas)," from *With His Pistol in His Hand: A Border Ballad and Its Hero* by Americo Paredes, copyright © 1958 University of Texas Press.

"The Sheepherders"; "Los Caballeros de Labor y Los Gorras Blancas"; "The Pioneer Women"; from *We Fed Them Cactus* by Fabiola Cabeza de Baca, copyright © 1954 University of New Mexico Press.

"The Campesinos," from *The Plum, Plum Pickers* by Raymond Barrio, copyright © 1969, 1971 by Raymond Barrio. Reprinted by permission of Harper & Row, Publishers, Inc.

"The Bracero" and "The Roots of Migration," from *Merchants of Labor: The Mexican Bracero Story,* copyright © 1964 by Ernesto Galarza. Reprinted by permission of the publisher, McNally & Loftin, Publishers, Santa Barbara.

"Folk-Lore of the Texas-Mexican Vaquero," by Jovita Gonzales, from *Texas and Southwestern Lore,* edited by J. Frank Dobie, Texas Folklore Society.

"To the Texas Colonists 'Mexican' Is an Execrable Word" and "The Fall of the Alamo" from *The Siege and Taking of the Alamo* by General Miguel A. Sanchez Lamego. Reprinted by permission of The Press of the Territorian, Santa Fe, New Mexico.

"After We Took Them to Our Bosom, They Destroyed Us," from *The Mexican Side of the Texas Revolution,* edited and translated by Carlos E. Castaneda, P. L. Turner Company, 1956.

"What Child Will Not Shed Abundant Tears at the Tomb of His Parents" by Governor Juan Bautista Vigil, from Archives of the State of New Mexico.

"The Treaty of Guadalupe Hidalgo," from Guadalupe Hidalgo Treaty of Peace, published by Tate Gallery, 1969, Truchas, New Mexico.

"Revolutionaries Are Also Sons of God," from *The Memoirs of Pancho Villa,* University of Texas Press, copyright © 1965 by Martín Luis Guzmán.

"An Emigrant's Farewell" and "Deported," from *Puro Mexicano* (Austin, 1935). Reprinted by permission of the Texas Folklore Society.

"El Coyotito," translated by Alice Corbin, first appeared in *Poetry,* copyright 1920 by The Modern Poetry Association. Reprinted by permission of the Editor of *Poetry.*

"La Cucaracha," from Publications of the Texas Folklore Society, IV (1925). Reprinted by permission of the Texas Folklore Society.

"Our Allegiance Is to the Land" and "Mother of All Life—The Earth," from *La Raza: The Mexican Americans* by Stan Steiner, Harper & Row, Publishers, 1970, copyright © 1969, 1970 by Stan Steiner.

"My Cow, She Was Almost Arrested"; "The Women of La Raza"; "La Madre de Aztlan"; "The Church and La Raza"; "Jesus Christ as a Revolutionist"; "El Plan Espiritual de Aztlan." These pieces originally appeared in *El Grito del Norte* and are reprinted with the permission of the publishers. "La Cooperativa," by Valentina Valdez Tijerina, *Motive,* March, 1971, Vol. XXXI, No. 5.

"La Jefita," by Jose Montoya, Quinto Sol Publications, 1969.

"Musica de Machete" by Benjamin Lune, *La Raza,* Los Angeles, Vol. I, No. 9, February 1968.

"The Land Grants," from *Land-Grant Problems Among the State's Spanish-Americans,* by Clark S. Knowlton, University of New Mexico Bureau of Business Research, *New Mexico Business,* June, 1967.

"Notes on Chicano Theater"; "El Teatro Campesino"; "Bernabe"; by Luis Valdez, copyright © 1970 by Luis Valdez.

"The Organizer" and "A New Cross," by Abelardo Delgado, copyright by the author.

"The Story of Vato"; "The Brown Berets"; "La Junta"; "Los Comancheros del Norte: For Machos Only"; "We Demand"; "El Grito"; "La Raza Unida." These pieces originally appeared in *La Raza Yearbook,* September, 1968, and are reprinted with the permission of the publishers.